More Praise for
The Art of Original Thinking–The Making of a Thought Leader

With the passing of Peter F. Drucker, the consummate thought leader, we all need to read Jan Phillips' book and adopt as our own her challenge to free ourselves from illusions and create a better life and business.

KEN SHELTON, CHAIRMAN AND EDITOR-IN-CHIEF
Executive Excellence Publishing

In a world of inevitable chaos and complexity, The Art of Original Thinking– The Making of a Thought Leader *helps show that social consciousness and corporate performance can be simultaneously managed. Paradoxes of profit and people, growth and continuity, learning and heritage, collaboration and competition may be sources of tension that thoughtful leaders face and manage. The principles in the book can be used by leaders at all levels to generate new insights into old problems.*

DAVE ULRICH, PH.D.
Professor, Ross School of Business, University of Michigan

Jan Phillips' wonderful writing style together with powerful content in The Art of Original Thinking–The Making of a Thought Leader *has made me take a hard look at business as usual in America. She debunks the myth that profit-making and social consciousness are poles apart. Brava, Jan, for asking the right questions!*

STANLEY WESTRIECH
Capital One Financial, Board of Directors; Partner, Westfield Realty

What sets apart The Art of Original Thinking–The Making of a Thought Leader *is the deep reservoir of hope that underlies the powerful ideas and message. Referencing leaders in many fields, Jan Phillips shows how creativity and original thinking can help heal our businesses and planet.*

FREDERIC LUSKIN, PH.D.
Director, Stanford Forgiveness Projects; Author of *Forgive for Good*

At last, a book that unites the web of commerce with the web of life and provokes the unsettling questions that all true leaders need. What more could a leader want than to know how to leave a legacy of creative contribution!

EILEEN MCDARGH, CSP, CPAE
President, McDargh Communications and The Resiliency Group

The Art of Original Thinking–The Making of a Thought Leader *is a must read for anyone wanting to expand their thinking about work and life. Jan Phillips' practical insights will help you re-examine the assumptions by which you think and enhance your sense of life purpose.*

RICHARD CHANG, CEO, RICHARD CHANG ASSOCIATES, INC.
Author of *The Passion Plan* and *The Passion Plan at Work*

Jan Phillips has truly captured the essence of being a thought leader. By zooming in on prominent aspects of today's business world, Phillips accurately and efficiently demonstrates the NEED for innovative thought and leadership. Her flowing and easy-to-understand writing style appropriately inspires readers to embrace the fact that they too can become a successful thought leader. The Art of Original Thinking–The Making of a Thought Leader *articulately maps out the steps necessary to seize one's ideas and transform them into desired knowledge. I recommend this book to motivate the inventive thinker in all of us.*

KEN LIZOTTE, CMC
Chief Imaginative Officer, Emerson Consulting Group, Inc.

Captivating stories, compelling examples and creative content. You will absolutely learn something new and original from reading this enjoyable book.

DR. TONY ALESSANDRA
Author of *Charisma* and *The Platinum Rule*

Several thousand books on leadership have been written in recent years; this is one of the best. Jan Phillips describes the courage, actions and behaviors of creative thought leaders who get exceptional results by building trust and relationships combined with clarity of vision, purpose and core values to inspire people who see their work as something far beyond themselves. The uniqueness of the book is that it effectively addresses the dimension of successfully meshing corporate profit and goals with those of our global environmental and resource issues.

RICHARD A. MCNEECE, LEADERSHIP CONSULTANT
Former Chairman and CEO, First National Bancorp

Jan Phillips is the ORIGINAL original thinker. Her powerful book will stir your gray matter, shift your paradigms, and allow you to experience a new way of thinking. Everything you do, see and contemplate will be changed as a result of reading this inspiring and thought-provoking work. Read it as if your life and the life of our planet depended on it.

JENNI PRISK, CEO, PRISK COMMUNICATION
Founder and President of Voices of Women

I love the spirit of this book. It is greatly needed at this time in human history. The challenges we face are daunting and discouraging, but Jan Phillips gives us a high energy, uplifting vision of how we can all see beyond the false dualities such as sustainability and profit, and makes us believe that each of us can make our unique contribution to the "original thinking" required to turn that vision into reality. Not only does she inspire, but she gives us a practicum through her own thought leadership!

JIM ZULL, PH.D.
Author of *The Art of Changing the Brain*

I was struck by three things. First, she knows what she's talking about. By integrating the works of giants like Peter Drucker, Peter Senge and Paul Hawken she makes a strong case for leadership based on individual, original thinking that inspires the community to follow her lead. The humble, generous, self-offering leader leads by deed.

Second, she is an engaging storyteller. She understands the power of an anecdote to reinforce her main points. She says it well: "If a story can move you from thought to action, then you know the power of a well-told tale."

Third, Ms. Phillips makes a persuasive case that the best leaders in the 21st century will be individuals from organizations that understand that it is in their grandchildren's best interest to maximize the triple bottom line. These thought leaders will inspire and motivate the human capital within their organizations to maximize economic profits while leaving no footprints in the sand.

In conclusion, Ms. Phillips thinks outside the parallelogram. I will recommend this book to my students.

DR. CURTIS L. DEBERG, FOUNDER OF SAGE
Professor of Business, California State University, Chico

Jan Phillips has done her homework in taking this giant step forward in reshaping our world view. Clear, concise—a true horizon of hope.

MARILYN J. MASON, PH.D., PRESIDENT, MASON & ASSOCIATES
Author of *Igniting the Spirit at Work: Daily Reflections*

Jan Phillips mentors leaders at all levels with her forthright advice, her deep personal experience and her ability to draw on a vast array of resources and references to educate her readers and amplify her points. The author makes a very unique contribution to what has already been placed on the vast list of leadership books. Thank you, Jan, for providing such a vivid picture of what the modern leader must do to impact others in their own organization and beyond its boundaries as well.

DR. BEVERLY KAYE, CEO/FOUNDER, CAREER SYSTEM INTERNATIONAL
Author of *Up is Not the Only way*; coauthor of *Love 'Em or Lose 'Em*

I was immediately drawn into the stories, examples and cutting-edge research. Jan easily moves between age-old wisdom and provocative thinking. She shows that you can use original approaches to win on all fronts. A must-read for anyone interested in authentic leadership!

BONNIE ST. JOHN, MANAGING DIRECTOR FOR SPECIAL PROGRAMS, THE LEADER'S EDGE
Author of *Succeeding Sane: Making Room for Joy in a Crazy World*

The Art of Original Thinking *is a timely and important book. It truly engaged me and sparked a shift in my thinking – how I view myself, my business and just how connected we all are in this global community we are creating.*

JACQUELINE TOWNSEND, CEO, Townsend, Inc.

The Art of
Original Thinking

| The Making of a Thought Leader |

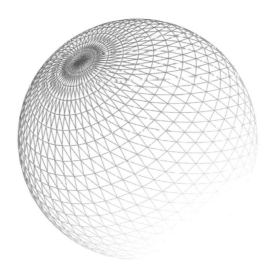

Jan Phillips

The Art of Original Thinking – The Making of a Thought Leader

FIRST EDITION

10 9 8 7 6 5 4 3 2 1

Published by 9th Element Press
6215 Ferris Square, Suite 210
San Diego, CA 92121
www.9thelementgroup.com

9TH
ELEMENT
PRESS

Thought Leaders in Print
A Division of 9th Element Group

ISBN # 0-9774213-0-9

Printed and bound in the United States of America.
9th Element Press strives to use the most environmentally sensitive paper stocks available. This book is printed on acid-free, recycled paper.

Cover design by Greenleaf Book Group LP
Author photograph by Tiger Lee
Interior design and illustrations by Thomas Gaebel

To Annie Bridget O'Flaherty,
for being the Muse that you are to me.

The Art of
Original Thinking

| The Making of a Thought Leader |

CONTENTS

Acknowledgments

I acknowledge and give thanks to the Original Source, from whom these thoughts and all thoughts derive.

I acknowledge and give thanks to my partners and sisters at 9th Element Group: to Ruth Westreich, Janet Clemento, Jackie Townsend, Marty Palecki, Michelle Price, and Annie O'Flaherty for the very idea of this book, for the resources you shared in making it happen, and for the gifts of your wisdom, your joy, and your visions.

I give thanks, as well, to Thomas Gaebel for your support of this project from its conception to birth, and for the brilliant creativity you brought to its design and layout. And I also give thanks to Stanley Westreich, for your early readings, your guidance, and your inspired responses.

I extend my thanks to all of you in my circle of support who feed me light and lift me up in so many ways, and to every person, organization, and business mentioned in this book for transforming your insights into action that makes this world a safer, saner place.

Masterpieces are not single and solitary births; they are the outcome of many years of thinking in common, of thinking by the body of the people, so that the experience of the mass is behind the single voice.

VIRGINIA WOOLF

Introduction

Calling this book *The Art of Original Thinking—The Making of a Thought Leader* is a way of acknowledging that originality is a practice that can be learned, or rather rediscovered, reclaimed, with a certain amount of attention and surrender. As with any creative endeavor, originality in thinking, in being, requires a heightened state of alertness, a bridging of the poles, a show of fearlessness and willingness to forfeit the known for the unknown, the learned for the experienced. It requires a trust deeper than the sea, for what it asks for is a letting go, an unmooring from the safe harbor of certainty for a journey into the mists of mystery and possibility.

The compass is not the mind, but the heart, and the journey takes us away from what was and toward what can be. The old adage "Leaders are born, not made" represents a style of thinking that's dualistic, argumentative, polarizing. It's an either/or, right or wrong proposition. Someone decides it's one way or the other and you have to choose. It's that kind of thinking we're leaving at the shore as we sail toward the possibility of unitive thinking: that leaders are born *and* made.

The premise of this book is that we are here to advance the evolution of thought, of human sensibility, of our own personal potential to be more than anyone ever said we could be. Its intention is to inspire thought leaders who are willing to be visible, vocal agents of evolutionary thinking for global good. Its reach is both deep and wide. It will guide you on a journey into your own thought patterns and processes, helping you free yourself from obstacles to original thinking. And once you begin to think from your genuine center, once you begin to experience your own pure, uncontaminated thoughts, you will feel rising up from within you a calling, a challenge to be of use, an idea that needs you in order to become real in the world. And it is this idea, your own original thought, that will guide you, empower you, enable you to take your place as a thought leader and catalyst for creative action.

Those who came before us did the best they could do, educating us to conform, to honor tradition, to study and sing and recite the appropriate creeds, anthems, and pledges. The instruction was never how to think, but what to think. Millions of us grew up believing everything we were told by people we trusted, abdicating our power to the proper authorities, and allowing our own creative powers to atrophy. Only now is it becoming clear to us what happened and what a distance we must travel to rediscover and reawaken our own originality.

This book is a road map for that journey. I am approaching it as an artist, hoping to create something that will envelop you in the experience of a new awakening, so that it is not just your mind that is fed, nourished, altered, but the entirety of you. I address you as an artist because I agree with Margaret Wheatley who says, "Start with the assumption that people, like all life, are creative and good at change." You are an artist at life and whatever you're making of it is the masterpiece you are working on. So I offer you the best of the poets and artists throughout history who have created words, images, stories to guide us, heal us, nudge us forward on this path of illuminating discovery: the discovery of our very own essence and the embodiment of our very own thoughts.

And I confess to this one desire: that as we each take this journey, we allow ourselves to become synthesizers of each others' thoughts, and in that wild jumble of imaginations, in that glorious dance of unity and wholeness, we become the thought leaders for a new kind of planetary citizenship. That as we unwind and unfold our own creative DNA, as we unearth our own wisdom, that very act will awaken us to our commonness and common needs. And from that place, with that awareness, we will step into our power to create businesses, organizations, and institutions that thrive because they serve the common good. The solutions to the crises of our time do not lie dormant in one individual. They live like seeds in every one of us. It is not a savior who will rescue us from the plight and perils we face, but a communion of saints who go by our names.

This book is an attempt to awaken in all of us the memory of our vocation, our purpose—that we are here to advance life, to transform every experience into an uttering that is unique, that has never been heard before, that is a clue to the others, a warning, a leading. To be an original thinker is to be a scout on new horizons, an adventurer into new domains, a perpetrator of inspiration, a leader of thought and heartfelt action.

As the philosopher Beatrice Bruteau once wrote: "We cannot wait for the world to turn, for times to change that we might change with them, for the revolution to come and carry us around in its new course. We *are* the future. We *are* the revolution."

This is the time, and we are the ones. Godspeed to us all.

| Releasing the Past |

Freeing Ourselves from Illusion

Myths: Dispelling the Old, Defining the New

The Nature of Change

Questioning Our Assumptions

What the World Needs Now

Freeing Ourselves from Illusion

People, like all forms of life, only change when something so disturbs them that they are forced to let go of their present beliefs. Nothing changes until we interpret things differently. Change occurs only when we let go of our certainty.

DEE HOCK

As leaders we must help people move into a relationship with uncertainty and chaos.

MARGARET WHEATLEY

Illusions are false beliefs. They are notions and ideas that we have inherited from our culture, our families, and almost every institution with which we've been associated. Illusions take up residence in our minds because we receive them, for the most part, when we are young, impressionable, trusting, and open to the ideas being handed down to us. They are part of our social conditioning, but they do not serve us. Illusions are, in fact, the only cause of our unhappiness.

To be thought leaders in any arena, we need to be free and original thinkers, capable of focusing on how we are thinking as well as what we are thinking. The Indian philosopher Sri Aurobindo said, "In order to see, you have to stop being in the middle of the picture." This means we have to step outside of ourselves, put some distance between ourselves and our thoughts, so we can assess their heritage and test them for authenticity. Because the consciousness of a leader has a tremendous impact on the consciousness of the organization, every leader must do the deep and personal work of clarifying his or her own thoughts, so that when we speak, every word has a ring of clarity, every statement has a purpose and air of authenticity.

This requires a looking inward that both grounds and balances our outward actions. When we look within and mine our own experience for feelings that not only mesh with our message, but are actually the source

3

of the message, then the delivery itself carries an integrity of authorship that is convincing, compassionate, and compelling. When we manage to rid ourselves of inherited voices and speak from the heart, our very speaking is a force that can change minds, lives, and the direction of any community to which we belong.

Freeing ourselves from illusion may seem like an esoteric concept that has nothing to do with leadership, but that's because one of the biggest illusions we suffer from is the notion that what goes on inside us has little to do with who we are on the outside. We've become so good at compartmentalizing our lives that we think our corporate selves are distinct from our private selves, that who we are on the golf course has nothing to do with who we are at home, or that the persona we project in the board room ought to be different from the persona we project in the family room.

My best friend in high school became a chief executive for a multi-national company in Australia and when I went to visit her she talked about how sad it was that she couldn't be friends with any of her employees. She felt so isolated. I'd started a few businesses in the States and said to her that they had been successful *because* I'd made friends with every employee, and her response was that in big business you just couldn't do that. "You can't be personal with people you supervise." That, to me, was an example of an illusion, an inherited notion, a handed-down tradition. She honored it like it was a holy corporate commandment, and perhaps it was, but organizations are living things, like evolving organisms. They only thrive when they adapt to their changing environments.

Anthony De Mello, a Jesuit priest, psychotherapist, and retreat director, taught that all our negative emotions are caused by illusions that we allow to obstruct our thinking. If we're sad or angry, it's because there is some underlying illusion preempting our natural state of joy. He says: "When the eye is unobstructed, the result is seeing; when the ear is unobstructed, the result is hearing; when the palate is unobstructed, the result is tasting. When the mind is unobstructed, the result is wisdom and happiness. Drop your attachments and you will be free. Understand your illusions and they will drop."

It is awareness, not effort, that dissolves the illusions. When we experience an upset, if we look to see what underlying belief or attachment is behind it, we can begin to see what illusions have us in their grip. If I make the mistake of thinking someone else is responsible for my happiness, I'll discover this when I back up and begin to explore my negative feelings about their behavior. Why am I upset? Because he didn't do so-and-so. Why should he have done so-and-so? Because it would have made me happy, and he's responsible for my happiness. That is my illusion.

I was in India during the monsoon season, living for awhile in a community founded by a man who'd lived many years with Mahatma Gandhi. One morning I woke up to discover this was the day we were going to begin the construction of a barn. Women, men, and children were forming a line from the creek bed to the site of the building, about a quarter of a mile away. Teenage girls were assembling at the site where there was a pile of huge rocks. As I took my place in the line, I asked Nayan Bala, the woman next to me, what in the world was going on. "We're transporting the mortar materials from the creek," she said, as the first tin bowl came my way. "Here, pass this on." The bowl contained a little water, some gravel and small pebbles. I passed it to the woman next to me, and as soon as I turned around, there was another bowl coming at me. I handed that one over and another one came. And another, and another.

It was 98 degrees and the humidity was hovering at about 90 percent. After passing bowls for an hour, I thought I might like to change places with the girls up at the site. "What are they doing with the rocks?" I asked. "They carry them on their head and deliver them to the men once the mortar is in place," said Nayan Bala, passing me another bowl. I decided to stay in line. But the heat was unbearable, and I was getting irritable. There has to be another way, I thought, as I scanned the horizon looking for some way out of this predicament.

I saw several oxen lazing around further down the creek, a tractor off in the distance, and a flat bed trailer up near the rock pile. "This is ridiculous!" I said to Nayan Bala, whose face was as drenched with sweat as mine. "Why don't we hook up those oxen to some carts, and get that tractor hitched to the flat bed. There's no reason why all these people have to be killing themselves passing these little bowls. Let's mechanize this process. Don't you know time is money?"

As much as I'd prided myself on not being an "ugly American," there it was, right out in the open. Even as those last few words tumbled out of my sorry mouth, I knew I had crossed some boundary, created some new cultural divide with the power of my own words. I wanted to shrink into non-existence. But Nayan Bala was a mountain of kindness. She put the bowl down that was coming my way, wiped her hands on her sari, and placed them on my shoulders. "Maybe you haven't been in India long enough to understand something important about us. Every person is in line here because they want to be. In ten years, or twenty years, when this barn is built, they will bring their children here, their grandchildren here, and they will tell them the story of how they helped build this barn. They are proud to be doing this, and they will be proud every time they tell the story. Do you think we should deny them this?"

That was the moment for me when, as Dee Hock, founder and CEO Emeritus of Visa, says, I was "forced to let go of my present belief." Time wasn't money for these people—nor for me, actually. That concept was an illusion I had carried with me like an extra bag on my journey. It was an illusion that led to stress and anger. It didn't serve me. It wasn't mine, really. It was an inherited thought, not an original one. I was simply thinking something I was taught to think. It was the American way, but not the right way—not for this time and place.

Nayan Bala's graciousness allowed me to look at my thoughts and to see that they weren't mine at all. But it took an upset like that to set me apart from my own thinking. According to philosopher and integral theorist Ken Wilber, when we're looking at our thoughts, we're not using them to look at the world, so there's a moment of freedom there, a moment to be open to a new awareness. Is this thought really mine? Am I the author of it? Has it passed the test of my own experience? The poet Kabir writes, "If you haven't experienced it, it's not true." We can only speak powerfully from our own experience.

To be a thought leader, an original thinker, we have to move and think and speak from our own personal knowing. Our power comes from our ability to transform what we have felt into what we know. It's an alchemy of sorts, where we acquire the skill of transforming the lead of our experience into the gold of our wisdom. Each of us knows what no one else knows because no one else has lived our lives, seen what we've seen, felt what we've felt. The great Persian poet Rumi writes, "The throbbing vein will take you further than any thinking." This is a great clue.

Who are the speakers who have really inspired you? Who are the ones who have changed your thinking, altered the course of your own life? Are they not the ones who speak and write from the heart? Are they not the ones who stand before you, not with notes and memorized speeches, but with the courage to be simply who they are, to share their visions, their struggles, their fears? This is the stuff of leadership—this transparency, this risking, this willingness to say it's a new frontier here, and not one of us has a map, but with what we know together, we can surely make it.

In an interview in *Worthwhile* magazine, Jeff Dunn, former COO of Coca-Cola North America offers a clarifying image of this kind of transparency when he describes why he named his new business, Grassy Lake Partners, after a lake. "When you look at it from a certain angle, it reflects like a mirror. But then when you're on it, you can see all the way to the bottom." To Dunn, this is a symbol for how he wants to be as a leader: reflective enough to help others see their gifts and beliefs, and clear enough to allow others to see his own. There's a certain openness to this mode, a level of vulnerability that signifies confidence, an inner strength, a willingness to be seen "all the way to the bottom."

People these days are longing for that kind of openness. We really want depth. It's the root of relationship from which stems all human possibilities. And yet our society perpetuates the illusion that this kind of intimacy is unsafe, unwise, unprofessional. So we skim across the surface of our workdays like water spiders, never revealing the most essential information about who we are, what we feel, and what truths we hold. That is the greatest gift we could offer, for we all find ourselves and our meaning in each other's stories.

Margaret Wheatley, one of the most innovative thinkers of our time, writes in *Finding Our Way: Leadership for an Uncertain Time:*

> It is crucial to keep organizational purpose and values in the spotlight. The values come to life not through speeches and plaques, but as we hear the stories of other employees who embody those values...It is essential that the organization sponsor processes that bring people together so that they can learn of one another's perspectives and challenges. Processes such as conversation and storytelling help us connect at a depth not available through charts and PowerPoint presentations.[1]

Whether in the workplace or our personal lives, deep dialogue is a practice that can be learned and cultivated. It is essential to original thinking because it is a tool for helping us discover what we value and why. As soon as you speak of your values, your visions, your fears, my mind begins a search to discover its own beliefs in the matter. We are hardwired to compare and contrast, to scan for differences and similarities, to take in and synthesize and evolve ourselves forward. According to Dr. Richard Moss in *The I That Is We*, we define ourselves through problems, which are statements of contrast, not absolutes. And in order to arrive at these statements of contrast, we need to hear each other's stories. They are the grist for our mills. Your deep telling feeds my deep knowing. Or as the enigmatic nineteenth century French poet Paul Valéry expressed it: "Nothing is more 'original,' nothing more 'oneself,' than to feed on others. But one has to digest them. A lion is made of assimilated sheep." The truths we cling to are based on the stories we've been told, and they are altered and enlivened by the stories we continue to hear. We take something in, we digest it, we decide what to keep and what to let go of. Sometimes we change our thinking. Sometimes we don't.

Original thinkers delight in this process. They are not frightened by opposing ideas; they welcome them as an opportunity to clarify and redefine their own meanings, which is the very activity that keeps them fully charged, awakened, illumined. This is the practice that allows one to dismantle the shackles of conditioned thinking. It's why diversity works. Being in the presence of others whose experiences are vastly different from ours causes us to see ourselves and our beliefs in a new light.

When Ray Anderson, founder and former CEO of Interface, Inc., a carpeting manufacturing company, read Paul Hawken's book, *The Ecology of Commerce*, Anderson's deeply held ideas about business, profitability, and corporate responsibility were seriously challenged. When a group of designers asked what his company was doing to protect the environment, he was stymied. But he remained open. He did not dismiss them, put them in a box called "tree-huggers," and go on about his business. He inquired within. He allowed for an interplay of ideas. He synthesized what he knew from his personal experience with the new information presented to him and an old illusion—that he had to choose between the environment and profits—dropped away.

Because of his openness, his willingness

> *If we want our world to be different, our first act needs to be reclaiming time to think.*
> MARGARET WHEATLEY

> *True compassion is more than flinging a coin to a beggar; it comes to see that an edifice which produces beggars needs restructuring.*
> MARTIN LUTHER KING, JR.

> *The measure of leadership is not the quality of the head, but the tone of the body.*
> MAX DE PREE

> *Give every task as much time as it needs to be completed.*
> ALGONQUIN ELDER

to adapt and incorporate the new, he experienced an epiphany of consciousness which he writes about in his book *Mid-Course Correction*. Questioning himself and his values in a new light sparked an insight, the discovery that "when you find two opposites, you don't try to choose between them but to find a third place that reconciles them. In business, that third place is doing well by doing good." Believing that "unless somebody leads, no one will," Anderson committed to his business being 100 percent sustainable, having zero environmental impact by the year 2020. With manufacturing locations on four continents and offices in more than one hundred countries, this announcement caused quite a stir and met with a great deal of skepticism, but eventually everyone came on board and the company has reduced total greenhouse gas emissions by 54 percent since 1994. Today, they dominate the carpeting industry worldwide, with 19 percent sales growth in 2004, including 29 percent in the non-corporate office segments. In Asia-Pacific, profitability is growing at a record pace, with 2004 sales up about 50 percent, according to their 2004 annual report.

> The more consciousness you have, the more potential you have to create.
> DEEPAK CHOPRA

In an interview with Narelle Hooper for *BOSS* magazine, published by the *Australian Financial Review*, Rob Coombs, President and CEO of Interface Asia-Pacific, said that another benefit came along with the sustainability effort—the engagement and motivation of its staff rose considerably. As they turned more to nature to learn some lessons, their ability to retain and attract staff increased. According to Coombs, the sixty-two-year-old chief engineer at their Picton plant in New Zealand gained a new lease on life and the plant is performing better than ever. "It's a philosophy that seems to have resonance with people—the idea that it is important how you make money, not just how much of it you make," said Coombs.

> Things which matter most should never be at the mercy of things which matter least.
> GOETHE

> There is one thing stronger than all the armies in the world, and that is an idea whose time has come.
> VICTOR HUGO

> We are breaking mind patterns that have dominated human life for eons.
> ECKHART TOLLE

To make Interface the leader in industrial ecology, Ray Anderson and his colleagues let go of old notions, dropped their illusions about profitability and sustainability being at odds with each other, and took brave steps into the unknown to finally discover that it is possible to do well by doing good.

To do this, they had to engage in original thinking. There were no manuals to read on the subject. They had to turn inward to their own creative sources. They met in diverse teams, took field trips into the natural world in search of new solutions, they shared their insights and their feelings, they built global partnerships to create a shared under-standing of sustainability, they engaged key players in the global environmental effort to help them prioritize challenges, and they created networks of connectivity to keep themselves informed and inspired. And all the while they're recording it, posting their milestones on their website, and encouraging other corporations to follow their lead. Many have, and many more will, because this is the nature of conscious evolution.

Thought leaders inspire leadership. They ignite imaginations, explode old myths, and illumine paths to the future that others may follow. One of the oldest voices embedded in our cultural consciousness is the voice that says, "If s/he can, I can." Our confidence is buoyed by the fact that someone else did it before us. No matter how dangerous or outrageous or innovative, if someone did it, we know it's possible, and that endeavor becomes a challenge, then, for others to meet or surpass. By going first, thought leaders provide the basis for change. They abandon outmoded traditions with the same alacrity as one dispenses with a pair of old hiking boots or an outdated pair of spike heels.

We let go of the old to discover the new, as we let go of illusions to discover the real. The way to awareness is the way of subtraction, of letting go, one by one, of our fears, our doubts, our prejudices, our judg-ments, our inherited notions of how it should be, who deserves what, who is to blame. What's happening in the world is a result of our collec-tive input. The morning headlines are the news that we are making as a whole human family, by what we do and what we fail to do. Each one of us is a co-creator of the very culture we are immersed in, and if we want to see change, we can make change by changing ourselves, our thinking, and our destructive habits.

Blame is not useful. Polarization is not useful. Bitterness and nega-tivity are not useful. What's useful in these perilous times is deep thought and dialogue. What's useful is a willingness to speak from our hearts, to say out loud what we hunger for, what we're willing to live for, and what it is we can no longer abide. We are attendants at the wake of the old way, and each of us—through our actions, our thoughts, our work and relationships—is midwifing a new world into existence. This is our destiny, our meaning, our purpose, and when we come to our days with this awareness, when we fully wake up to this tremendous privilege, when we sense the oak in the acorn of our beings, then we will have the energy to move mountains and shift the tides.

It is an illusion that we are powerless. It is an illusion that someone else is responsible. It is an illusion that we cannot transcend these dualities and differences that are making a mockery of democracy. We are the people. This is our world. And every movement that ever led to any change in this ever-evolving civilization grew like a seed from one person's imagination. And what did that person have—a deeply rooted sense of what's right; a commitment to truth-telling, to heart-sharing, to bridge-building; an ability to inspire, to breathe life into the hearts and minds of others. No matter how brilliant our attempts to inform, it is our ability to inspire that will turn the tides.

Transformation originates in people who see a better way or a fairer world, people who reveal themselves, disclose their dreams, and unfold their hopes in the presence of others. And this very unfolding, this revelation of raw, unharnessed desire, this deep longing to be a force for good in the world is what inspires others to feel their own longings, to remember their own purpose, and to act, perhaps for the first time, in accordance with their inner spirit.

Dee Hock writes in *Birth of the Chaordic Age*: "If your beliefs are based on the old model of top-down command and control, specialization, special privilege, and nothing but profit, your organization will, in time, turn toxic. It will become antithetical to the human spirit and destructive of the biosphere." What he advocates is a leadership rooted in purpose and principles, organizations that have, at their very heart, concerns that engage and enliven the human spirit, that call forth from the membership the essence of their fertile imaginations.

As we have evolved beyond the mechanics and rigidities of the industrial age in our buildings and businesses, so have the workers evolved into beings who seek more purposeful lives, workplaces that require and inspire relationships, collaborative processes that stimulate originality and culminate in a sense of meaningful community. People want to engage with others, to feel the thrill of creative combustion, the joy of originating new solutions, like spelunkers in a cave, illuminating the unknown with the floodlight of their diverse wisdom and experience.

Every thinking person on this planet feels in their heart the toll of compassion and the weight of complicity. On some deep level, we are aware that our choices have an impact on others, that there is some ineffable connection between our lives and the lives of our sisters and brothers in Rwanda, Calcutta, Uzbekistan. We sense the inequities and a deep sorrow runs through our nervous system day and night. We are frozen in our silences, numbed by our distractions, waiting and yearning and praying for war to end, hunger to end, poverty to end. Many of us cry out silently in the night, but the time has come to be public with this pain, to speak of its relentlessness, its unbearableness, for it is only when we release it that we become free to address it, to embrace it, and, ultimately, to heal it.

As individuals, the greatest courage that is called for is the courage to be real. When we are real, it melts the frozen places in ourselves and others. It opens the passageways between our hearts and our minds, thaws the blockages that constrain our imagination, and carries us down to our wellsprings of wisdom. The solutions to our crises are already here. They exist in our relationships, in our stories, in our unfolding forgiveness, and it is through the expression of these things that we will one day live into the answers we seek at this time.

The leadership that is required at this moment in history is a leadership of generosity, of humility, of self-offering. To lead, we need not know the answers. We must only convene the circles, articulate the questions, frame the conversation, and direct attention to the issues that matter. It is the community that will rise up in response to our calling—joyful to be invited, heartened to be involved—and it is the community that will lead us past our illusions, beyond our fears, and into a reality brighter and bolder than all imaginings.

To be free to offer the gifts of your heart, to be free of what others might think, to be a truth-teller, a catalyst, a voice in the dark: these are the fruits of original thinking, and these are the signs of leaders of consequence.

TWO

Myths: Dispelling the Old, Defining the New

To change our realities we have to change our myths.

RIANE EISLER

We cannot change our politics until we first change our perceptions.

BEATRICE BRUTEAU

Some of the greatest thinkers today are in agreement about the power of our consciousness to alter our circumstances. From biologists to business leaders, mystics to medical professionals, philosophers to philanthropists, individuals are speaking out about the role of our thoughts in the unfolding of our realities. Simultaneously, the world of quantum physics is seeding our fertile mindscapes with findings that propel us beyond all known imaginings.

Quantum nonlocality, or nonseparability, is asking us to completely alter our ideas about objects. "We can no longer consider objects as independently existing entities. They are interconnected in ways not even conceivable in classical physics," writes theoretical astrophysicist Victor Mansfield in *Synchronicity, Science, and Soul-Making.* Quantum nonlocality teaches us that particles that were once together in an interaction continue to respond to each other no matter how many miles apart, and at a rate faster than the speed of light. Physicist Menas Kafatos writes: "Nature has shown us that our concept of reality, consisting of units that can be considered as separate from each other, is fundamentally wrong." Since we are composed of cells, molecules, atoms and sub-atomic particles, this makes *each of us* part of one indivisible whole, interconnected and interdependent.

This is hard to put our minds around since we have constructed a society based on myths of duality and separation. Myths are the great overarching stories that we are born into—stories that help us know our place, understand our nature. They are universal in scope, leading us to believe that *this is how it is* for humanity. According to the mythologist Joseph Campbell, myths are stories that bridge our local consciousness to "Mind at Large." The images they give us reflect our relationship to the eternal, to the earth, and to each other.

In the Neolithic era, people were guided by the creation myth of a Great Mother Goddess who ruled over the natural world and presided over all their earthly activities. Men and women considered themselves children of the Goddess, as they were the children of the women who headed the families and clans. The myth of the Great Mother Goddess connected them to the eternal and guided them in the creation of their culture, art, and social order. Archeological excavations from these cultures have not unearthed weapons and instruments of war, but an abundance of art and artifacts indicating a pervasive reverence for the Great Goddess.

The myths of the Garden of Eden and Cain and Abel reflect the cataclysmic cultural change that erupted when the Bronze Age warriors from the north invaded the peaceful, matristic societies of Mesopotamia, writes Riane Eisler in *The Chalice and the Blade*.[1] With the arrival of these soldiers came male dominance, weaponry, and a war-like mentality. As societies that conceptualized the Goddess as the supreme power in the universe were conquered, the story of the Great Mother was rewritten, and the image of her replaced with one of a wrathful, bearded sky-God.

The myths of dismissal from the Garden, separation from the Divine, and murdering brothers have been the inheritance of Western civilization, and they have had an impact on the creation of our society, just as the Goddess myth had an impact on our Neolithic ancestors and the creation of their society. But myths can and do change over time, and at this time in history, we are undergoing an upheaval every bit as profound as the uprooting of the Goddess and the seeding of patriarchy.

"Humanity is being taken to the place where it will have to choose between suicide and adoration," wrote the Jesuit priest and paleontologist Teilhard de Chardin. The fate of the world, of every child in the world, is in the hands of those of us who populate it, and we are each at that choice point, each responsible every day for actions that move the tipping point one way or another. The matter of original thinking now is an urgent one, as it is time to think anew, to weave the findings of science—of our true interconnectedness, our profound and universal indivisibility—into new myths and stories that feed our souls and inspire acts of adoration.

One of the most revered scientists of all time, Albert Einstein, believed likewise. He wrote:

> A human being is part of the whole called by us universe, a part limited in time and space. We experience ourselves, our thoughts and feelings, as something separate from the rest. A kind of optical delusion of consciousness. This delusion is a kind of prison for us, restricting us to our personal desires and to affection for a few persons nearest to us. Our task must be to free ourselves from the prison by widening our circle of compassion to embrace all living creatures and the whole of nature in its beauty. The true value of a human being is determined by the measure and the sense in which they have obtained liberation from the self. We shall require a substantially new manner of thinking if humanity is to survive.[2]

And the thinking that is required is original thinking, conscious thinking, courageous thinking that inquires into the whole body for its insight, that engages the spirit in its process, and that considers the whole of humanity in its conclusions.

"It's all a question of story. We are in trouble just now because we are between stories," wrote the historian Thomas Berry several years ago. But we are making strides and turning tides as we challenge the old, conjure the new, and pass on ideas like batons in a relay. "Our stories are changing from the old hero's journey to people cooperating, understanding passionately, creating collectively," said visionary philosopher Jean Houston in a recent interview. "We are all now the agents for the next dispensation, the inspiration for the bringing of culture and consciousness to its next possibility."

The true leaders of this time are the ones who are not just imagining, not just hoping for and waiting for the new dispensation to arrive, but actively bringing it into existence. They are stepping out of the old roles, refusing to do *business as usual*, abandoning practices that do not serve the common good. The myth-makers and change-makers of this era embody peace, practice reconciliation, and are undaunted in their service to higher standards. They are the Mahatma Gandhis, the Nelson Mandelas, the Rosa Parks, and the Harriet Tubmans of our time, not looking to be heroes, but acting heroically in the face of massive opposition.

Rising above popular opinion, social conditioning, conformist behavior, thought leaders of today are daring to speak the unspeakable, as Copernicus did, as Galileo did, as the mystics and poets and scientists throughout the ages did, guiding us into fuller awareness, deeper imagining. To bring anything into existence, to be a creator of circumstances, we have to *imagine* the new, then *speak* the new, then usher it into reality with the *power of our intention, the passionate force of our belief in it.* There are hundreds of books that have been written but not published because the writers imagined them well enough, wrote them well enough, but failed to believe in them enough to propel them into reality. If our founding fathers did not have faith in their words, if they were not fervent in their beliefs about a more perfect union, they could not have succeeded in shaping the initial contours of these United States.

And so with us, to bring about a world of unity, a planetary community, we must begin to image it, speak it, and believe it into existence. To end war, we must begin to say war is obsolete, and it is time to ban it, just as we banned slavery, child labor, witch-burning. To protect the planet or the poor, we must begin to say—convincingly and collectively—that corporations can profit as they wish, but not at the expense of the environment, of human rights, and of the communities in which they do business. This is not a revolution against corporate tyranny, as was the Boston Tea Party. This is an evolution for corporate consciousness, and it will lead to higher profitability and more goodwill because it is the right action for this time, and we, as a people, reward actions that hearten us. And we all want to engage in lives and work experiences that are heartening as well.

In *Finding Our Way: Leadership for an Uncertain Time,* Margaret Wheatley writes that "people don't step forward in order to support greed or egotists or to benefit faceless entities such as shareholders. Meaning is the most powerful motivator of human behavior. People gain energy and resolve if they understand how their work contributes to something beyond themselves."[3]

When John Akehurst, CEO of Woodside Petroleum, Australia's largest oil and gas exploration and production company, found out that people were ashamed about working with nonrenewable resources, the company made a decision that they were only going to do things if they could be proud of them. "This really caught the imagination of the workforce," said Akehurst in an interview for *What Is Enlightenment?* magazine.[4] "Someone would say, 'Wouldn't it be exciting to go into

16

another country, produce their first oil and gas and do it in a way that is profitable and actually enhances the unspoiled environment and the economy of the nation?' Then people would get really excited, realizing they could make a real contribution to humanity."

Woodside Petroleum is not some upstart, ideal-driven company. It operates more than seventy-five joint ventures in Australia, Africa, and the United States, has a market capitalization of more than $14 billion, and a staff of twenty-five hundred. Since their decision to be a force for good in the world, their sales revenue has continued to soar. This is how the new story begins to take root in the world. A few companies do the work of imagining, engaging every employee in the process, as the body engages every cell in its daily processes. The inquiry is not simply "How can we profit more?" but "How can we work in such a way that we profit for ourselves *and* contribute to others?" It is this second question that opens the gates to deep meaning and vitality for people. We *want* to be of use. It is our heart's deepest desire, as was manifested so graphically in the wake of September 11th, the Indonesian tsunami, and Hurricane Katrina.

And once we inquire into this deeper question, open ourselves to the gifts of our imagination and explore new ways to work together, be together, create together, then the solutions will arrive, as they arrived for Woodside, for Anderson Carpet, and for every other company committed to doing well by doing good. The new myth is a story of collaboration, and it will grow from our circles of conversation, our communities of dialogue. And we will learn, as others share their stories and successes, that this is the time to let go of the old, to walk toward each other and begin to speak, unfolding our wisdom in the lines between our words.

This is the time to set aside our old notions of separation— from our creative source, from each other, from our own potential for greatness— and construct a new worldview based on the fact that we are, in a very real way, *one;* and not one as Americans, or Africans, or Iraqis, but one as planetary citizens; not one as a heart cell with other heart cells, or as a lung cell with other lung cells, but one as *a whole body* which needs all its cells and systems working in alignment, for the sake of the whole.

If the body's organs competed with each other like corporations compete, like nations and individuals compete, for what they believe to be limited resources, the body would collapse. It is only able to thrive when every cell responds to messages from other cells with an immediate impulse to be of use, to share its life force and send its energy and nutrients where they are needed. Tumors get their start when cells isolate themselves and start multiplying independently of the normal laws of growth. When cells in a certain area reproduce unchecked, serving no physiologic function, they can interfere with vital body functions, absorb nutrients needed elsewhere, and destroy surrounding normal tissues. It is no stretch to apply this analogy to what is happening around the world today.

We do damage to the entire human family when we make decisions that serve certain individuals but not the whole. A worldwide anti-globalization movement emerged in the 1990s to call attention to the potential dangers of unchecked corporate expansion. Hundreds of social movements came into alignment to issue a warning about the impending negative consequences of global trade agreements on the poor, the environment, and world peace. Their response of massive protests and demonstrations was like the body's immune system which produces antibodies to defend the body against substances identified as potentially harmful. Interaction between cells at this stage is critical in eliminating infection. But because of our dualistic patterns, our divide and conquer mentality, we tend not to interact, but to oppose.

> *There is no reason why anyone would want a computer in their home.*
> KEN OLSEN, FOUNDER DIGITAL EQUIPMENT CORP.

> *We must raise prodigiously the threshold of our awareness so that we see ourselves for what we really are: individual cells in the immortal body of humanity.*
> NORMAN COUSINS

> *When the forms of an old culture are dying, the new culture is created by a few people who are not afraid to be insecure.*
> RUDOLPH BAHRO

Being against globalization is like being against wind. It is a force that is upon us, and it is presenting us with the greatest challenge of our lives—to tame the beast, to catalyze ourselves into a force greater than the force of greed, to shape a social mandate so genuinely moral, so unequivocal, so vigilantly protective of the rights of the whole body politic that it will be indisputable. Like wind, globalization can be a source of great destruction; but if we harness it intelligently, it can provide the very power we need to reshape our many parts into a fully functioning whole.

The art of original thinking is the art of thinking beyond dualities. It is the art of immersing ourselves so thoroughly in the idea of oneness that the creations, the visions, the solutions we offer the world are in the service of the whole human family. This, itself, is countercultural, given that we have all been born into a world where duality has reigned. But we know from science now, if not from our own faith and spiritual awareness, that the notion of separateness is fundamentally wrong, as was the notion of a flat earth or of the earth being the center of the universe. These findings caused a great tumult in the societies called upon to accommodate them, for it is never easy to realign a worldview. And our society now is undergoing a similar upheaval as we witness and bear the breakdown of nearly every system we have created—from health care to defense, education to entertainment, politics to religion. The old ways are disintegrating before our eyes, as well they might, rooted as they were in the soil of separateness. Profit before people is a concept that will soon be history, for it fails to stand up to the tests of *this* day. *Is it good for the whole? Does it harm the system?*

We are standing on the edge of a new world, on land created like virgin soil from the lava flows of an exploding volcano. There has been an eruption of consciousness and never has anyone stood in this place. The thinking that is called for now is truly original—not revolutionary or reflexive, but evolutionary and reflective. These times call for a confluence of ideas from all avenues, and for a courageous sharing of purpose and perceptions.

Peter Senge writes in *The Fifth Discipline*, "The discipline…starts with turning the mirror inward; learning to unearth our internal pictures of the world, to bring them to the surface and hold them rigorously to scrutiny. It also includes the ability to carry on 'learningful' conversations that balance inquiry and advocacy, where people expose their own thinking effectively and make that thinking open to the influence of others."[5]

For individuals invested in shifting the tides of global consciousness, in truly co-creating a higher order of planetary priorities, it is particularly important to convene with others, to unfold one's images in the presence of others, to invite the unfolding of theirs, for it is out of our collective imagining that the new ways will be revealed to us.

And because we are dealing with an entirely new worldview, with the creation of a new myth, based not on separation and a fall from grace, but on oneness and ascendancy into our true

> The overall number of minds is just one.
> EDWIN SCHRODINGER

> I know war as few other men now living know it, and nothing to me is more revolting. I have long advocated its complete abolition, as its very destructiveness on both friend and foe has rendered it useless as a method of settling international disputes.
> GEN. DOUGLAS MACARTHUR

> To control a nation, you don't have to control its laws or its military, all you have to do is control who tells the nation its stories.
> GEORGE GERBNER

potential, the revelations of our collective wisdom will take some time to supersede the old myths and methods. They will meet with opposition, cynicism, and a wild clamoring against change. Since so many are profiting from things as they are, and since we collectively fear letting go of the known, the forerunners of change will be addressing minds that are closed and frightened. And this is the great challenge for any emergent thought leader—to know that one's ideas will be criticized and resisted, and yet to dare to speak, knowing that these thoughts are the only building blocks we have to a new and safer world. As the poet Audre Lorde reminds us:

> We have been socialized to respect fear more than our own needs for language and definition, and while we wait in silence for the final luxury of fearlessness, the weight of that silence will choke us...The transformation of silence into language and action is an act of self-revelation and that always seems fraught with danger. We fear the very visibility without which we also cannot truly live...and that visibility which makes us most vulnerable is that which is also the source of our greatest strength.[6]

Thought leaders do not wait in silence. Nor do they wait for others' minds to be opened, or for safe places to speak into. Thought leaders are the openers of minds, the modern day prophets who dare say "we," knowing their words spring from a place of unity. Muhammad Yunus, founder of the Grameen Bank and microcredit pioneer, is one such leader. In an interview with Marco Visscher for *Ode* magazine, Yunus states that "poverty is a creation of a complex system of conceptions, rules and attitudes we have thought up ourselves. Therefore, if you want to eradicate poverty you have to go back to the drawing board, discover where we have planted the seeds of poverty and make changes there."[7]

After a famine in 1974, Yunus met with banks to try and get loans for the poor who needed just a pittance to make a new start for themselves. Universally, the response was negative: the poor are too big a risk; they're illiterate, not creditworthy, have no collateral, and will never repay the money. Every banker was so trapped in the old myth, it was impossible to imagine anything new. So Yunus dipped into his own pockets and came up with $35 US for forty-two people—loans for such things as a cow, a pair of scissors and comb to start a haircutting business, a sewing machine. Very little was required for these people to get back on their feet, and they all lived up to the terms of their contract.

What started as a seed in Muhammad Yunus's imagination grew into a reality that is benefiting the lives of millions of Bangladesh citizens today—and millions of poor in countries around the world where microcredit programs have taken root. Because he believed when others didn't, because he had a new vision and the courage to act on it, because he understood his kinship with the poor in his community, Muhammad Yunus became a force for good that ignited a unique, successful, and replicable response to poverty.

Grameen Bank now serves 3.7 million families in 46,000 villages in Bangladesh, and is owned by the rural poor whom it serves. Borrowers of the Bank own 90 percent of its shares, and with a few exceptions, the bank has turned a profit every year. As of May, 2005, Grameen Bank disbursed $4.8 billion in loans to 4.6 million borrowers, 96 percent of them women, with a repayment rate of 99 percent. It currently lends out about two million dollars a day in tiny loans averaging around $200. To encourage the children of the borrowers to stay in school and perform well in academics, Grameen Bank offers over six thousand scholarships each year to these children, and gives student loans to students in professional schools to become doctors, engineers, lawyers, and scientists.

Today, the hot new item in the microcredit program is a mobile phone. A hundred thousand women across Bangladesh, known as "phone ladies," have invested in cell phones and are making a good living by renting them out to villagers in their communities. They charge the market rate for calls, pay half of that to the Grameen Phone Company, and take home the rest. They are all Grameen Bank members who have a good record of loan repayment, and they are proving to the world that it pays to invest in the poor. Not only are they earning a living wage, but the villagers they serve are increasing their earning potential because of their expanded access to information. Instead of traveling by foot from village to village to compare prices for grain or negotiate with prospective buyers, they can save time by doing it on the phone.

And as for Grameen Phone, an offshoot of Grameen Bank, their success has far exceeded their expectations. Marco Visscher reports in *Ode* magazine that Grameen Phone "had expected to have around 70,000 subscribers by 2002, but already had 100,000 two years earlier. It reached the one million mark in 2003 and today has some 2.5 million subscribers around the country. By 2003, the company had booked a net profit of $75 million US and has 62 percent of the Bangladeshi mobile phone market."[8]

Yunus has held to a vision that the business world would contribute to the creation of a humane society, and for the development of "non-loss" social business enterprises which would use the market mechanism to stay profitable while they engage in solving social problems. In an acceptance speech for the Inaugural Petersberg Prize, awarded by the Development Gateway Foundation to Grameen Bank for its Village Phone Project, Yunus spoke of the creation of a "social stock market" to bring the social business entrepreneurs and social investors into contact with each other. In his mind's eye, he envisions rating agencies for social business enterprises, a methodology for evaluating their successes and failures, and the development of training curriculum for social MBAs.

While he is aware that the goal of capitalism is not to improve society but to maximize the personal wealth of the capitalist, Muhammad Yunus advocates for companies that manage to do both; and he is proving, through the success of microcredit programs the world around, that it is possible. Daring to share his visions and imaginings with others, he has spoken them into existence and sparked a movement of Himalayan proportions, culminating in the UN declaration of 2005 as the International Year of Microcredit.

Yunus' stories and the stories of others who have seen the poor lift themselves to unimagined heights are the very threads of the new myth we are weaving together. They are allowing us to release ourselves from the grip of outmoded thoughts and free our imaginations to create the new. His actions lend us images that blend with our knowing and expand its parameters. His work enables us to think more broadly, as Matisse, van Gogh, Kadinsky taught us to see more broadly, and Bach, Beethoven, Tchaikovsky to hear more broadly.

"The images on which we feed govern our lives," writes Jungian therapist Marion Woodman. There is a great power in imagery, as any advertising agency will attest to, and images have helped shape the constructs of the culture we're immersed in. What we believe is possible for ourselves comes from the images and stories that have entered into our consciousness. Just think of how the images you've seen—on television, in magazines, in movies, in your own imagination as you read fiction—have shaped the contours of your mind. We are a synthesis of what we absorb, as our bodies are a synthesis of sunlight, water, and nutrients.

When a whole generation of people grow up watching *Father Knows Best, Leave it to Beaver,* and *Ozzie and Harriet* their values and their thinking cannot help but be informed by the images and scripts of those television programs. So we end up with a culture created by and composed of people who were literally "programmed" to believe men know better, women should be concerned with looking good and taking care of everyone, the poor and people of color don't exist, or at least are not a significant part of "our" world.

While very few families resembled the Andersons, the Cleavers, or the Nelsons, theirs were the ideals being projected to an entire nation of youth who have since grown up and perpetuated these values in their families, companies, classrooms, and churches. And now we are entrenched in a deep cultural pathology because these notions are wrong, exclusionary, provincial, sexist, and harmful. To properly dislodge them, we have to "remount the slope of thought," in philosopher Henri Bergson's words. We have to return to the roots of our values, backtrack to their point of origin, assess which values serve the common good, and consciously release those that do not foster love and respect for ourselves and others.

Consider what you learned when you were young about authority and who should have it; what you were told about being a male or a female; about people of other cultures, colors, and religions; about the poor; about your body; about your sexuality. Get a visual image of all those moments, when all those values were handed to you, and when you, in your state of pure innocence, received them like commandments carved into stone. No one meant us harm. They were handing down values that were handed to them in the same way, with the same good intentions.

Our parents, our teachers, our ministers, priests, and rabbis were shaping us in their image so that we would fit in, conform to the contours of the established culture. They wanted us to be safe. They were not promoting original thinking, not engaging us in questions of why and how. They were attempting to contain our imaginations so that we wouldn't venture out too far beyond the fold. And step by step, many of us have had to teach ourselves how to think independently, how to let go of harmful beliefs, how to establish our own values based on our life experiences. This is an ongoing process and one that involves a whole systems approach—our minds, our bodies, our feelings, our faith.

With the onslaught of images and information coming our way on a daily basis, original thinking has become an aerobic exercise. It requires a constant opening of the heart which tends to close down in the face of inhumanity. Wanting to protect ourselves from images of starving children, terrorized nations, crime-ridden cities, we resist looking. Our emotions recede into a safer place, denial jams our channels of expression, choking our imagination, and our thoughts become hostage to fear.

The only access we have to our authenticity is the pathway through the heart, and we must keep this channel open, at all costs. We must look deeply into our world, into its heartbreak, into the eyes of our sisters and brothers, and let these images awaken our senses, expand our awareness, and jolt our memories back to the truth of our oneness. It is not altruism, not charity, not selflessness that will open the gates to our own magnitude, transform our propensities for greed into principled generosity. It is awareness. And when awareness is fleshed out in the experience of our lives, it culminates in the event of relationship, of community, and of cooperation.

This is true even in the natural world, as is illustrated by the behavior of slime mold amoeba who live out most of their four-day life spans as single-celled animals in search of bacteria. Since they only move half an inch in twenty-four hours, they quickly devour all the food within reach, so their next strategy is to excrete a hormone-like substance that sends out chemical pulses about eight minutes apart. Other amoebas sense these distress signals and start emitting their own as they move toward the source. As many as a hundred thousand amoebas stream toward each other until they merge into a multicellular "slug" where they share their DNA and create the next generation of offspring. The new amoeba hibernate in spores until they receive signals from nearby food molecules that it is time to end their hibernation and enter the world as single-celled amoebas again. Isolation is death. Relationship is survival, resilience, regeneration.

It is our relationships that sustain us personally—heartening us, empowering us, comforting us. It is our relationships that ground us, support us, inspire us—even in the darkest times. And collectively, as we search for solutions to our global undoing—the poverty that eats at us, the health crises that are decimating populations, the grave imbalances between those who have and those who have not—it will be in relationships that our answers will unfold and our fears subside.

We learn from science, from religion, from the arts that we are intricately connected, but how is this reflected in our myths? Where are the stories of this? Where are the pictures we need to see of ourselves? Where are our mirrors? We are blasting images of American culture around the world that few of us subscribe to or align with. We are saying to the hungry, to the hordes of unemployed, to those we have never helped to educate: "Look here, see how rich we are, see how liberated we are, see all the stuff we have, all the power we have," with no regard, no insight as to what impact this might have on the spirits of those people.

Our world was turned upside down on September 11, 2001, and we cannot right it with old thinking and old behavior. We cannot look behind us for answers. They do not live there. We must *imagine* ourselves forward, envision the world we want to create, and feel the new reality in every cell of our beings *in order to bring it about*—for it is our feelings, our heartfelt emotions, that will inspire the new choices and open our minds to the new solutions. The question is not *what is wrong and how can we fix it?* The question is *what does the world we want to live in look like?*

Until we get a picture of it in our minds, we cannot manifest it. "The image is the device for escaping from the established grid and exploring alternatives," writes philosopher Beatrice Bruteau. If we see it and desire it fully, imagine it fearlessly, hold to it wholeheartedly, despite criticism or opposition from others, then we create the possibility for its being. We become the vessels for its expression, and through us the new will arrive.

Joseph Campbell, in *Myths to Live By*, offers an image for our new myth. He writes:

> We are the children of this beautiful planet. We were not delivered into it by some god, but have come forth from it. We are its eyes and mind, its seeing and its thinking. And the earth, together with its sun, came forth, we are told, from a nebula; and that nebula, in turn, from space. No wonder then, if its laws and our laws are the same. Likewise our depths are the depths of space…We can no longer hold our loves at home and project our aggressions elsewhere; for on this spaceship Earth there is no "elsewhere" any more. And no mythology that continues to speak or to teach of "else-wheres" and "outsiders" meets the requirement of this hour.[9]

The requirement of this hour is an awareness of our oneness. It is openness to a new story that will surface in our lives, our families, our companies, and our communities when we circle together and speak from our hearts. It is a willingness to see ourselves as co-creators of the very world we are immersed in, and to shape with our minds, our hands, our words, and our passions, a world that we want our children to live in. Like the slime mold amoeba, it is only in our merging that we will find our safety, only through communion that we will survive and thrive.

THREE

The Nature of Change

"Spiritual" is not necessarily religion. A spiritual impulse draws a person towards inner meaning, toward the intangible, toward the enhancement of consciousness and the search to serve the dignity of mankind.

JACOB NEEDLEMAN

A new system of philosophy will only be built up by the collective and progressive effort of many thinkers, of many observers also, completing, correcting and improving one another.

HENRI BERGSON

A while ago, I was asked to give a short talk at the opening reception at a hospital where four doctors were exhibiting their photographs. The woman who invited me to speak did so because I have a book entitled *God Is at Eye Level: Photography as a Healing Art,* and she thought it was a good link. A few days before the opening she called to give me a heads-up. "A couple of the doctors are upset because they don't want anyone bringing religion into the picture, and they say their photography has nothing to do with healing. You might want to be careful what you say," she warned.

I arrived at the reception early enough to view all the photographs and was stunned at how moved I was by each body of work. One was a series of black and white images from the same Himalayan mountain range I had trekked in a decade earlier. One group was color landscapes from my favorite place in this country, Canyon de Chelly on the Navajo reservation in Arizona. One was an array of dazzling close-ups of flowers, and another was a series of vibrant murals and portraits from a Hispanic barrio in south San Diego. Every photograph in the exhibition spoke to my heart, aroused my emotions, awakened my joy, and reconnected me to the whole.

When I started to talk, I looked out at the doctors, their arms crossed, their faces stern and inanimate. I was mindful of speaking only about my own process of photographing, not wanting to make any of them uncomfortable. I spoke about photography as my way of grounding myself in the present, about how it's the most healing thing I do, because it roots me in the now, and when I'm there, truly present to just what's before me, I feel a oneness with life. I'm untouched and unfettered by anything past or future—no regrets, no fears, no anxieties—just a kinship with what's at hand. I spoke of my belief that the Divine dwells in the present moment, and when I'm there, I'm safe and I know it.

I shared my reactions to each of the doctor's photographs, commenting on how they awakened my senses, conjured up memories, ignited my imagination and joy. Their images made me feel connected to my world, in awe of its mystery, in love with its flowering. And this, to me, was a holy thing because it made me feel *whole*. And when we *feel* whole, we speak with our whole heart, and what emanates from our being then is a love and authenticity that breaks through any obstacle on its way to the heart of the another. Or as Coleman Barks so poetically puts it, "All the particles of the world are in love and looking for lovers. Pieces of straw tremble in the presence of amber."

As I spoke, I watched the doctors move forward in their seats. I saw their faces soften, their eyes widen. They never knew the power of their work, the healing potential of their images. They never knew that something they created had the power to bring another into wholeness, but when I spoke of it, when they could see that my energy had been affected by their work, something shifted in their thinking. After the talk, one doctor came up to me, took me aside, and said "I could never talk about spirituality in my practice before, but your talk opened something up for me. I saw you come alive when you spoke about the spiritual, about how our photographs actually moved you. It was like a light going off. Your honesty was so compelling and it made me wonder, 'Why do I need to keep that part of me locked up?' I don't think I do anymore."

In turn, the other doctors approached me, one at a time, and said very similar things. They were afraid to talk of the sacred, afraid to use the G-word, afraid of how they might be misunderstood, so they kept silent in the matter. For all those years they followed the rules without questioning, but that evening opened a chink in the wall and another possibility came into being.

Transformation involves a major shift in consciousness that results in a new way of being and acting in the world. It leads to embodied and enacted insight—it is deeper than a revelatory idea which may remain cerebral and particular to the thinker. Transformational thinking is cellular, non-local. It belongs to the whole; it is in service to the whole. Transformation is a human family affair.

It does not happen because we will it or work for it. It comes gratuitously when we clear the passageways between our minds and hearts, when we trust and act upon our bodies' messages, and when we master the art of transcending duality, which simply means that instead of resisting what appears to be "other" we embrace it, bring it into ourselves, and see what transpires when the poles unite. Jungian psychologist and scholar Marie-Louise von Franz wrote: "If we can stay with the tension of opposites long enough—sustain it, be true to it—we can sometimes become vessels within which the divine opposites come together and give birth to a new reality." This is the essence of transformation.

All our lives we have been trained to look for differences, to rebel against ideas that are the opposite of our own, to seek out people who are like ourselves. Who is "the enemy" but someone whose ideas are contrary to ours? This is ordinary thinking and it has gotten us just where we are today. Original thinking is the only thing that will transport us beyond our current state, and it calls for discipline and diligent practice. Original thinking is a thought process that seeks out the opposite in order to incorporate it, to understand it, to embody it, knowing that it is a fusion of the two that creates the new.

The poet Baudelaire said that "true genius is the ability to hold two contradictory thoughts simultaneously without losing your mind." This is step one in the process of transcending duality. You won't lose your mind, but you do have to *use* your mind. Just as we have to exercise and retrain our muscles after periods of non-use, so do we need to exercise and retrain our minds, when they have atrophied into a state of habitual duality. When new learning occurs, it literally changes the architecture of the human brain; hence, the phrase "neurons that fire together, wire together," which is a well-established catch phrase in developmental neuroscience. What we're literally doing when we unite the opposites is rewiring our brains, creating new neural networks, new pathways in the brain, which will re-route us from knee-jerk reactions to heart-based responses. But "the new intelligence, rather than being encoded, forms only by our doing," writes Joseph Chilton Pearce in *The Biology of*

Transcendence.

Rethinking is an important step in the process of transformation, and aligning our feelings and actions with this higher intelligence is equally important. Thought leaders do not present new ideas in a dry, intellectual fashion. They themselves are transformed by the dance of heart and mind, and what ushers forth is an excitement, an energy of confidence that is contagious and convincing because what they are communicating is vital, alive, and most pertinent to these times. Ideas that are born from the union of thought and feeling, that originate out of a desire for synthesis, a diligence to rise above duality, contain within themselves the DNA of transcendence. Carl Jung called emotion the chief source of consciousness. "There is no change from darkness to light or from inertia to movement without emotion," he wrote. The practice of uniting the opposites involves opening the heart as much as the mind. It means feeling our way forward even as we're thinking our way forward, for it is our feelings that rise up like red lights, alerting us to the crossroads of old habits and new choices.

There is a momentary discomfort as we try to find the rightness in another's thinking or perceive the "enemy" as our self. It goes against everything we've ever learned, and it involves the same kind of emotional withdrawal symptoms that come with every attempt to give up an addiction. We are addicted to dualism because every institution of our lives has promoted this kind of thinking, but none of us can call ourselves free until we have rid ourselves of this dangerous habit. The ability to hold two contradictory thoughts simultaneously is not just a matter of true genius; it is a matter of true freedom. If we cannot hear an opposing idea without a negative emotional reaction, we are not free. We are bound to an ideology that we have most likely inherited and never thoroughly examined.

Authentic thought leadership follows on the heels of this kind of radical re-thinking. It is a leadership that is sourced from and rooted in

> *Desire is the need of every unit to extend its experience by combining with its opposite.*
> ALEISTER CROWLEY

> *Opposites are not always contradictions—rather, they may be complementary aspects of a higher truth.*
> LEONARD SCHLAIN

> *Every great idea starts out as a blasphemy.*
> BERTRAND RUSSELL

> *I suddenly realized it's all one, that this magnificent universe is a harmonious, directed, purposeful whole. That we humans, both as individuals and as a species, are an integrated part of the ongoing process of creation.*
> EDGAR MITCHELL

the merging of opposites. Just as a battery is charged by the union of positive and negative forces, just as a child is conceived by the union of a male sperm and female ovum, just as a thought issues forth from the union of right and left brain, so does original thinking emerge from the practice of joining "us" and "them" into a "we." Our imaginations are the most potent engines of change in the universe, and there is no doubt that we can convert our patterns of destruction once we replace our dualistic habits with thought processes that aim at convergence and are informed by compassion.

In this matter, emotions are essential. They are our guide, our body's means of instant messaging to the brain. *Yes, this decision is wise. No, that choice is unwise.* Our bodies are hardwired for survival of the species, and if we listen deeply to them, if we are wise enough to trust the feelings they emanate on our behalf, then we will find the clarity necessary to make inspired choices that are as good for the whole as they are for the one, which is an absolute prerequisite for thought leadership today. And because the work of transforming our own thought processes is so evolutionary an act, it requires the total engagement of body, mind, and spirit. This is not business as usual. This is re-orienting to a new star. Parts of us will balk at the letting go of the old, but it is the only way forward. And when we feel our emotions ruffling at this new attempt toward unity, we should rejoice, actually, for it is a sign that we are fully alive and fully engaged in the great work of trans-formation—personal, at first, but ultimately global.

The following quotations are simple examples of thinking that connects the opposites. See if reading them brings up any feelings. Notice if they cause you joy, or comfort, or if they create a sense of dissonance. Notice if you identify with them, or if they cause you to change your thinking. Try and get used to feeling your feelings to identifying where they are in your body, and imagining what they are trying to communicate to you.

> *Don't aim at success— the more you aim at it and make it a target, the more you are going to miss it. For success, like happiness, cannot be pursued; it must ensue . . . as the unintended side effect of one's personal dedication to a course greater than oneself.*
> VIKTOR FRANKL

> *Nature is not a force over which we must triumph, but the medium of our transformation.*
> MARILYN FERGUSON

> *Emergent consciousness is essentially dialogic.*
> JAMES O'DEA

RELEASING THE PAST

"My barn having burned to the ground, I can now see the moon."
JAPANESE SAYING

"In the depth of winter, I finally learned that within me there lay an invincible Summer." ALBERT CAMUS

"When the ax came into the forest, the trees, upon seeing its wooden handle, said, 'Look, one of us.'" HASSIDIC SAYING

"You gotta have a swine to show you where the truffles are."
EDWARD ALBEE

"Two boys arrived yesterday with a pebble they said was the head of a dog until I pointed out that it was really a typewriter."
PABLO PICASSO

"The opposite of a correct statement is an incorrect statement, but the opposite of a profound truth is another profound truth."
NIELS BOHR

"Participate with joy in the sorrows of the world."
BUDDHIST PRINCIPLE

"The question of bread for myself is a material question, but the question of bread for my neighbor is a spiritual question."
NIKOLAI BERDYAEV

"The dividing line between good and evil passes, not between the other and me, but right down the middle of my forehead, between my left side and my right." LANZO DEL VASTO

"In spite of everything I still believe that people are really good at heart." ANNE FRANK

"Pay attention to what they tell you to forget."
MURIEL RUCKEYSER

Transformation is like the opening of a prison door, allowing us to see what we could not see before because we were locked into certain beliefs and habits. Millions of women experienced this during the days of consciousness-raising when they suddenly realized that the personal is political; that who they were and how they felt about themselves was shaped by cultural, political, and religious institutions that benefited from keeping women in certain roles. It wasn't until women started meeting in small groups and sharing their stories that they discovered the problem was more external than internal, and as systemic as it was local. "The enemy has outposts in our heads," was an oft-repeated phrase.

Women's very thought processes had been infected and the remedy was two-fold: first came the telling of the stories, the careful listening, the incremental shifts from self-censorship to self-expression to self-aware-ness to self-determination. Next came the action, the mobilization, the campaigns to equalize the power and bring some yin to the yang of the corporate and cultural table.

This, of course, met with resistance, and the media made a mockery of these women whose resolve to create a better world for everyone was belittled and undermined by such phrases as "bra burners," and "angry feminists." Forty some years later, many women hesitate to call them-selves "feminists" because that very term is a label that pushes buttons and puts up walls, but it cannot be denied that what came to life out of those living room gatherings—out of all those stories and sobs and anger and disenchantment—was a full-blown social movement that led to an overhaul of American consciousness.

And it is this kind of transformation, of social evolution, that we are in the midst of now, though it is more oblique, more implicit and unquantified, because it is happening in the inner milieu of ideas, values, perceptions, emotions. As a culture, we have not developed many tools for measuring the inner realms, though it is there that every move-ment for change is conceived and gestates until it is delivered into the world as an embodied idea, an independent force with its own shape and substance.

In the late 1990s, a number of various social organizations came together in protest against global trade agreements that they feared would exploit the poor and harm the earth. What drove them together was a shared value, a commitment to keep the body politic and our home planet from harm. They were not against profit, not against progress or the international exchange of technology and talent. They were taking a stand against thoughtlessness, against greed, against the implementation of regulations that might pave the way for corporate abuse or irresponsibility. To cite an example from nature, their actions were akin to the oyster's when a foreign substance, such as a grain of sand, enters its body.

To protect its soft inner body against intrusion, the oyster takes defensive action and its cells secrete a smooth and hard substance, called nacre, around the irritant. This nacre is composed of microscopic crystals, and because each crystal is aligned perfectly with every other one, the light passing along the axis of one is reflected and refracted by the others to produce a rainbow of light and color. For years, the oyster continues to secrete this crystalline substance around the irritant until it is totally encased and ultimately transformed into a lustrous gem called a pearl.

The protesters were like the nacre, bringing their consciousness to bear on deliberations that could affect the lives of billions of people. As they circled the building where the trade agreements were being discussed, they were encasing the irritant, which was, to them, an imbalance of representation and a governing body with no checks or balances. What they were calling for is inclusion in the conversation, the ability to add "*people*" and "*the planet*" to an agenda they feared was solely about "*profit.*"

If we carry the analogy further, imaging these protesters as those microscopic crystals, aligning perfectly, passing their light along from one to another, reflecting and refracting ideas in such a way that they become a rainbow of luminous thought, then we can envision the possibility of this light force transforming what was once an "irritant" into a "pearl of great price." It is this kind of imagining that surfaces in the act of original thinking. There is no longer the old "we're right, they're wrong" conclusion, but a stretching into wholeness that surpasses duality. Original thinking employs the opposites; it starts with duality but doesn't stop until it has brought the two forces together, culminating in a creative combustion that dissolves dissonance and creates a higher order.

Transformation ushers forth from the reconciliation of opposites. What caused the shift in thinking for the doctor photographers? When they came into the room, they were stone-faced and resolute, resistant to the notion that their work had anything to do with healing or spirituality. When I talked about the impact of their work on me, I said how healing it was *because* it moved me spiritually and emotionally. And because I talked about my feelings, they trusted and believed me—their work *was* healing and it *did* have a spiritual quality. The unfolding of this awareness is what caused their bodies to relax, their faces to loosen up. This collision of oppositional ideas sparked a transformation not just in their minds, but in their bodies as well. And in their actions, for each of them mentioned it, and thanked me for it.

And it was a similar collision of ideas that led to the transformation of all those women who unified and became a social force that turned American culture upside down. Initially, the inner voices were cruel and self-defeating: *I'm not good enough; I don't deserve happiness; I'm not powerful or smart; I don't deserve equal rights, equal pay.* We heard these lines over and over until some women started saying just the opposite, in books, in speeches, in public, and at great risk. And when the force of these bold statements met with the force of their own self-deprecating statements, there was a combustion powerful enough to spark a revolution.

A revolution in compassion began in San Diego, California after the murder of a twenty-year-old Muslim man, Tarik Khamisa, by a fourteen-year-old gang member. International financial consultant Azim Khamisa said that the news of his son's death was like the detonation of a nuclear bomb inside his heart. "What is different about this story is that while I obviously had compassion for my son, somehow in my heart I felt compassion for the fourteen-year-old who took my son's life. There were victims at both ends of the gun—Tarik, a victim of Tony, and Tony, a victim of society," said Khamisa in a recent interview.

Nine months after losing his son, Khamisa started a foundation in his son's honor, and at the first meeting, the assistant District Attorney who had handled his son's case was present. Khamisa asked the ADA to be introduced to Ples Felix, Tony's guardian and grandfather, and they eventually met in the Public Defender's office. "I told him I didn't feel any animosity toward him or his grandson, that I was concerned about him and all the other kids who are growing up in this violent world, and that I started this foundation to help provide some solutions. I invited him to the second meeting and we've been working together now for ten years," said Khamisa.

"The first feeling I had was really jubilant rejoicing because it was the answer to my prayers," said Felix, a former Green Beret who did two tours of duty in Viet Nam. "When I first found out that my grandson was responsible for murdering an innocent soul, I began immediately to pray for the Khamisa family, and for the opportunity to meet them so I could express my sympathy and commit myself to them, to help in any way I could with the loss. When the time came, I felt nervous and uncertain, but when I looked into Azim's eyes, I didn't see hatred, or any of the things you'd expect to see from a man who lost his son at the hands of my grandson. He shook my hand, told me his plans for the foundation, and asked if I would join him."

Since then, the Tarik Khamisa Foundation has worked with over 350,000 gang-age youth teaching them conflict resolution and alternatives to violence. Tony and Azim have met face to face and Azim has offered him a job at the foundation when Tony gets out of prison. Both Ples and Azim write to Tony frequently, and so do hundreds of schoolchildren who write to say that seeing him take responsibility for what he did has helped them to re-think violence, to stay away from gangs, and to make better choices.

"By saving Tony, which in my heart of hearts I know we will, think about how many kids Tony will save," said Khamisa. And it is not just children, but adults as well, who have been similarly transformed by the actions of these two men. When they went to receive the prestigious Common Ground Award in Washington, D.C., Azim was approached by a woman whose son was also murdered. "How do you forgive them?" she asked, admitting that she was struggling to find compassion in her heart.

Azim responded by saying there were three major parts to forgiveness: first, acknowledge that you've been wronged; second, give up all the resulting resentment; and finally, reach out to the perpetrator with love and compassion. "Then the woman met Ples and you could see the electricity," he said. "Later the woman wrote me, saying it was because of Ples and you that I have reached out to the family of my son's perpetrator. Thank you for the healing."

This is transformation. This is thinking originally—saying no to conditioned responses that keep us ensnared in the trap of duality, and saying yes to what appears to be "other." It is the synthesis of the two that will fire up our neurons and carve new pathways in our global brain. As the great mystic Meister Eckhart wrote: "The whole scattered world of lower things is gathered up to oneness when the soul climbs up to that life in which there are no opposites." It is a Himalayan climb, to be sure, but there are millions on the path, and what a view.

Questioning Our Assumptions

No one person can answer the question of meaning in this world today. It is in thinking together, under strong conditions of serious search, that a new understanding can be approached. Group communication, group pondering, is the real art form of our time.

JACOB NEEDLEMAN

If we cannot express our assumptions explicitly in ways that others can understand and build upon, there can be no larger process of testing those assumptions and building public knowledge.

PETER SENGE

An American businessman was visiting a Mexican coastal village and encountered a fisherman on the dock. He had just unloaded his stash of tuna for the day, and the businessman asked him how long it took him to catch them.

The fisherman said, "Just a little while."

The businessman then asked why he didn't stay out longer and catch more, to which the fisherman responded he didn't need more. He had caught enough for his family's needs.

"But what do you do now, with all the rest of your time?" asked the businessman.

"I take a nap, I play with my children, take siesta with my wife, Maria, and I walk to the village in the evening, sip a little wine, and play music with my friends," said the fisherman.

The American scoffed. "I am a Harvard MBA and could help you. You should spend more time fishing and with the proceeds buy a bigger boat. With the proceeds from the bigger boat, you could buy a fleet of boats and open your own cannery. You would control the product, processing, and distribution. You would need to leave this small village and move to Mexico City, then Los Angeles, and eventually New York, where you would run your expanding enterprise."

When the fisherman asked how long all that would take, the businessman said, "Fifteen to twenty years. And then you could sell your company stock to the public and become a millionaire."

"But what then?" asked the fisherman.

"Then you could retire, move to a coastal fishing village, fish a little, nap a lot, play with your kids, enjoy time with your wife, and go to the village at night to play music with your friends."[1]

This is an example of how our assumptions tumble out of us, beckoned or not. We enter into a situation, assess it from our own personal worldview, and generously offer suggestions for improvement that were never invited in the first place. In *The Fifth Discipline*, Peter Senge writes: "Mental models are deeply ingrained assumptions that influence how we understand the world and how we take action. We do not "have" mental models. We "are" our mental models...The discipline of working with mental models starts with turning the mirror inward; learning to unearth our internal pictures of the world, to bring them to the surface and hold them rigorously to scrutiny."

Turning the mirror inward is a required discipline for original thinkers, since the primary labor of originality is to unearth the insight that is unique to us. Our experiences and relationships are the wellsprings of our embodied and embedded wisdom. The piece of knowledge that we hold is different from what anyone else holds since none other has felt our feelings, loved what we loved, suffered what we suffered. And once we learn to mine these experiences, to process them with an understanding that they have led us to where we are today— once we are willing to forgive what we must forgive, to clear ourselves and others of guilt or blame—then we are free to harvest the jewels of insight that await us like butter within the cream.

Most of us don't even know what our assumptions are until we see what actions emerge from their engagement. If anyone had asked the businessman on the dock what were his assumptions, he probably wouldn't have had an answer. But from his actions, we can see that he assumed he knew more than the fisherman; he assumed the fisherman wanted to make more money; he assumed that the life the fisherman had created for himself and his family was somehow lacking or broken, and he knew how to fix it.

Underpinning every action we take is an assumption that we've incorporated from somewhere, consciously or not. The common phrase "you can't fight city hall" comes from an assumption of personal powerlessness and bureaucratic impenetrability. It is neither true nor empowering, but it is such a part of our social vernacular that many people have come to believe it. And once we buy into a belief that supports our own powerlessness, something dies in us. Our vitality diminishes, our imaginations dull, the excitement of experiencing ourselves as creators of our circumstances turns to a dread and fear of being victims of our circumstances.

Individuals, organizations, and businesses operate on assumptions that are rarely conscious, but that affect their outcomes in major ways. Questioning our own assumptions or the assumptions running rampant through our organizations is key to understanding why we're getting the responses we're getting from the people we encounter, our employees, or our customers. To think this has nothing to do with the bottom line is naïve and short-sighted. Robert Reich, former Secretary of Labor, spent a lot of time visiting different businesses and talking with the employees. "When they used the word 'they,' I knew it was one kind of business," said Reich. "When they used the word 'we,' I knew it was a whole other kind of business."

"You can see the corporation as a machine for producing money, or you can see it as a human community," according to Senge, but if you prefer the community idea, you want people to be saying "we." And in order to foster this sensibility of community, every leader in the organization has to believe it, feel it, be it, and speak it. And underneath this must be a foundational assumption that is so rooted in reality that no one can mistake it. If you *do* assume that people are honest, that they give their best when they are most encouraged, that any expenditure of resources for their well-being will result in work and attitudes that benefit the organization, then those assumptions will be apparent in your actions and you will be seen as a person of integrity. If those are not your assumptions, but you try to act as if they are, your dishonesty will be discerned immediately.

We become the most powerful communicators when every word and action is consistent with our root assumptions, so for us to be clear on what they are, and to help others clarify what theirs are, is a critical part of thought leadership and original thinking. When Socrates said, "The unexamined life is not worth living," this is the kind of unraveling and examining he was talking about. It's coming to terms with what you think is true about human nature, about your own possibilities, about your power in the matters of cause and creativity. Believing is seeing, and what we believe to be true ends up being the very reality we enter into. In the play *My Fair Lady*, the transformation of Eliza Doolittle was directly related to Henry Higgins' dual assumptions: one, his own power to make a difference; and two, her power to make a change. This phenomenon plays out in every classroom, living room, and boardroom as we enable or disable the people in our midst based on the assumptions that fuel our words and actions. Here are a few questions that will help you see some of your underlying assumptions:

Do you believe that what you do really matters?

Do you believe you're doing your fair share to make this a better world for everyone?

Do you believe if something goes wrong there's someone to blame?

Do you believe that it's profitable for businesses to be socially responsible?

Do you believe that people have faith in you?

Do you believe that someone else is responsible for your successes or failures?

Do you believe that people can see your values by watching what you do?

Do you believe that your words and actions can empower or disempower another?

Do you believe that your children are well-served by the choices you make?

Do you believe that if you died tomorrow, you would go with pride knowing you had done the best you could have done?

These are the kinds of questions that help us unearth our assumptions so we can rout out those that were imposed upon us, or that we once held to but no longer believe. We are organisms in a constant state of flux, exposed to an ever-changing environment, and the more we inquire into our own state of consciousness and notice the evolution of our own ideas, the more aware we become of our place in the family of things. As a civilization, we are shifting out of an industrial, assembly-line mindset of isolated units into an organic, knowledge-based network of communities. There is a tectonic shift of consciousness occurring and an evolutionary tendency away from the mechanical and back toward the natural. This may be seen as Mother Nature's mid-course correction. As the thinking neurons of the planet, biologically oriented toward survival, we are finding ways of connecting and communicating with unimaginable speed and precision. Someone has calculated that we can globally transmit the contents of the Library of Congress across a single fiber optic line in 1.6 seconds. Science and nature have announced their engagement.

In his book, *Birth of the Chaordic Age,* Dee Hock, founder of the largest commercial enterprise on earth—Visa International—writes about the founding of an organization that is owned by 22,000 member banks who both compete with each other for 750 million customers and cooperate by honoring one another's $1.25 trillion in transactions annually across global borders and currencies. The resistance he encountered in the early stages was the equivalent of "city hall," but Hock did not hold the assumption that he couldn't fight it. "When it becomes necessary to develop a new perception of things, a new internal model of reality, the problem is never to get new ideas in, the problem is to get the old ideas out," he writes. "The future is not about logic and reason. It's about imagination, hope, and belief."

Dee Hock is a visionary whose assumptions, commitments, and successes inspire people to think about the whole, to act like our actions matter. He reminds us that parts have meaning only in reference to a greater whole in which everything is related to everything else. "Never again should management accounting be seen as a tool to drive people with measures. Its purpose must be to promote inquiry into the relationships, patterns, and processes that give rise to accounting measures." It is time to envision and implement new forms of ownership and financial systems; time to address the "gross maldistribution of wealth and power, degradation of people, and desolation of the ecosphere, or our stories will be increasingly immoral and destructive," Hock writes.

Every original thinker today is urging a rethinking of the entire system, a retooling of the corporate imagination and the organizational mind so that the products and processes we develop and export around the world support growth, not just financially, but personally, socially, and spiritually. A self-renewing organization is created and sustained only by self-renewing individuals, self-renewing relationships, and self-renewing cultures. The question upon us is not whether our problems are personal, organizational, or systemic. They are all of the above, and the real challenge is to stay mindful of their connectedness.

Part of the evolutionary thrust toward wholeness is a dissolution of borders—the borders between our body, mind, and spirit; the borders between our colleagues and ourselves; the borders between organizations, businesses, nations. Newtonian science and the Industrial Revolution turned the whole into a jigsaw puzzle of parts, and the quantum science of today is reassembling the pieces. In tandem with the rising globalization of industry is a burgeoning globalization of intelligence that is committed to serving the whole. When any part of the corporate body acts out of alignment, this network of intelligence sends out an alert and millions of cells mobilize—just as it is in our individual bodies. If you cut your finger, every system and cell activates to initiate pain relief and healing. With globalization, we are witnessing a living example of a whole systems approach to the well-being of the body politic.

While there once was an assumption that corporations could fly safely under the public radar, we now have a global posse of networked bloggers, citizen advocates, writers, and activists tracking down culprits of corporate misbehavior and posting their crimes in the non-local press of the World Wide Web. Instantaneously, news of transgressions passes across every border like lightning, and action campaigns are mounted at the drop of a hat. While this looks adversarial at first glance, we can also view it as an evolutionary self-healing function. If the survival of the whole organism is at stake, these are self-correcting actions of the parts.

Consider the concept of Corporate Social Responsibility (CSR). It's an age-old topic, but there's a new momentum growing as the band width of the global brain expands and a regard for the environment and all things human seems only smart and worthy of attention. According to the *Christian Science Monitor*, almost one in three of America's top one hundred companies reported on their social progress this year, up from the handful of five years ago. The United States, however, still lags behind Britain, where 71 percent of top companies presented social-progress reports, and more than half of those came with an assurance from an independent monitor.[2] Only one in a hundred American reports was submitted with verification from an independent auditor, which is an expensive proposition, but a true indicator of corporate character.

Today, the Corporate Social Responsibility Newswire Service (csrwire.com) announces many weekend-long CSR conferences in Sydney, Frankfurt, Denver, Jakarta, Chicago, Quebec, Paris, New York City, Boston, Washington, DC, and Bedford, UK and those are just between August and November. There's a Corporate Social Responsibility Academy in London (csracademy.org.uk) with a running repertoire of companies who've attended that reads like a "Who's Who" of successful businesses.

The Social Investment Forum published a *Report of Socially Responsible Investing Trends in the United States* in December 2003 that revealed a total of $2.16 trillion under professional management involved in socially responsible investment strategies—nearly four times the $639 billion that the Forum identified in 1995.[3] Stephen J. Schueth, President of First Affirmative Financial Network, LLC, writes in the newsletter *SRI in the US* that the growth of socially screened portfolios has risen over 183 percent in the last two years. "Wall Street did not cook this one up," he writes. "The impressive growth of socially responsible investing is primarily consumer-driven."

Schueth attributes this to a variety of factors, including the erosion of trust in corporate leadership, the growing reach of social research organizations that has led to more informed investors, a yearning among investors to integrate personal values into all aspects of life, the growing availability of socially responsible investment options, and the rising influx of women in the workforce who, he says, "have brought a natural affinity for the concept of socially responsible investing with them."

Perhaps most significant is the recent evidence challenging the assumption that socially responsible investing is linked with underperformance. In fact, the reverse is true. According to an article in a recent *Business Ethics* magazine, research is showing that "a lack of social responsibility has a negative effect on stock price."[4] In 2004, a meta-study of fifty-two studies over thirty years proved a significant positive association between corporate social performance and financial performance.[5] An international social research firm, Innovest Strategic Value Advisors, found that forest and paper products companies with above-average environmental performance had 43 percent better share price performance over four years than competitors with below-average environmental ratings. And in the oil and gas sector, the top environmentally rated businesses outperformed others in share price by 12 percent over three years.

In academia, social issues are making inroads into business school programs and some universities are offering joint masters degree programs between their business and environmental schools. Nine of the top ten business schools organized conferences and seminars on social issues, ethics, and leadership. One graduate from the University of Michigan Business School just landed a job as "corporate social responsibility associate" at Ford Motor Company. Thirteen hundred MBA students around the nation have founded one hundred chapters of Net Impact: New Leaders for Better Business, a business student organization dedicated to social and environmental responsibility.

Milt Moskowitz, co-author of the annual *Fortune* magazine survey, "The 100 Best Companies to Work for in America," has been writing about CSR since 1968. In an article for Trillium's 2005 Summer Newsletter, he brought to light two recent reports that bear witness to the impact our thoughts and actions are having. GE's 2005 Citizenship Report includes announcements that GE will not pursue business opportunities in Myanmar because of this country's "history of human rights violations." Moskowitz notes that one-third of GE's officers and 40 percent of its senior executives are women, US minorities, and non-US citizens, which is in itself, a sign of inspired leadership. GE is also requiring its suppliers to comply with environmental, health, safety, and labor standards, and they have terminated two hundred suppliers for failing to improve performance in these areas.

Accolades also went to Nike, a company that initially stonewalled protests against its factory working conditions in Asia when they first surfaced. Nike employs over 650,000 workers in Asia and has since developed a Code of Conduct that bars child labor, respects the right of employees to form unions, and requires factory owners to provide safe and healthy workplaces—all signs that public opinion matters in

The leadership we need next cannot try to escape the complexity of the world but has to develop a capacity for effectiveness that acknowledges that the fundamental reality is one of inherent unity. That's why the primary revolution that we need is a spiritual revolution as opposed to a political or economic one.
LEO BURKE,
DIRECTOR OF EXECUTIVE EDUCATION, UNIVERSITY OF NOTRE DAME

Wall Street should judge companies on the kind of world they support, not just financial returns.
JOAN BAVARIA,
CEO TRILLIUM

Our destiny is not the accumulation of money; it is the expansion of soul.
THOMAS BERRY

the long run.

Why all these examples? Because original thinkers are up against a wall of cynicism these days, and stories of success are a good antidote to knee-jerk negativity. In the past few weeks, I have encountered no less than ten businessmen who have resolutely proclaimed the following: "Forget about making change. The only thing people care about is money. You can't trust a corporation to do the right thing. Money is the bottom line. You might as well get used to it. Corporations are poisoning the planet. There's nothing real about CSR; it's just a façade. The world is not going to make it."

These are the kinds of assumptions that are blowing across the cultural landscape like the prevailing westerlies, and we need to prepare ourselves for them just as we would prepare for the onslaught of a hurricane or tornado. Our response to the unrest in the world has been one of fear and tension. The greatest mystery of our age—our own inhumanity toward each other—cannot be solved by science and is sadly often perpetuated by religious zealots. The tragedy of this is so profound and inexplicable, that multitudes of people are simply closing down to the possibility of turning it around. Forgetting their own power as agents of change, they are hardening their hearts against the pain and unconsciously perpetuating it with phrases like, "That's just the way it is. There's nothing you can do about it." A host of others are caving in to feelings of anxiety and powerlessness and relying on medication for relief.

I sat at a table with four highly respected professional women the other night and three said they were now taking anti-depressants just to "take the edge off." A study published in *Psychiatric Services* claims that pre-schoolers in the US are the fastest-growing market for antidepressants. At least four percent of them, over a million, are clinically depressed.[6]

What are we to make of these turbulent times? Some of us lash out, some of us recede, some of us cry, others of us shout—but the greatest resource any of us have is the resource of

Consider that man may be defined as a being who is constructed to receive a gift of unfathomable immensity and is, at the same time, obliged to pay for that gift with unfathomable commitment and service.
JACOB NEEDLEMAN

It is our responsibility to design social systems that are in alignment with the tendency in nature toward higher consciousness, greater freedom, and more synergistic order.
BARBARA MARX HUBBARD

What we might like to call the truth is often made up of several truths, including the first thing we thought, its opposite, and something in between.
MARY GORDON

our own awareness and the stories we can hold to that remind us of the light. To look upon our country, our communities, our neighborhoods with an awareness of everyone's vulnerability is a great gift and service. To speak to this, to speak *of* this, is an even greater service. We need to hear the story of how we've been here before, at a precipice like this, and always managed to make it home safely. This is our nature. We survive on our stories.

So let us remember the history of our making. Let us recall, in public, our power to enchant, to inspire, to attract, to transform. Let's say to each other, "Tell the one about…" and "Don't forget the time…" Let's forget the assumptions that betray our hugeness. Let's have a great story in our pocket for every time we meet a naysayer or encounter a soul who's lost in the dark. And let's pile them up like nickels and dimes, currency against the forces of fear.

Let's remember the photographer Dorothea Lange, who passed right by that sign *Migrant Camp* on her way home from work, exhausted as she was and lame in one leg. Let's remember how she drove on another twelve miles, until she turned around and headed back, thinking something might be there that could make a difference. And how that photograph of the mother, harried and worn, with her kids clinging to her, made it to the wall in some museum and was spotted by a writer named John Steinbeck. And how moved he was by the Dust Bowl story that Dorothea told frame by frame—so moved that he wanted to pass it along and wrote the famous *Grapes of Wrath*. And how, when this book was in the hands of movie director John Ford, it led him to think it ought to be a film, so he found a screenwriter and made it happen. And once the film was seen by America, its heart was broken to see its own face so creased and saddened. So the theater-goers rallied, they appealed to Congress, they said "something must be done," and they made it happen. Legislation was enacted that turned the tides for the Dust Bowl farmers and the families who were starving through the Great Depression.

And there's the story of Peter Gabriel watching the video footage of Rodney King. In an article in *Yes!* magazine, writer Dana Hughes unfolds the tale in a way that inspires the reader as much as informs. When the British musician saw King being beaten by Los Angeles police officers on the evening news, he thought of other abuses around the world and how video could be used to spread the word that something must be done. Together with Human Rights First (formerly Lawyers Committee on Human Rights) and the Reebok Human Rights Foundation, Peter

Gabriel launched Witness, an organization that provided cameras and assistance to people willing to record human rights violations in their own communities.

Witness started with a budget of $150,000 and a staff of two. In 1996 they helped Global Survival Network produce *Bought and Sold,* a documentary on the Russian mafia's involvement in the trafficking of women from the former Soviet Union. Footage of this was picked up by ABC, BBC, and CNN and became a front page story in the *New York Times.* In response, President Clinton allocated $10 million to fight violence against women, with special emphasis on trafficking. Secretary of State Madeleine Albright put it on the agenda in her meetings with heads of state, and in 2000 the United Nations passed a transnational protocol to prevent trafficking. The US Congress also passed the Trafficking Victims Protections Act that year.

Following the success of the *Bought and Sold* campaign, Witness, under the directorship of Gillian Caldwell, installed a full-time production and editing facility on site and the number of its in-house productions increased from three to thirty in two years. Their website (www.witness.org) features "Rights Alert," webcasts that highlight footage from partner organizations with accompanying narratives and suggestions for action. They have gone from one hundred hits a month in 1998 to 1.5 million hits a month today. As the group's visibility has increased, the number of Witness partners has grown by more than forty in the past four years, and they have expanded their focus from civil rights to include social, economic, and cultural rights as well.

Dorothea Lange, one person. Peter Gabriel, one person. And what was the source of their inspiration? Tragedy. They were witnesses to the inhumane, face to face with the brokenness of individuals that revealed a deeper cavern of decay in the culture at large. But they did not deny it; they did not run from it; they did not fold their arms and pontificate about how it's always going to be like this. They took the tragedy into themselves and transformed it into another form—a piece of art, a collaborative vision, a work that would go on working. And what they created has changed our world.

This is the very work of a thought leader—to look out at our beautiful world and see the paradox that resides there, and to be, in the face of that, a builder of bridges. It is to hear the skepticism all around us, to listen to the critics and not be silenced, because underlying everything is the most basic of assumptions: *that who we are and what we do does matter.*

If a story can move you from thought to action, then you know the power of a well-told tale. If another's action has ever inspired you, then you know that your action can inspire another. This is a knowing that carries a force, for it comes from the crucible of our own experience and cannot be undone by another's doubt. To live from this place, to exude this confidence, to see the light on the near horizon and harvest great stories from the daily news, this is the challenge of original thinking, and these are the talents of a true thought leader.

FIVE

What the World Needs Now

The more evolved you are, the more of the universe is in your view.
YASUHIKO KIMURA

We receive the light, then we impart the light. Thus we repair the world.
KABBALAH

In 1982, a group of five activists in Syracuse, New York sat around a card table in the living room of Dik Cool and asked themselves, "What can we do? What's needed now? What do we want for ourselves?" The nation was awash in anxiety as the superpowers amassed massive arsenals of nuclear weapons, outdoing each other's capacity to destroy the world many times over. The group of thirty-somethings had experience in corporate America, religious communities, publishing, the peace and women's movements, the art world, and the local university. They considered themselves agents of change. There was no doubt that they could make a difference, but where did they want to make it, and how did they want to work together?

After a few sessions, the group organized itself as a publisher and distributor of artwork that would offer an alternative vision to a world besieged with images of destruction. They named themselves the Syracuse Cultural Workers (SCW), and on good-faith credit from a local print shop, they published three thousand Peace Calendars, with images of demonstrations for disarmament that were occurring around the world. With those proceeds, they paid the printer and went on to publish artistic posters, datebooks, and note cards that drew attention to global issues of social justice. They compiled a catalog of these items to announce themselves as publishers in the business of peace and justice, and put the word out to artists across the country that they were looking for and paying for "art with a social conscience."

SCW asked artists to incorporate into their creative processes an awareness and sensibility about our global relatedness. A list of issues went out in a call to artists to stimulate their thinking and prime their creative pumps, and soon artwork addressing every global issue started filling the mailbox. Work poured in that put a face to apartheid, racism, child slavery, the Sandinista movement, the Israeli-Palestinian conflict, environmentalism, endangered species, pollution and water issues. Syracuse Cultural Workers had created a need for a body of artistic work that said something about our world, responded to its urgencies, and imagined something different in the place of war and hunger and violence.

The business was a muse of mindfulness to artists around the country, asking them to conjure up imagery based on the political and cultural particularities of the time. They were invited to create, from within their own depths, a vision of another way, another world. And now, there are artists around the world in the SCW network imagining differently, looking at the world through different lenses, and producing images that bear witness to the tragedies and triumphs of the human family.

What the Syracuse Cultural Workers wanted for themselves was to create work that was as inspiring to them as it was to the world. They wanted work that engaged their whole beings, that served them as it served others, and that filled a need that was not being met. And twenty-four years later they are still at it, only now in their own building and with a full time staff of sixteen cultural workers. At their weekly meetings, before every agenda review, they take time for personal sharing, so that everyone has a chance to be heard, to acknowledge any difficulties, to show up in their entirety and know they are being seen. As important to them as the production of artwork is the creation of a community that feels like home. "We're in business to do well, but we also know that the wellness of the group is intrinsic to our success," said Dik Cool, president of SCW, in a recent interview. He quoted Daniel Ellsberg who said during the anti-war days, "Most of what you do will have little effect on ending the war, but it is essential that you do it."

"There's no way to quantify the impact we're having, but from all the letters that come in every day, I know we're making a difference," said Cool. "Everyone who works here believes deeply in what they're doing, and that's what defines our corporate culture. We're working collectively to contribute to a better world, responding to a need that is real, and I think our success has everything to do with the power and passion of that commitment."

SCW has a policy where the highest salary cannot be more than two times the amount of the lowest salary, and they pay one hundred percent of every employee's health premiums. Contrast this with the current CEO-worker pay gap of 458 to 1. What is it in our collective consciousness that allows an executive to earn so much more than the employees of a company, even when those employees live with the threat of being outsourced and shareholders' dividends diminish by the week? From 1980 to 1990, the gap only doubled, from 45:1 to 90:1. What has caused this hundredfold leap in twenty five years? Author and journalist Holly Sklar reports that Yahoo's CEO Terry Semel earned more than $4 million a week in 2004, even though Yahoo! is on the *Lou Dobbs Tonight* list of companies outsourcing American jobs. "It would take the pay of 7,075 average American workers to match the pay of Yahoo's CEO," writes Sklar. And the CEO of the nation's leading insurer, UnitedHealth Group, made enough to cover the average health premiums of nearly 34,000 people. Adjusting for inflation, American workers earned eleven percent less than they made in 1973, though their productivity rose seventy-eight percent in the same time period.[1]

Facts like these are grist for the creative mill. They are signs of our national waywardness, invitations for a kind of thought leadership that addresses the unacceptable inequities that abound in our culture and establishes a pathway to a higher, level ground. The art of original thinking calls for equal portions of humility and courage, introspection and outward action, self-awareness and self-transcendence. It is an art whose form is openness and whose function is service. Original thinking takes us back to our common roots and forward to our common needs and rights and responsibilities to each other as citizens of a great nation and planet. It is not the task of thought leaders to know the answers, but to articulate the questions we face as a people and to call us together to create our solutions.

This is the potential of corporate America—to re-think their structures and processes in such a way that they become furnaces of inspiration, centers of creative ingenuity, arbiters of a culture conscious enough to bring the whole human family into the picture. The profits from such an endeavor—materially, culturally, spiritually—could over-whelm the most skeptic imagination. In a recent article, Howard Bloom, author of *Global Brain* and *The Lucifer Principle*, writes:

> Imagine what it would be like if at every staff meeting you were expected to put the care of the multitudes we mistakenly call "consumers" first. Imagine what it would be like to go to work each morning in a company that saw your passions as your greatest engines, your curiosities as your fuel, and your idealism as the pistons of your labors and of your soul. Imagine what it would be like if your superiors told you that the ultimate challenge was to tune your empathic abilities so you could sense the needs of your firm's customers even before those customers quite knew what they hankered after.[2]

Notice your response to these suggestions. Did you toss them off as ludicrous? Did you think they could never work in the business world? Did you feel enlivened at the prospect? One characteristic of original thinking is the ability to entertain new ideas with an open mind and an open heart. Openness is the operative word, since that is where the line is drawn between traditional and original thinking. Thought leaders open themselves to new questions. They come at challenges from the future, not the past. They are not asking, "How can we get more?" They are asking, "What is needed now? How can we give more?"

Thought leaders do not think in terms of "me" and "mine." They think in terms of "we" and "ours." They do not *think* outside the box, they *live* outside the box. No matter what their address, they think of themselves as global citizens, responsible to the earth, responsible to the human family, and aware that their well-being is tied to the well-being of others. They are balanced and in tune with their own inner life, and they are awake to the immense possibilities that erupt when the inner lives and imaginations of their colleagues are fully engaged.

People today are looking for meaning, for work that matters, for ways to be of use. We want our hearts to be engaged as much as our minds and hands, and this happens through relationships, in creative communities where the questions about what to produce and how to produce it are influenced by the deeper questions of what is needed and who needs it. It doesn't matter if you're the CEO of a multinational corporation, an inner-city teacher, a religious leader, or a traveling sales-person—you take in the world every day through your five senses and it is telling you something. You are hearing the needs of your community, your family, and your world on a daily basis, and the meaning you are searching for in your life is directly related to your response to these needs.

Viktor Frankl, Holocaust survivor and author of *Man's Search for Meaning*, writes: "We needed to stop asking about the meaning of life, and instead to think of ourselves as those who were being questioned by life—daily and hourly. Our answer must consist, not in talk and meditation, but in right action and in right conduct. Life ultimately means taking the responsibility to find the right answer to its problems and to fulfill the tasks which it constantly sets for each individual."[3]

The tasks which are set for us now, as co-creators of this global civilization, are the tasks of doing no harm, of using the natural resources of our energy and creativity for the common good, and of uplifting the poor in whatever ways we can. These are the moral imperatives of this time, and thought leaders in all professions are incorporating these mandates in the agendas they are promoting. Right action and right conduct leads us directly to the right answers that Frankl refers to. We are not being naïve when we ask ourselves: *What is life asking of us today? What do we have to contribute? How can we make this offering in a way that sustains us as it enlivens others?* We are not being liberal or conservative. We are opening ourselves to the greatest imaginative challenge, increasing our chances of success exponentially by matching our gifts with the needs of the world. This is the work that inspires greatness, engages the soul, and transforms the workplace from a labor camp to a laboratory of human possibility. Someone once said that "we are not hungry for what we are not getting; we are hungry for what we are not giving." Reframing our questions around what is needed offers us a smorgasbord of ideas to feast on.

When it comes to uplifting the poor, it turns out that businesses, with their drive for efficiency and cost-effectiveness, often do a better job of bringing the underprivileged into the world economy than the slow-moving bureaucracies of government and international aid programs. Many corporations are finding win-win solutions as they retool their imaginations in an effort to market their goods and services to the four billion poorest people on earth.

In an article in *Ode* magazine, Senior Economist C. K. Prahalad and World Resources Institute vice-president Allen L. Hammond suggest that "turning the poor into customers and consumers is a far more effective way of reducing poverty."[4] Helping the poor to participate in the global market is a way of offering them choices they never had. Teaching people how to fish is much more effective than handing out halibut, and while perpetuating a culture of consumerism is not the goal, there are thousands of ways to build relationships with the poor that are rewarding—politically, psychologically, and economically—for everyone involved.

Thanks to a network of Internet-connected computers established by the Indian firm ITC in 2000, rural farmers in Madhya Pradesh were able to negotiate better prices for their crops, track soy futures on the Chicago Board of Trade, and buy seeds, fertilizer, and soil-testing services. Building on their success in Madhya Pradesh, ITC expanded the network of computers, known as "e-choupals," from 6 to 1200 linking 1.8 million people in 6,500 villages. "The purpose of the e-choupal is to empower farmers with real time information on weather and prices so that they are prepared to face the ever-changing climate conditions and price fluctuations," said Y. C. Deveshwar, ITC chair and president of the Confederation of Indian Industry, who sees the networks as a strategic tool for value creation and rural empowerment, capable of distributing a wide variety of products such as insurance, micro-credit, health services, etc.[5]

At present, ITC operates aqua-choupals in Andhra Pradesh, coffee-choupals in Karnataka, soya-choupals in Madhya Pradesh, and wheat-choupals in Uttar Pradesh. The success of the e-choupal initiative has attracted the attention of Harvard Business School and Kellogg's School of Management, and both are taking it up as a case study in their curriculum. The e-choupal network, which is enabling the poor to increase their productivity and incomes, has not only brought consumer market power to life at the poorest level of Indian society, it is serving as an example that much can be gained when we ask ourselves "what is needed and who needs it?"

Another innovation that came about as a result of inquiring into a community's needs happened at Hindustan Lever, an Indian subsidiary of Unilever. The managers there were

What if we discover that our present way of life is irreconcilable with our vocation to become fully human?
PAULO FREIRE

The question of bread for myself is a material question, but the question of bread for my neighbor is a spiritual question.
NIKOLAI BERDYAEV

Perhaps today, when faced with one decision or another, we should also step out of what we perceive to be inherent necessities and consider whether what we are doing can stand up to the judgment of history – or to that of our children.
KLAUS LEISINGER

used to serving wealthy urban citizens and never thought of marketing to the poor. A competitor came up with the idea of selling laundry detergent in single-use packages that the poor could afford, and they were a huge success. In response, Hindustan Lever came up with a new brand of detergent that was modified to work well in rivers and public water sources, where the poor most often do their laundry. They also devised a new distribution system to sell this product and created a host of new jobs in poorer rural areas. Both manufacturers currently have nearly 40 percent of the market.

In Thailand, when Information and Communications Technology Minister Surapong Suebwonglee wanted to extend the benefits of technology to the poor, he challenged the Thai computer industry to come up with a $260 personal computer and laptop. In exchange, he guaranteed a market of a half million computers. The Thai company could meet the price, but they would have to forego the expensive Microsoft operating system and go with the open-source Linux system instead. When Microsoft heard this, they agreed to cut their price to $38 in Thailand, so the computers were produced, some with Windows and most with Linux. Projected first year sales are for one million machines.

> We have to demand the impossible in order to achieve the possible.
> HERBERT MARCUSE

These are the kinds of alliances that can emerge when we change our questions from "What can we gain?" to "What can we give?" Businesses have always been on the cutting edge of creative innovation, and finding ways of bridging their bottom line concerns with the basic needs of the poor opens up whole new avenues for win-win solutions. Research shows that poor households spend most of their income on housing, food, health care, education, finance charges, communications, and consumer goods. The market for goods and services among families with an annual income of $6000 or less is enormous, as is the opportunity to create empowering partnerships that lead to dignified and well-paid work, improved health care, and educational opportunities for the whole community.

> Sometimes it takes darkness and the sweet confinement of your aloneness to learn that anything or anyone that does not bring you alive is too small for you.
> DAVID WHYTE

> Because we find as our interdependence increases that, on the whole, we do better when other people do better as well - so we have to find ways that we can all win, we have to accommodate each other.
> Bill Clinton

Prahalad and Hammond submit these statistics in their article:
- The eighteen largest emerging and transitional countries include 680 million poor households, with a total income of $1.7 trillion
- Brazil's poorest citizens alone comprise nearly 25 million households with a total annual income of $73 billion
- India has 171 million poor households with a combined $378 billion in income
- China's poor account for 286 million households with a combined annual income of $691 billion[6]

There is a tremendous opportunity here for commercial enterprises that balance commerce with compassion, that reframe "the poor" from a category of charity to a category of collaborator, and that imagine new ways of working with and in these communities so that everyone benefits.

A few months ago, I facilitated a workshop in Big Rapids, Michigan and the producers took me on a drive through the countryside. "Oh, you should see Fremont," they said. "It's a tiny town, fewer than five thousand people, but they've got a state of the art library, a fabulous performing arts center, and a hospital that's been on the top hundred list of American hospitals for the last three years." When I asked how they managed to pull all that off, they said "It's Gerber. Fremont is where Gerber Foods started and they donated so much to the community, they have everything they ever wanted."

I later spoke with Ron Vliem at the Fremont Chamber of Commerce, who verified Gerber's contributions to the city, acknowledging that the award-winning Gerber Memorial Hospital was the second largest employer in town with a staff of over five hundred. It turns out that in the 1930s and 40s, Jacob Andrew Gerber, his wife, and a few other visionaries bequeathed a few hundred thousand dollars to a charitable fund for the well-being of Newango County, Michigan. Their motto was, "for good, for ever." Ultimately, these funds, along with the contributions of others, secded the Fremont Area Community Foundation which is one of the largest community foundations in the nation on a per capita basis, serving a population of nearly 50,000 with assets around $165 million. They award about $10 million in grants each year, and have contributed more than $110 million to the community since its inception.

Imagine the global impact that corporations could make if they committed to uplifting the communities in which they do business. In my research on Gerber, I found an example of one company who is doing just this, and finding that the benefits far outweigh the costs in the long run. In 1994, Gerber Products merged with Novartis of Switzerland, which is creating its own legacy of global community involvement with their Novartis Foundation for Sustainable Development.

Novartis is a world leader in the research and development of products to protect and improve health and well-being, with core businesses in pharmaceuticals, consumer health, generics, eye-care, and animal health. Dr. Klaus M. Leisinger is president and CEO of the Novartis Foundation, and in celebration of the foundation's twenty-fifth year, he wrote about an encounter with former CEO Samuel Koechlin in 1972. Leisinger was a student, working there during the summer vacation. When Koechlin asked him what he was doing, Leisinger told him he was studying economics and doing his dissertation on Socioeconomic Development in the Third World.

Koechlin then asked him, "So? What do you think, are we doing the right thing in Africa?" to which Leisinger responded, "No, definitely not. There's a lot one should be doing differently." He writes:

> Samuel Koechlin challenged me. "It's not enough to criticize," he said. "If someone wants to be taken seriously, he has to show what, why, and where things should be done differently." I set to work full of idealism, a rucksack full of theories and not an ounce of practical experience. I called amongst other things for the Africanization of all management positions, a majority shareholding for local partners, training on all levels beyond what was necessary for the company's own purposes and a company policy which endeavors "to solve problems and not only sell products."[7]

While the company leaders did not act on all his ideas, they did decide to develop a corporate policy for the Third World and to engage in development assistance. Leisinger refers to this action as "enlightened self-interest," a concept that Alexis de Tocqueville discussed in his work *Democracy in America.* It was his opinion that Americans voluntarily join together in associations to further the interests of the group and, thereby, to serve their own interests. From his text: "The Americans… show with complacency how an enlightened regard for themselves constantly prompts them to assist each other, and inclines them willingly to sacrifice a portion of their time and property to the welfare of the state."[8]

RELEASING THE PAST

Enlightened self-interest holds true for business, as well. In its work in 140 countries around the world, Novartis has focused on finding allies, building coalitions, and creating synergies. Through their foundation, several millions of leprosy patients have been cured—about three million alone since Novartis started distributing all medicines for multi-drug therapy *free of charge*. More than five million people in rural sub-Saharan Africa have access to better seed varieties, and hundreds of thousands of women and children in poor communities have benefited from Novartis's commitment to empower women. In 2004, the Group's businesses achieved sales of $28.2 billion and a net income of $5.8 billion. *Furthering the well-being of the whole serves the interests of the parts.*

This is another countercultural idea, but it is being proven again and again, and people are catching on because we are evolving. We are becoming conscious enough to see that our own well-being is tied to the well-being of others. We are learning, not from religion or education or culture, but from the intimacy of our own experience, that *giving is receiving*. The phrase, "What goes around, comes around" is as clear as it gets. Or as the poet Rumi says, "The rule that covers everything is: How you are with others, expect that back." The very same generosity that we extend to the world is the generosity that returns to us—materially, emotionally, physically, and spiritually—and we are each learning this at our own pace.

In *New Traditions in Business,* Ken Blanchard wrote about a study done by the Ethics Resource Center in Washington that examined twenty-one companies with a written code of principles stating that serving the public was central to their being. As it turns out, if you had invested $30,000 in a composite of the Dow Jones thirty years ago, it'd be worth $134,000 today; whereas if you had invested the same amount in those twenty-one companies, it would be worth $1,021,861, almost nine times as much.[9] *Serving the public is serving ourselves.*

Anais Nin wrote that "there are very few human beings who receive the truth, complete and staggering, by instant illumination. Most of them acquire it fragment by fragment on a small scale, by successive developments, cellularly, like a laborious mosaic." Evolution is happening through us as surely as autumn happens through the maple leaf and spring through the budding rose. Fragment by fragment, we are moving away from our old notions of separateness and tuning into the reality of our complete and indivisible oneness.

Though we are all at different locations, all seeing things from different vantage points, all having different experiences and reaching different conclusions, we are all participating in the evolution of one nature, all components of one family, all cells of the One Mind. We appear to be separate in the same way one's fingertips look like five separate circles when placed on a frosty window, but behind that is the hand, the arm, the body. When John Updike wrote, "Chaos is just a local view of things working out in general," this is what he was referring to—the bigger mystery behind us, around us.

An understanding of this oneness is what leads people to ask the questions, "What do we need? What shall we do to be of use?" It is an evolved thinking, an intuitive awareness that a decision is only good for me if it is good for others. I had a friend who was a founder and president of a steel company in the Northeast. He was quite a philosopher, and a man of many opinions. When I asked him how he came to his decisions, how he deliberated in his political choices, he said, "Before I vote for something or make a decision, I always ask myself, 'Is it good for the Jews? Is it good for the blacks? Is it good for the poor?' and if it is, then I know it's good. It's got my vote." He was clear on his standards. Clear about his connection to others, and clear that his choices had everything to do with the lives of others.

This was a conversation of consequence. He revealed something important about his values and his process of discernment. And doing that, he helped me to clarify my own values. He never said his path was right for anyone else, or that those were the questions we should all be asking ourselves, but he dared to say, from his standpoint, that those were the considerations that were important to him.

As thought leaders, our job is to have this kind of clarity about our own thinking processes. To be able to say, to ourselves at the very least, these are the values that guide me, this is my personal bottom line, this is the impact I am making with my life. It's important for us to come to terms with what we are doing with our time and energy, with who is benefiting, and with the consequence of our existence—for these are the questions life asks of us. These are the questions that help us redirect if we have gone off track, refocus if we have glazed over and happened into someone else's creation instead of our own. There is nothing complex about these questions. They do not call for genius, but rather for the ability to imagine the wake we are leaving in our path.

As a result of you being here, who is being served?
Who feels more capable, more confident, because of your presence in their lives?
What difference are you making?

RELEASING THE PAST

Where are you casting your light?
What joy is being created out of your service?
What deep desire do you have for your life?

We participate in our own evolution; *we cause it to progress,* as we engage more and more consciously in these questions and begin to shape our lives around them. We find our purpose and the means to fulfill it at the place where our deepest desires meet the world's deep needs. This is the wellspring of our vitality—this intersection of self awareness and self-giving. It is as Rumi describes it in his poem, "The Far Mosque":

> The place that Solomon made to worship in,
> called the Far Mosque, is not built of earth
> and water and stone, but of intention and wisdom
> and mystical conversation and compassionate action.
>
> Every part of it is intelligence and responsive
> to every other. The carpet bows to the broom.
> The door knocker and the door swing together
> like musicians. This heart sanctuary *does*
> exist, but it can't be described. Why try!
>
> Solomon goes there every morning and gives guidance
> with words, with musical harmonies, and in actions,
> which are the deepest teaching. A prince is just
> a conceit until he *does* something with generosity.[10]

And what can we *do* with generosity, as original thinkers, as thought leaders, as instigators of compassionate action? We can take a few minutes to reframe our world. We can look at it through eyes conscious of our connectedness, and with our hearts open to its pain and the possibility of change. We can sit for a moment and bear witness to the fact that nearly three million people are trying to survive each day on what we spend for a cup of cappuccino. We can imagine that one of the eleven million children who die annually from preventable diseases is *our* child—and that the daily toll of these 30,000 deaths is equivalent to sixty jumbo jets filled to capacity crashing every day. We can imagine that one of the six thousand people dying today from HIV/AIDS could be our brother, or that one of the fifteen million children orphaned by this disease is our grandchild. We can imagine that our mother is among the 40 percent of the world's population who live without proper sanitation.[11]

We can reflect on the fact that the US military budget request for Fiscal Year 2006 is $441.6 billion, and that does not include money for the Afghan and Iraq wars ($49.1 billion for Fiscal Year 2006), or Homeland Security funding ($41.1 billion for Fiscal Year 2006). We can also take note that the US military budget was six times larger than the Russian budget. Combined, Russia, China, and the seven potential "enemies" of the US spent only 34 percent of the US military budget in 2004.[12]

We can take into account how little it would cost to bring relief to the rest of our human family. If we can help countries reform their aid policies and improve their service delivery, the World Bank estimates that an additional $40 to $60 billion a year would be sufficient to achieve the UN Millennium Development Goals by 2015. A rough breakdown of these costs are $10-30 billion for education, $20-25 billion for health, and $5 to 21 billion for the environment.[13]

We can contrast this with the $25.3 billion that ExxonMobil earned last year; or the $17 billion that Citigroup earned after taxes. And we can mull over the fact that corporate taxes are at the lowest level in twenty years, and that nearly 95 percent of corporations pay less than 5 percent of income in taxes, despite a tax rate that officially stands at 35 percent.[14]

If we can sit with these facts for a little while, perhaps we can make some sense of the puzzle. It may just need a little time, combined with the right amount of courage and humility, for the answers to begin surfacing through the minds of ordinary people who love deeply and hear a call to justice. The creative process is a process of putting the pieces together. These are the pieces of our world, waiting for you and me to hold them in our hands, press them to our hearts, and fit them together, like a work of art, a mosaic, a family, at last.

Embracing the Present

From Truth to Transformation: Starting with Ourselves

Asking the Right Questions

Between Chaos and Clarity: Dwelling in the Mystery

The Creative Enterprise

Prophets and Profits: Capitalizing on Wisdom

SIX

From Truth to Transformation: Starting with Ourselves

In a room where people unanimously maintain a conspiracy of silence, one word of truth sounds like a pistol shot.

CSESLAW MILOSZ

Only by investing and speaking your vision with passion can the truth, one way or the other, finally penetrate the reluctance of the world.

SØREN KIERKEGAARD

What makes a thought leader a thought leader? It is the ability to speak with enough passion and credibility about something to influence another's feelings, assessments, and actions. Thought leaders inspire change—personal change, social change, cellular and systemic change. They are not redirecting traffic on the old thoroughfares, but building superhighways of communication that transport people to destinations of heightened awareness, broadened perspectives, and a truer, deeper sense of their place and purpose in life.

Thought leaders are modern-day prophets who speak with the authority of embodied wisdom. What they know is in their flesh and bones, harvested from the experiences of their daily lives. They have learned to pay attention, to mine conflicts for the jewels they offer, to embrace the darkness with the dawn, the tragedies with the triumphs. Thought leaders walk heart first into every challenge, knowing that it is their *energy*, as much as their words and thoughts, which touches the other and clears the way for communion and clarity.

What makes us real to each other, important and useful to each other, is our ability to share the essence of who we are, what we have felt, what we have learned. The greatest gift we have is the gift of our story, and the greatest stories we can tell are those that contain the seeds of our own learning. These are the stories that engage the listeners, that reward and honor their time and attentiveness with a gift of insight, an illuminating point, an "aha" that opens them to further trust and continued courage.

Every one of us, every moment of our lives, is engaged in the unfolding of a human drama. We have come here to learn things and we draw toward us people and events that lead us into that learning. This is our creation. It is not a neat, pain-free, mindless phenomenon, given our complexities and idiosyncrasies, but an intriguing and compelling play that we write, direct, star in, and review every day.

I once started out in my Honda Civic on a cross-country trip through the small towns of America. I was a young photo-journalist, intent on interviewing ordinary people about their social and spiritual values. I left from upstate New York and headed south, excited and afraid at the same time. I drove right through Pennsylvania, lacking the courage to talk to anyone. My great idea didn't feel so great anymore. I had a yellow legal pad on the passenger seat and kept adding questions I wanted to ask people, and while my list grew longer, I grew shorter on confidence by the day.

In this age, the mere example of non-conformity, the mere refusal to bend the knee to custom, is itself a service.
JOHN STUART MILL

They may forget what you said, but they will never forget how you made them feel.
CARL W. BUECHNER

Story is the most dynamic and versatile tool available to us humans for the exploration of meaning and mystery.
DIARMUID O'MURCHU

Finally, I drove into a Waffle House parking lot in Virginia and pumped myself up. I would walk into the restaurant and look around. If someone made eye contact with me, I'd simply ask if I could interview them. I took along a copy of my book, *Making Peace: One Woman's Journey Around the World,* for the sake of credibility, and of course, my yellow legal pad with all the questions.

One man in the back caught my eye when I came through the door. He was wearing a denim jacket and a Playboy baseball cap. And he was the only one in the place making eye contact with me. So I approached him, said what I was doing, showed him my book, and asked if he had a few minutes. "Yes," he said, so I sat down. When I pulled out my pad of questions and focused in on the first one, I looked right into his eyes and asked, "Where did you get your values?"

He stared right back at me with a deep, vacuous look, and after several long moments, said, with a very southern, two-syllable drawl, "Wha-ut?"

I panicked for a second, and then heard a little voice in my own head whisper "Go first." Realizing I could be helpful by giving an example, I went first and told the story of how my mother always told me, when I passed a person on the street, to look that person right in the eyes, give them a big smile, and say "Hi," as friendly as I could. I told him it was difficult at first, since I was young and very shy, but then it got easier and now I do it all the time, because it's just part of me. "So being friendly is one of my values," I said. "And I got it from my Mom."

He kept nodding his head and chewing on his toothpick, until he finally asked: "Is it like this? When I was little and my daddy used to whup me when he'd get a drinkin', I'd go out on the back porch wantin' to cry and my Grandaddy would be there. He'd look at me and say, 'Son, looks like you've got some big feelings goin' on. Why don't you get yourself a pad of paper and go down under that oak tree and write yourself some poems. That'll help you with them big feelings.' So I did, I wrote a lot of poems. I still do, when I need to work out my feelings. Wanna hear one?"

He recited a poem by heart, and then wrote it down in my journal. And we sat in that plastic booth for another hour and a half while he told stories he had never told to another person—about his own anger, his big dreams, his pickup truck and double-wide, his drinking problem, his fear of being in love and messing it up like his dad. And every story he told me illuminated my own darkness, taught me something I never knew, and opened my heart to bigger love and deeper courage. He found parts of himself that had been long lost, simply because I was there to hear and receive them. And the same was true for me. When we left that restaurant, we were two different people from the ones who had walked in, alone and afraid.

What I learned that day was the importance of "going first." I didn't know, all those years ago, that the word *leadership* comes from an Old English word meaning "go first." It came like a whisper from the Muse, a nudging that caused me to open and share in such a way that the other knew it was safe for him, as well. My story was a gift to him. It was a tale of the passing on of

> *You were allowed to see the truth under agreement that you would communicate it to others and therefore, if you have seen, you simply must speak out.*
> KEN WILBER

> *The sin of inadvertence, not being alert, not quite awake, is the sin of missing the moment of life—live with unremitting alertness.*
> JOSEPH CAMPBELL

> *Speak truth in a million voices. It is silence that kills.*
> CATHERINE OF SIENA

values, wrapped in a few paragraphs, a little history, and some visual images. And yet, it was powerful enough to evoke his own history, his own creative wisdom, and the courage to speak of his fear and dark nights. And from that intimacy and vulnerability grew a new story, a universal story, the story of Going First.

I now know, from that one experience, that I can be the cause of a profound conversation, if I dare to go first, if I share something personal and meaningful, if I ask of another a question that matters, and listen like our lives depend on the answer. Since I value such conversations, and rely on them for my joy and sanity, I've been practicing this for many years now, learning more from others' lives than I could from any book. And it's because of that energy exchange that a vitality rises up when two people open the pages of their hearts, share their wonderings, find their commonness. That is the energy of transformation. It whisks us away from our sense of aloneness, draws back the veil between one and another, and rustles up, like a gentle wind, newfound feelings and age-old knowing.

Our most original thoughts are unearthed in the process of mining our lives, entering into the depths and caves of our personal history. We know what we know because it has been imprinted upon us in our cycles of growing and becoming. Our very cells have been informed by the mountains we've climbed and the forests we've walked in. If you traced an outline of your foot on a piece of paper and made notes or symbols for all the earthly places your feet have carried you, there would be a record of the paths you've walked, the trees you've climbed or planted or photographed, the seas and rivers and streams you've delighted in, the city parks, the country roads, the bayous, the dunes, the meadows. And if, in any of these places, you were paying attention, they spoke to you in a language you understood, they taught you the nature of things. And your body and mind know this still; but you must go back to the memory, find the story, conjure the images, define the contours of that space and look deeply enough into it to see what truth you hold in that memory.

Trace the outline of your hand and make note of the moments you remember touching or being touched in a profound way, moments of great or humble giving and receiving, times of reaching out, times of hunger and longing when someone took your hand and led you home. Return to that story to find its elements—the conflicts, the drama, the resolution—and sit with it until you discover the learning that was born from your labor. Remember that you created it to advance your own awareness, and until you have mined it for its gems of understanding, you will not have finished your work. While we are characters in these stories of our lives, we are also their authors, and it is this knowing that sources our authority.

What I know serves me well enough, but the story of how I know it can serve others in unimaginable ways. The story is an art form that does what all good art does—it suspends us in a space of freedom and possibility. It opens the gateways to our creative energy, awakens our drowsy imagination, and helps us see and feel our connectedness to each other. In the distilled expressions of our stories, we give form to the revelations that are unique to us, and of value to others. The artist Wassily Kandinsky writes, "That which belongs to the spirit of the future can only be realized in feeling, and to this feeling the talent of the artist is the only road." The solutions to the complex challenges of these times will emerge from our deepest feelings, when our hunger for resolution, our longing for an end to poverty and war outweighs our apathy. Social engagement begins when our sorrow takes flight and transforms into service. As Marge Piercy writes in her poem, "The Low Road":

> It goes on one at a time,
> it starts when you care
> to act, it starts when you do
> it again and they said no,
> it starts when you say *We*
> and know who you mean, and each
> day you mean one more.[1]

Just like poetry, music, films, and plays, stories—*my stories, your stories*—transmit an energy. They cause a movement in the synapses of the brain, the sinews of the body, the molecules of emotion. They can shed light, heal the spirit, provoke thought, evoke action. They are the tools of transformation, available to every one of us, for what is our life but a series of stories waiting to be lived, mined, shaped into form, and shared with others?

As we hone and harvest our own experience, recalling the details of what we've learned and how we've learned it, so do we clarify our wisdom, crystallize its essence, and fulfill its meaning. Becoming an authority is an organic process. It is not merely mindful, but soulful, sense-full, purposeful work that begins in the fertile region of feelings and extends outward. Feeling is the context of our learning. None of us study or seek what does not delight us. We follow our hearts, our emotions, our bliss and in the midst of what moves us, we find our voice, our strength, our reasons to act.

This is the place we lead from—this place of delight and determination—for as we're inspired, we inspire. This is how we repair the world. It is not facts and formulas, but the simple refining and telling of our stories that will spark a rethinking in the minds of others—for the hunger in this Information Age is not for more information, but for the fire and light of stories that reveal us to ourselves. As Marget Wheatley writes in *Finding Our Way: Leadership for an Uncertain Time:* "What we ask of the tellers of the new story is their voice and their courage. We do not need them to create a massive training program, a global approach, a dramatic style. We only need them to break their silence and share their ideas of the world as they have come to know it."

National Public Radio (NPR) has invited anyone who wants to contribute an essay called *This I Believe* to their ongoing archives of American stories. Fifty-five years ago, people sat by their radios and listened to the voices of politicians, cab drivers, baseball players, and secretaries tell the stories about the core values that guide their daily lives. Today, those essays are still accessible, along with many more. From Albert Einstein to Jackie Robinson, Helen Keller to Helen Hayes, Newt Gingrich to William Buckley to Gloria Steinem, we can read their words and listen to the stories of the well-known and lesser known.

And to guide the writer who wants to contribute, NPR has published some suggestions about telling a story right on their website. "Be specific. Take your belief out of the ether and ground it in the events of your life. Consider moments when belief was formed or tested or changed. Think of your own experience, work and family, and tell of the things you know that no one else does…Make your essay about you; speak in the first person…edit it and simplify until you find the words, tone and story that truly echo your belief and the way you speak."[2]

These are great guidelines for all of us as we wind our way inward, picking up the treasures. They're all there, in our own depths, waiting to be shaped into story, waiting for us to sit down with another and just Go First.

SEVEN

Asking the Right Questions

What is faith worth if it is not translated into action?

MAHATMA GANDHI

Far better than a precise plan is a clear sense of direction and compelling beliefs. And that lies within you. The question is, how do you evoke it?

DEE HOCK

When I was in elementary school, I learned to attach importance to things based on one's willingness to die for them. The whole idea of heroes usually involved a sacrifice of someone's life. Being willing to die for your country was the essence of patriotism. And as a young Catholic child, the chance to be a martyr for my faith was something I could only hope and pray for.

I have an eighty-year-old uncle who still brings up World War II every time I see him because it was in the throes of that experience that he found his meaning. Whatever else he has done with his life—owning his own business, fathering eight children, giving blood to the Red Cross at every opportunity, showing up at the funeral of everyone he knows in his small upstate New York town—these, in his mind, pale in comparison to the great heroism he experienced as a paratrooper in the Philippines. What he was willing to die for has colored his conversations for sixty years.

When I teach photography workshops and ask people to share their favorite images of themselves, they often bring in photos where they were doing things one might describe as risky—skydiving, mountain climbing, skiing in the Alps, or standing at the edge of the Grand Canyon. The photos convey their courage, and they are proud to introduce themselves as courageous people.

EMBRACING THE PRESENT

We have learned to associate courage with risk, and with the question, "What are you willing to die for?" But what if we ask, "What are you willing to live for?" If we determine for ourselves exactly what we choose to give our lives to, where we will direct our energy, what crises we'll work to ameliorate or prevent, then we set ourselves on a trajectory that takes mountainous courage to sustain. We need to refuel constantly to stay the course, to avoid obstacles, to overcome resistance from ourselves and others.

When I was working as a freelance photojournalist, I attended a workshop given by a panel of photo editors from several mainstream magazines. There were four hundred photographers in the room and we were all trying to figure out how to get *our* photographs into *their* magazines. After the editors talked about their publications and what they were looking for, it was time for questions from the audience.

I started to ask my question, which I thought was fairly astute, but I could tell from their body language that we didn't share the same opinion. I continued on, asking what the protocol would be if I was both writing the article and shooting the photographs for illustration. "Should I send the query letter to the articles editor or the photo editor?" I asked. I could tell by the rolling of their eyes that they were disgusted for some reason, but didn't know why until one editor said to me, with a hint of disdain: "Look, honey, you can't be a photographer and a writer. You have to choose one or the other. And if you choose to photograph, you have to decide *what* you're going to photograph. We have our dog photographers, our cat photographers, our architectural photographers, our car photographers, our fashion photographers. You have to pick one and stick with it, or you'll never be taken seriously." The other panel members nodded their heads in agreement.

I felt like the country bumpkin in the palace. It was a humiliating moment and I slid out the side door as fast as I could. "Let's see," I asked myself, walking down the long corridor of the Jacob Javits Center. "What shall I photograph—dogs, cats, houses, cars?" I didn't get too far down the hallway before realizing my mistake. I was trying to fit into *their* rules. In order to become a photographer of *one* thing, I would have to give up what I was living for, which was photographing people *and* events *and* places *and* animals *and* everything I saw that gave me pause. I was living to see it all and capture as much as I could through my lens.

Even though I already had one book of photographs and stories published by a prominent press, because of the photo editors' comments, I questioned myself immediately. "They must know better," I thought. "They're the decision makers." But by the time I reached the exit door, I had reached my conclusion. Their box was too small for me, and their rules way too confining. What if someone had said to Michelangelo, "Look, buddy, you have to make a choice between painting and sculpting. You can't do both." We'd have the Sistine Chapel or David, but not both.

Instead of encouraging me to expand my vision, these "experts" wanted me to narrow it. The question was, "What was I willing to give up?" Whereas it should have been, "What was I willing to give?" I felt throttled and stifled in response to their question. The upshot was that I abandoned the freelance profession and went on to create work that was true to myself and worth living for.

As thought leaders, it is our business to be asking questions—of ourselves as well as others—that help us all redefine what we are living for and why. The generation that is stepping up to leadership is a generation looking for curricula and challenges that have an impact, that engage the whole of their fertile imaginations in bridging the gaps we have failed to bridge thus far in our shaping of a culture. When Mahatma Gandhi was asked what he thought of Western civilization, his response was, "I think it would be a very good idea."

In the wake of Hurricane Katrina, what's surfacing from the muddy waters is a clear awareness of our national and cultural shortcomings. Our conversations about morality have detoured into the realm of private and personal choice, while we neglect the most basic moral questions confronting us: How can we use our immense resources to balance the inequities in our own nation? What has to happen to feed the 12.9 million American children going hungry every day, to secure health care for every citizen, and to create affordable housing for the working poor and the 35.9 million people living below the poverty line in America?[1]

What we're in need of is thought leadership that leads people in two directions: first, into their own deep recesses where they can access their feelings, their desires, their most basic human instincts, and identify what it is they are truly called to. This is a leadership of creativity and imagination that frees people from their social conditioning, familial expectations, religious and cultural programming long enough to enable their unique originality to surface. It is a process of self-definition, a washing away of all that is not authentic, a clarifying of one's essence. The questions are personal:

What activities bring you joy and peace?

EMBRACING THE PRESENT

To what do you aspire?

What do you perceive as obstacles to your success?

What inspires you?

*If you could imagine yourself capable of fixing one broken thing,
or creating one thing that doesn't yet exist, what would it be?*

When you were a child, what did you want to be when you grew up?

What did you imagine that profession would give you?

What would have to happen for you to have that now?

In a radio interview the other day, the host asked me, "How do you help people know what they want?" I once thought that was a silly question, but have since realized that most of us need help clarifying our deepest desires. Since our education was more a matter of *what* to think than *how* to think, many never learned the process of inner inquiry. By default, we end up being perfect consumers, going into debt for what advertisers tell us we need and want when maybe what we'd really like is to work less and have a little lakeside cabin on a mountain—which would be absolutely possible if we weren't paying for all those other things we really didn't want.

So a crucial part of original thinking is the clear-cutting of all thoughts that are not our own, and the answering of our own deep questions. If you aspire to lead, then you will need to do this for yourself first, then find ways to help others engage in the same process. The more self-awareness each individual has, the greater the potential of the group to succeed. When everyone comes to the table from a place of total freedom, with an unadulterated willingness to serve, with full access to their feelings and inner resources, and an awareness of the group's mission and power to fulfill it, then that circle of individuals will be capable of achieving whatever they can imagine.

The Swiss psychiatrist Carl Jung wrote: "In the last analysis, the essential thing is the life of the individual. This alone makes history, here alone do the great transformations take place, and the whole history of the world ultimately springs to a giant summation from these hidden sources in individuals. In our most private and subjective lives, we are not only the passive witnesses to our age, but also its makers." We are only able to access those hidden sources when we take the time to ask ourselves the proper questions and go deeply into the places where our genuine answers lie. This work is a prerequisite for thought leaders looking to shape a culture of compassion and engage others in the transformational work that such an endeavor requires. Finding the answers to our questions is the first step on that journey.

The next step is to move toward fulfillment. Any deep inquiry into the self will lead to a heightened sense of our interconnectedness and interdependence on each other. Who we are, in essence, is revealed to us through our interactions. What we value is revealed to us through our relationships with others. What gifts we have, what talents and abilities we possess, only become real when they are enacted in community. The very meaning of our lives only becomes apparent to us in our service to others. Given this, our next questions are directed outwardly. They pertain to the ways we manifest the gifts we discovered in our self-inquiry. They are questions that help us determine what to make of our talents.

As an individual, how can I do what I love while being of use to others?

As an organizational leader, how can I create a forum that calls forth the ingenuity of individuals and assists them in applying that toward communal solutions?

As a business leader, how can I deliver profits to the shareholders while rewarding fairly all those who made those profits possible?

As an educator, how can I make learning relevant and engage the students in real-life problem solving?

Here are a few examples of how some people are responding to these questions and what it's leading to:

Author and educator June Gould, Ph.D., has been offering memoir writing workshops to a group of eight women, ages seventy and older at The National Council of Jewish Women, New York Chapter for the last three years.[2] What motivates Gould to do this work is her belief in the power of creative expression and the potential for change and growth that individuals have no matter what their age. "Despite our problems, we also have a passion to shape personally meaningful lives, to understand ourselves and the world around us, and to grow and branch out in positive directions," she says.

As for the changes that occurred, Gould comments: "I watched them transform themselves into a real community. They began to genuinely like one another. Several of them said they had never shared so much of their 'real lives' with anyone before and this sharing helped them feel nurtured and appreciated."

The women found themselves and each other through June's classes, in writing their own stories and hearing the stories of others. The writing revived them, invigorated them, and once they experienced themselves as authors, as women of authority, the next step was to take this new energy and insight out into the world. Two women participated in international writing conferences. Several women who had poor or no relationships with their children called them, wrote to them, and resolved old conflicts. For the first time in their lives, they each got up at a microphone and read from their work at the National Council head-quarters. And then they published their own book, *Important Women: Extraordinary Lives,* and they are doing readings and signings throughout the community. This is the difference that one individual made in many peoples' lives once she became clear about how to share her gifts with others.

Ten years ago, in a Subaru factory in Indiana, a few individuals decided to work together to reduce the impact their plant was making on the environment. Within ten years, they became the first auto manufacturer to reach zero landfill status. They recycle everything that comes into their plant, and, as a result, use less electricity while increasing productivity. This did not happen because a CEO had a bright idea and decided to enforce it. It happened because a few conscientious employees decided to take responsibility for doing the right thing.

One organization that is inspiring its members to become active co-creators is the World Future Society (WFS)[3], a nonpartisan, nonprofit educational and scientific association with 30,000 members in over eighty countries and chapters in a number of cities. WFS acts as a

Don't keep searching for truth. Just let go of your opinions.
SENG TS'AN

Each soul takes upon itself a particular task. . . Whatever the task that your soul has agreed to, whatever its contract with the Universe, all of the experiences of your life serve to awaken within you the memory of that contract, and to prepare you to fulfill it.
GARY ZUKAV

Compassion is an unstable emotion. it needs to be translated into action, or it withers.
SUSAN SONTAG

neutral forum and clearinghouse for ideas on future trends, and partners with several organizations to facilitate discussions of strategies for a better future at the global, organizational, and individual levels.

One partnership they've developed is with Global SchoolNet (GSN)[4], a nonprofit network of more than 90,000 online educators in 194 countries dedicated to helping young people become literate and responsible global citizens. GSN uses a variety of project-based approaches focusing on collaboration and community-building. In partnership with WFS, Global SchoolNet sponsors an annual web-based CyberFair which engages students from 582 schools in 109 countries in preparing for the future by thinking about their own future plans, the conditions that will affect the future of their community, and future issues of global importance.

This year's top projects originated from Taiwan, Australia, Cyprus, the Netherlands, Singapore, Hong Kong, and the United States, and the winners are featured at the annual World Future Society Conference. Now in its tenth year, the contest has involved more than one million students from 4,500 schools in 194 countries and is the longest running international cyber event for schools. Both World Future Society and Global SchoolNet inspire innovation among their members and are architects of programs that extend the reach of their creativity into the community at large. What makes them both so exemplary is their ability to partner with organizations, schools, universities, communities, and businesses to bring about the changes they want to see in the world.

In the business arena, one retailer that stands out as a leader in conscious commerce is the natural and organic food supermarket, Whole Foods Market, Inc. They first opened in Texas in 1980 when there were less than half a dozen natural food supermarkets in the United States and have since become a Fortune 500 company and have appeared on *Fortune* magazine's "100 Best Companies to Work for List" for eight consecutive years. The company currently has 171 stores in the United States, Canada, and the

How you do anything is how you do everything.
ZEN PROVERB

Poverty is not a culture to be understood, it is a condition to be eradicated.
GARRETT KEISER

The power that you gain by pursuing your interest will give you the ability to take upon yourself a greater challenge than you have taken on so far. We gain in power by pursuing our purpose in life.
HAZRAT INAYAT KHAN

United Kingdom.

A group of sixty employees, known as Team Members, drafted a Declaration of Interdependence that sits on their website (www.whole-foods.com) and helps to explain their phenomenal success. Some of the notable characteristics at Whole Foods include: staff are all stockholders in the company; the stores show their commitment to their local communities by supporting food banks, sponsoring neighborhood events, and compensating their team members for community service work. No one makes more than fourteen times the average salary, and they donate 5 percent of their after-tax profits to not-for-profit organizations.

They have created an Animal Compassion Foundation to provide education and research services to ranchers and meat producers around the world who want to remain economically viable while maintaining standards of excellence for animal welfare. To do this, they are partnering with animal welfare advocacy groups and the farmers and ranchers they do business with.

They have also established a Whole Planet Foundation which is partnering with EARTH University in Costa Rica, Universidad Francisco Marroquin in Guatemala, and Grameen Trust of Bangladesh to conduct a micro-loan program to help women in these areas develop their own micro-enterprises. Whole Foods is concentrating its efforts in the regions where it purchases pineapples, bananas, and coffee, and their goal is to assist up to 8,500 women in their efforts to become self-supporting entrepreneurs. They are beginning with an initial $2 million investment in 2005, but will continue to support the projects through the Global Five Percent Day, allocating 5 percent of all global sales on a designated day to microcredit loans.

In a recent interview for *What Is Enlightenment?* magazine, co-president Walter Robb attributed Whole Foods' success to their principle-driven culture. They see themselves as co-creators of the future, and their business decisions are made with that in mind. They do not sell sea bass anymore because it is not being fished in a sustainable way. And they discontinued tilapia when they found out hormones were being used in the production of the fish. Says Robb:

> We're not retailers who have a mission—we're missionaries who retail. At the very heart and soul of Whole Foods is the mission. We're here to make a real difference in people's health and well-being, in the health and well-being of the planet, and in creating a workplace based on love and respect. So we put our customers and Team Members before our shareholders. And if you compare our performance to other

publicly traded food companies, it's superior. A thousand bucks invested in Whole Foods at the beginning in 1992 would be worth well over thirty thousand now. Since we've been public, we've delivered a twenty-five percent compounded annual growth rate. Our return on invested capital is north of thirty-five per cent. Those are some of the strongest numbers in the history of food retailing.[5]

Original thinking in the world of education is leading to some global-wide innovations that are as heart-touching as they are eye-opening. Curtis DeBerg, an accounting professor at California State University at Chico, is founder and director of Students for the Advancement of Global Entrepreneurship (SAGE)[6], an international network linking university students from several countries to high school students and business leaders in their communities. DeBerg's mission was to create an infrastructure rooted in both problem-based learning and community service-learning that matched high school students with international college mentors and local business advisers. With the help of these mentors, the students complete projects related to entrepreneurship, community service, teaching others, civic engagement in a democracy, and environmental awareness.

According to DeBerg, poverty is more often the expression of low productivity than lack of resources. Through the SAGE network, high school students are learning how to galvanize their creative energies and design entrepreneurial projects that are profitable and socially-relevant. The economist Jeffery D. Sachs wrote, "The very hardest part of economic development is getting the first foothold on the ladder." SAGE and Rotary International are developing a partnership in Ghana to involve students there in helping Ghana get their first foothold of the ladder by empowering youth to create wealth with mentoring, advising, and support from the local community. The strategy is to prepare and empower Ghanaian youth through a youth entrepreneurship *and* community service program, while simultaneously emphasizing the importance of financial literacy, ethical business practices, civic engagement, and environmental awareness.

Students involved in the SAGE program come together annually for a World Cup Competition and each team has fifteen minutes to make their presentation in English before more than thirty judges from academia, nonprofit organizations and the business sector. The 2005 competition took place in San Mateo, California and included student teams from eight countries: the United States, Poland, Ghana, South

Africa, Russia, Tajikistan, China, and Ukraine. With a sophisticated audio-visual display as background to their presentation, the Ukraine high schoolers were judged the best. Among their award-winning projects were the publication of a four-color magazine, and the creation and management of a popular new music group in their home city of Odessa.

The high school SAGE teams from Shanghai, China, and Cape Town, South Africa, took second and third place, respectively. The US entry, from Northwestern Lehigh High School, New Tripoli, Pennsylvania, came in fourth. Willie Hopkins, CSU, Chico dean of the College of Business and a judge for the competition, said:

> The way they crafted their business plans, explained the operations of businesses developed from their plans and demonstrated the benefits that their respective communities derived from these businesses, made me feel extremely optimistic about the future of our world. Through this competition, these young high-school students have not only learned self-reliance and how to contribute meaningfully to their local and global communities, they have also learned the importance of operating business in a socially-responsible manner.

Fifteen SAGE students in Oakland were involved in the creation of the new Youth Empowerment School (YES), which is part of Oakland's Small Schools Initiative. They worked with Principal Maureen Benson to design a school that would help shape community leaders by engaging the students in the issues their local communities were dealing with. According to the plan, the school would start out with only 128 ninth-grade students, and each of them would go out into the community to gather data for an hour and a half each day. At the end of the ninth grade, based on that knowledge, the students would decide which issues they wanted to study further. From grades 10 to 12, they would work on projects that came from their needs assessment of the community. In a recent e-mail exchange, Benson reported, "We have 230 students, and are in our 3rd year. School is great, violence is down, and achievement is up! It really takes a village and our community has stepped up to it!"

There are exemplary programs in K-12 schools across the country, and one organization that is helping to spread the word about practices that work is the George Lucas Educational Foundation (GLEF). Disenchanted with what school had to offer him as a child, the filmmaker Lucas asked himself what he could do to improve creativity in today's schools and his foundation was the inspired answer. GLEF has thirty full-time employees, a $4 million annual budget and headquarters on the founder's Skywalker Ranch in the Marin County hills. It publishes *Edutopia*, a new magazine for a new world of learning (www.edutopia.org), a monthly must-read for teachers that celebrates the renaissance of originality that is changing the face of American education.

Lucas' goal is to document and disseminate information about effective, creative programs in K-12 schools to help these ideas spread nationwide. GLEF supports projects in both public and private schools, distributes an e-mail newsletter, and maintains an extensive website that contains all of the multimedia content they have published since 1997. They provide free downloadable teaching modules that were developed by education faculty and professional developers that can be used in the classroom, workshops, or meetings. Detailed articles, research summaries, and links to hundreds of relevant Web sites, books, organizations, and publications are also available to help schools and communities build on successes in education.

They have a robust collection of short, online documentaries on classroom innovations that allow visitors to visualize what these innovations look like, as well as a multimedia compilation of success stories in our nation's schools. The GLEF staff has also developed multimedia programs of interest to educators, community leaders, and policymakers interested in gaining deeper insights into community partnerships with business and nonprofits, curricula integrating technology and real-world projects, and new approaches to assessing student learning.

June Gould is just one individual among millions who is doing what she loves to do in the service of others. The World Future Society, Global SchoolNet, Students for the Advancement of Global Entrepreneurship, the George Lucas Educational Foundation—they are four of 1.5 million nonprofit organizations in the United States responding to the question, "How can we apply the resources of this group to the needs of our community?" The Youth Empowerment School is one among thousands of educational institutions stepping out of old traditions and creating new ones that inspire students to ask new questions, think originally, and engage with their communities in a meaningful way. Whole Foods Market is one of a myriad of businesses who are asking the questions: How can we serve our communities? How can we best respect and reward our employees? How can we maximize our positive impact on the planet while we maximize our profits?

The journey for all conscious citizens is a twofold journey: the

"That's where you went wrong," said the prophet. "You looked at the scriptures. You should have also looked into his eyes."

The mayor and the priest spent the whole night searching through the scriptures trying to decide what to do. Had they looked as well into their own hearts, or spoken with the man who was being hidden away, or polled the entire community, they may have reached a wiser conclusion. Instead, they relied on texts that, in the end, led them astray. In the face of a great challenge, they did not know how to, or perhaps even *why* to, summon forth a deeper wisdom, having learned to rely on their scriptures for the answers they sought. But it was their failure to do this that resulted in the tragedy.

The mysteries we face today are equally challenging. The welfare of villages around the world is at stake, and no amount of wealth or weaponry can defend against the terrorism that is loose in the world. A deeper wisdom is called for now, and as a collective body, we contain it. No leader knows the answer. No individual knows the answer. No sacred text holds the answer. We, as a body of global citizens, contain the blueprint for a peaceful future. As Ken Wilber says, "We are all right, only partly so." The wisdom of humanity is dispersed among its members, and the real leaders are those who can evoke that wisdom, summon the members to find their voices, and create a forum for them to be heard.

In his fascinating book *The Wisdom of Crowds*, James Surowiecki, the *New Yorker* magazine business columnist makes the case that large groups of people are smarter than an elite few, no matter how bright those few may be. "Groups are often smarter than the smartest people in them, and they do not need to be dominated by exceptionally intelligent people in order to be smart. Even if most people within the group are not especially well-informed or rational, it can still reach a collectively wise decision."[1]

Surowiecki cites the work of Scott Page, a political scientist at the University of Michigan whose experiments with computer-simulated problem solving agents revealed some interesting findings. Page set up groups of ten to twenty agents, each endowed with a different set of skills, and had them solve a sophisticated problem. Individually, some did well at solving the problem and some were less effective. What Page found was that "a group made up of some smart agents and some not-so-smart agents almost always did better than a group made up just of smart agents…Adding in a few people who know less, but have different skills, actually improves the group's performance."[2] Surowiecki asserts that "bringing new members into the organization, even if they are less experienced or capable, actually makes the group smarter simply because what little the new members do know is not redundant with what everyone else knows."[3] Diversity works.

Today's Internet is making it possible to get feedback from everywhere at warp speed. Television shows like *Dancing with the Stars* and *American Idol* are hearing from voters across the globe and trusting in *the wisdom of the crowds* to determine their winners. Even NASA engaged in a recent online experiment to see if the collective judgment of ordinary people might be helpful in finding and classifying craters on Mars. They called the experiment "Clickworkers," and anyone who wanted to could visit the site, go through a brief training session, and then register their ideas with the click of a mouse. As it turns out, the collective judgment of the group was "virtually indistinguishable" from that of a "geologist with years of experience in identifying Mars craters."[4]

While the priest and the mayor were stymied in the face of an awful decision, had they polled the villagers for a collective idea, most likely they would have arrived at a more inspiring solution. But they were not original thinkers. Perceiving themselves as the leaders, it did not occur to them to look beyond themselves and the Village Council for answers, especially to the common villagers. When they had exhausted their own mental resources, they turned only to their scriptures. They never turned to the man "who seemed kind and innocent and was loved by all." They resisted the complexities of human emotion, the challenge of engaging the entire community. A literal answer from the sacred text was the easy way out. "Look, it says it right here. It must be right. It's our sacred scripture." And this was the fatal flaw. They stopped there.

Answering the questions that are besieging us now calls for a plunging of our whole beings into the dilemmas presented in every morning newspaper. Relying solely on sacred texts is an invitation for chaos and polarization. There will always be those who want to "turn the other cheek" and those who want "an eye for an eye," and each will be "right" according to their choice. Fear is in the air now because each side is building a formidable case for its rightness, and the energy that might be spent on solving the problems is going into proving the other side wrong. The butterfly will never get off the ground if the right wing is at war with the left wing.

The answers that we are seeking lie *between* the right and left and the only way to access them is to move toward the other, to re-pair the opposites. But one look at our culture—from our religions to our media to our politics—reveals a history of opposition, a "divide and conquer" disposition. In her book *The Allure of Toxic Leaders*, Jean Lipman-Blumen writes, "Savvy leaders have long known that identifying an enemy— usually external—is a surefire method for uniting a group...With mind-numbing regularity, the visions of toxic leaders point to enemies and scapegoats as the wellsprings of all their followers' problems."[5] Somehow, if we know there is an enemy out there who's the source of our problem, we can relax a little. We know the military will fix it. Or the government will take care of it. Or science or technology will handle it. We don't have to reckon with a lack of certainty. We don't have to change our lives, change our minds, change our habits. The problem is out there. Global warming will get fixed. They'll figure out how to rebuild New Orleans. Someone will get food to those kids in Rwanda, or Pakistan, or those slums in New York or LA. It's not my problem.

"Culture, created by humans to reduce our existential fears, offers us security through clearly-prescribed norms for every aspect of life, from how we learn in school to how we select a mate, how we enter a career, how we become heroes, and how we choose a leader. Faced with a seemingly immutable culture, we commonly respond with knee-jerk reactions dictated by the norms of our particular place and time," writes Jean Lipman-Blumen. But those norms are rapidly changing. We have exported American culture to nearly every country in the world and people are getting a look at affluence. They wonder why they have to struggle so hard when Americans have it so easy, or so it seems. And there's the big mystery. Why *is* the gap so huge? Why *do* we allow such disparity in the distribution of wealth? What *do* we say to people who are starving—in our own country as well as abroad?

The Internet and the media are the nervous system of the global body and our synapses are more connected now than ever before. Years ago we had to rely on *National Geographic* for pictures of our brothers and sisters from far away, but now we see them every day on CNN. I have passed by bamboo huts in the middle of a rice field outside Bangkok and seen the flickering blue light of a television screen. We see them. They see us. Our glimpses into each others' lives are giving shape to the greatest questions of our times and we will not find our answers in books or facts or science or religion or anything than has been constructed by minds from another age. The problems we face can only be solved when we stop looking behind us for answers and begin looking within and around us. Our insights will come from communion and convergence, and this must happen both within ourselves and in our relationships with others.

Sister Joan Chittister, member of the Benedictine Sisters of Erie, Pennsylvania, has been one of America's key visionary spiritual voices for more than thirty years. A social psychologist and columnist for the *National Catholic Reporter*, she wrote in a recent article about how non-Americans are coming to view us in light of the Iraqi war and Hurricane Katrina. At a meeting with several international religious leaders, Chittister was informed that "being like America was not an ideal to which they aspired." The Korean representative said that their president had promised independence from US control, but was now being extorted into being part of "the coalition of the willing" with the threat of US boycotts and tariffs. The Taiwanese leader said Taiwan and China could develop peaceful relations if it weren't for the intervention of Western arms traders. The Indian said that it was US capitalism that was destroying India with its capitalist economy, value system, and culture.[6]

"It doesn't really matter at this point whether you and I and the rest of the United States believe what these people are saying or not. It doesn't make much difference whether we agree with them or not. It's not even very important whether they are right or not. What counts is that this is their perception of us," writes Chittister. "As far as the poor of the world are concerned, we are at the base of their problems. We have become the American Empire, which like the Roman Empire of old, is simply living off their resources, their slave labor, their tribute in cash crops and their future. We are the new economic colonialists who are sucking the economic blood out of them and destroying their cultures."

One deep mystery is how these ideas could be so prevalent around the world while our own national self-image is so different? An imam from Sudan said to Chittister, "After 9/11, the United States could have said, 'We will not destroy others as they have destroyed. We will seek to understand why this happened so that it can never happen to anyone again.' But instead, you became what you said you were not. And now we see you as you are. It is so disappointing—so frightening. In you we had hoped."

Because of the nature of our political system and the tendency of the media to emphasize our polarities, we, as a country, have become terribly divided. More walls are being built every day between the left and the right, at a time when we need to be building bridges and making new meanings from the mysteries of these times. Our challenge is to awaken, as individuals, from whatever trance we're in, and do what we need to reclaim our power, our voice, our culture.

It is time now to re-pattern our thought processes and disavow all notions of our powerlessness as individuals. It is the thoughts and actions of individuals that have created the world we experience today and it will be the thoughts and actions of individuals that create the world we will live in tomorrow. We are those individuals and this is our time to break through every wall that has kept us from wholeness, every border that has kept us from "the other," and every belief that has silenced and disempowered us.

The philosopher Henri Bergson writes of humanity laboring under the weight of its own inventions. It is as if we have grown too far ahead of ourselves, added to the body but not the soul, so that the extension of our physical capabilities and our technological advances are out of proportion to the refinement of our spirit. "Now, in this excessively enlarged body," he writes, "the spirit remains what it was, too small now to fill it, too feeble to direct it... Let us add that this increased body awaits a supplement of the soul and that the mechanism demands a mysticism."[7]

Mysticism is an experience of communion. It is an embodied awareness of oneness, an intuitive recognition that the whole is in all of the parts. If religion were intelligence, mysticism would be wisdom. If religion were the recipe, mysticism would be the meal. Mysticism is the outer brought inward. It is not the knowledge of something, but the experience of something. And what Bergson is saying is that it is time to journey as far inwardly as we have journeyed outwardly, to rebalance ourselves by supplementing our souls as we have supplemented our bodies. It is a matter of re-integration, of making a whole from the scattered parts.

What makes original thinking *original* is that it synthesizes the outer and the inner and arrives at a new awareness that encompasses them both. It is a dynamic process that incorporates—from the Latin *incorporare*, meaning to embody, to bring together into a single whole—thoughts we

> *Perhaps the ultimate enterprise of the twenty-first century will be the establishment of a tranquility base, not on the moon, but within humankind.*
> KENNETH R. PELLETIER

> *The physics of one era is the metaphysics of the next...The belief that there is only one truth and that oneself is in possession of it seems to me the deepest root of all the evil that is in the world.*
> MAX BORN

> *From now on, if we are to have any future, we must create that future ourselves.*
> BEATRICE BRUTEAU

receive from the outer world and insights we hold in our inner world, gleaned from our   experience, our intuitions, our sensibilities. Original thinking does not favor the letter of the law over the spirit of the law, or vice versa, but shapes a new and creative thought-form from the basic elements of the two. This is the alchemy of the creative process. It does not set hydrogen against oxygen, but incorporates the two and yields water.

A prerequisite for original thinking is the ability to dwell in mystery, to be comfortable in that space between the dissolution of old ideas and the emergence of the new. We need to be courageous and humble enough to suspend our "beliefs" long enough to incorporate, to bring into ourselves, the beliefs of others that differ from ours—for it is the blending of these two that causes the combustion of original thought. As Leonard Schlain reminds us in *Art and Physics,* "Opposites are not always contradictions—rather they may be complementary aspects of a higher truth."

Dissolving our mental barriers to opposing ideas is a heroic act. All our conditioning is against it. We are programmed to believe certain things and to defend these beliefs, but there is no absolute truth to defend. We have magazines that cater to the left and magazines that cater to the right, and both are busy proving the other side wrong. Facts are manipulated to serve the purposes of different constituencies, from the relevance of global warming to the needs of hungry children. Just as we can find opposing arguments in our sacred texts, so can we find opposing ideas in the scientific, economic, and political arenas—all based on the same facts.

There is no right or wrong on the level of the absolute. There is only the continual evolution of ideas, and if we want to participate in this evolution, become an agent in shaping it, then we have to become the vessel in which the opposites fuse and transmute into a higher form. Just as it takes centuries of heat and pressure to transform carbon molecules into precious diamonds, so are we refined in the friction and the fray of

Through our own efforts, we try to leave behind some small trace that makes a positive difference in the world, a difference that is based not on annihilating the Other but on enhancing the Other. In this way we enhance ourselves as well—by living up to the most noble part of our being.

JEAN LIPMAN-BLUMEN

Our deepest nature, our coded-in-every-cell primate nature is that we are at our most majestic when we do for others.

KENNY MOORE

human discourse.

In his book *Protean Self,* author and psychiatrist Robert Jay Lifton writes about the ability to take up emotional residence in the being of another. "Empathy is the feeling from which social trust is built," he writes. It requires that we include "the other's humanity in one's own imagination."[8] Most of us have never learned to do this. In fact, being in the company of "the other" often causes distress. We're outside our comfort zone, and can't imagine that something might be in it for us.

Years ago, when I was making a cross-country trip interviewing small town folks about their values, I made my way to the homestead of a friend's mother in Kentucky. Her name was Babe. She was seventy-two and lived with her brother, Arthur, who was eighty-eight. When I drove up the long driveway, Babe was sitting on the porch, rocking in her rattan rocker. She waved me up, fetched me a glass of lemonade, and regaled me with tales for the next few hours. When we went into the house, Babe showed me around, saying "This is Arthur's room," at the entrance to the living room. Arthur was out somewhere, so I hadn't met him, but as soon as I saw all the literature on his coffee table, I knew all I needed to know. This man was an ultra-conservative, militaristic, fundamentalist and I didn't want to have anything to do with him. In fact, I was glad he was gone.

Halfway through supper with Babe, in walked Arthur, big as life and gruff as a bear. Babe babbled on about how I was an author, writing this big article on values, and how he ought to talk to me. I nearly choked on my okra. The last thing I wanted to do was talk to Arthur, but he told me to meet him on the porch at eight o'clock the next morning, and he'd tell me whatever I needed to know.

Bright and early the next morning, I ventured out to the porch with my notebook and pen. Arthur was already there, with an old gray golfer's cap on his head and a hand-carved cane in tow. "Come on," he barked, setting off across the lawn. "Get a move on."

"I thought I was going to interview you," I said.

"Can't you walk and talk? Hurry up! Time's a wastin'."

Leaving my notebook in the chair, I took off after Arthur, agitated already.

He started talking about the lumber business he used to own, what kind of trees were on the property, how he knew the land like the back of his hand. The he stopped in his tracks and pointed at a tree with his cane. "Look over there at that walnut tree," he said. "Can you tell me how in the world that tree spits out those walnuts that are so hard I can't crack 'em with my hands? Even them squirrels have to crack 'em on a rock just to get 'em open. What power's loose in the world that can make that happen year after year?"

We walked a bit further, then he stopped again, pointing his cane at the nearby garden. "Look over there at those rows of corn. Why, I just planted those seeds a while ago, and now look, row after row of perfect stalks, with the silkiest golden tassels you ever did see. And do you know what you're gonna find when you pull off those tassels and husk those ears? You're gonna find row after row of golden kernels, all lined up perfect. You tell me, girl, what power's loose in this world that can make that happen?"

I was amazed. This was a man who I'd taken for my opposite. A man I didn't want to talk with. A man I'd boxed into the category "other," and written off as a person to avoid. And now he was ushering me around his land, opening his heart, unfolding the details of his love affair with nature. We walked for two hours, through the woods, down to the creek, across the meadows, and all the while Arthur spoke of the birds, the flowers, the maples, the oaks, as if they were miracles of life going unnoticed. My listening was a vessel for his secrets, a temple for his sacred thoughts. My questions drew the light from his deepest places. My laughter met his gruffness and turned it into joy. We were yin and yang, Arthur and I, and on that two-hour walk we fell in love.

He insisted I stay a few more days, and every morning we'd walk the land, as Arthur talked about trees and nature, his personal beliefs, his troubled life. We had taken up emotional residence in each other's being and it was no longer possible to think of him as "other." Arthur had become my brother in spirit, my friend, and a mirror to myself. His opinions, different as they were from my own, were easier to understand, knowing their context and how they were formed. I had to think more broadly with Arthur in my life, and for this I'm grateful.

Before I left, Arthur confessed to his lifelong dream of seeing the Great Sequoia trees out west. "I waited too long, it'll never happen now, but that's something I dreamed of since I was a boy."

"Arthur, it's not too late," I said. "You can still get there."

"No, it's too late," he insisted. "My own damn fault. I just waited too long."

After that, when I was on the road, I'd always look for postcards with pictures of trees. "Dear Arthur," I'd write. "It's not too late. There's still time. Get to the redwoods! Love, Jan." I must have sent him dozens of those cards.

EMBRACING THE PRESENT

Months went by, and I finally made it back to my home in Syracuse. When I collected my mail, what a surprise to find a postcard from Arthur, from the Sequoia National Forest. "Dear Jan, If it hadn't been for you, I'd never have made it. These trees make me cry like a baby. What power's loose in this world? I love you, Arthur."

My relationship with Arthur lasted a few years until he died, and it taught me one of my biggest lessons: that there is a great advantage to exploring the minds of people whose opinions are different from mine. While there is a kind of friction as opposing thoughts rub against each other, there is also the potential for creative fire that comes with that friction. And as original thinkers, that's what we're after.

CHAPTER NINE

The Creative Enterprise

Whereas moral courage is the righting of wrongs, creative courage, in contrast, is the discovering of new forms, new symbols, new patterns on which a new society can be built.

ROLLO MAY

I know artists whose medium is life itself, and who express the inexpressible without brush, pencil, chisel or guitar. They neither paint, nor dance. Their medium is Being. Whatever their hand touches has increased Life. They see and don't have to draw. They are the artists of being alive.

FREDERICK FRANCK

A few years ago I was visiting my friend Ruby Lee in southern Kentucky. When Sunday morning rolled around, we climbed into her 1972 yellow Oldsmobile and headed off to the Baptist Church. While we were waiting for the service to start, Ruby Lee leaned over and told me, in a hushed voice, to check out the woman at the organ. "She's the minister's wife," she whispered, "but he's having an affair with that blond woman in the second row of the choir. The wife's so mad she's spitting nails and she won't even look at him during the service anymore."

Next thing I knew, the organist was hammering out the processional hymn, her face starched into a sour scowl. The blond in the choir was radiant, singing her heart out and smiling adoringly at the minister as he took his place on the altar. The organist nibbled constantly at her bottom lip and avoided eye contact with anyone in the church.

The balding, overweight minister swaggered to the pulpit like he owned the world. "Brothers and sisters," he bellowed as he raised his arms in a welcoming gesture to the crowd, "today we're here to speak of our enemies, and to follow the Lord's call to love those enemies."

I wasn't sure yet who or what he meant by the enemy, but he said the word with such vehemence it gave me a fright. I looked over at Ruby Lee to see what she made of this, and she was nodding her head in zealous approval. Ruby Lee was seventy-two years old. She had spent nearly every Sunday of her life in this church, and for her, it was business as usual.

As the minister launched into his sermon, his deep voice rose to a fevered pitch and his robe billowed like a mainsail when he flailed his arms. The organist, by this time, was clipping her fingernails, and the blond was sitting on the edge of her choir chair, rapt in devotion to the minister of her dreams. I tried to follow what he was saying, but every time he roared out the word enemy, I just cringed in the pew. After awhile, it was all I heard—enemy this, enemy that.

It was hard for me to stay focused on the subject of enemies since I'd spent my whole life trying not to have any. What I really wanted to do was go up to that pulpit and tell people to get past the whole idea of enemies, because it doesn't serve us anymore. But I stayed where I was, wondering if anyone considered me an enemy, just because of what I think.

When we got into the car after the service, I told Ruby Lee what I was feeling. "Don't you think it's time to move beyond this enemy thing? Don't you think we have to get past what keeps us separate from each other and figure out what we have in common?" She threw her Olds into reverse and backed up right into the chain link fence. "Girl, you sure got some crazy ideas up there. Let's go git lunch."

We headed off to the local hospital for their Sunday brunch, but I couldn't get the minister off my mind. There he was with a captive audience and a chance to make a difference in people's lives. He had all the benefits of theater, with the music, the rituals, the stage of the holy altar. He took a reference from the Bible and created a performance piece on the theme of enemy, and each of us perceived it through our own filters. Had there been critics in the congregation, some would have panned him, others applauded.

On some level, we are all creators whether we intend to be or not. As we perform our lives, there are always people watching us, listening for clues, looking for differences, assessing our actions, our words. We constantly create environments which others enter into and feel either nourished or negated. We create waves of energy that wash over people in our presence—waves that can lull and comfort or lash and damage. We create what our days and nights look like, what work we do, what beauty surrounds us. And on a daily basis, we create the attitude we bring to life and choose whether the door to our heart is open or closed.

Like the preacher at the pulpit or the artist at her palette, we each create something for others to respond to, whether it is a sermon to ponder, a painting to look at, or something as intangible as a safe space to be in. And just like those church-goers, we are taking in everyone else's performance, listening for clues about what to think. The minister's agenda was to inspire the congregation to think about enemies as he thought about enemies. My agenda, had I had a chance at the pulpit, would have been to inspire people to think as I thought about enemies.

Years later, another approach comes to mind. That would be to address the subject in such a way that people could see both sides. Then they would have to tap into their intuition, draw from their personal experience, and synthesize this with the two perspectives to come up with a new and original thought on the subject. They would not abdicate their power to the minister or to me. They would use our thoughts to stimulate their own, and leave church that day with new insights gained from the merging of our words and their experience. This is the alchemy of creativity, the process of original thinking. It takes place in the realm of the imaginal—the inner frontier—which is the last and most fertile frontier to explore.

"Socially and economically the late-20th-century emphasis on information is shifting in favor of the imagination," writes Harriet Rubin, author of *The Princessa: Machiavelli for Women* and editor of some of the most influential business books of the decade. "Leaders who want to discover new markets or radically transform their industries or perhaps test their own mettle need to explore uncharted waters. They need to sail into the imagination." The work of thought leaders today, no matter what the arena, is to rouse people into consciousness, to awaken the drowsy imaginations of a sedated public and get them to turn on the lights of their own lives. And to do this for others, we need to know how to do this for ourselves.

We need to know how to resolve our own conflicts, how to manage our thoughts, how to dissolve the obstacles to our creativity. And as leaders, we need to know how to guide people through the portals of new possibilities—new ways of thinking, speaking, being. It is not our role to encourage people what to think, to convert people to our side, whether it is the right or the left. It is our role to become bridges between the two—to create a new thoroughfare for thinking that supersedes the binary and finds its strength in the whole.

To come to our challenges like an artist calls for a great letting go. It demands of us the willingness to replace a vernacular of blame and criticism with a language of openness and kindness. It demands a spiritual depth and an emotional breadth that enables us to honor another as our self. It demands that we embody compassion and speak like our words are the seeds of tomorrow.

It takes more than a vision to make a visionary. It takes a rigorous discipline of thought management and a meticulous undoing of old habits. It requires the capacity to not simply withstand the tension of opposites, but to become the mechanism for their transformation, to contain and direct the power that is generated as they fuse and ignite. Just as a battery cable needs to be connected to the positive and negative poles to give it the power to recharge a dead battery, so it is with us. If we learn to bring the opposites together in our own lives—to welcome ideas that differ, to embrace people from different cultures and creeds—then we learn, as well, the alchemy of creation. We become practitioners in the art of generating power—authentic, unitive power—which is the medium of leadership itself.

We're exposed to so many contradictions these days, it's hard to know where to turn for facts that are unadulterated by someone's spin. In researching for this book, I often found that just when I had accumulated a substantial file of information in support of an idea, on another day I'd find a treasure chest of facts that supported its opposite.

For three years, Enron was named one of the 100 Best Companies to Work for in America. It received six environmental awards in 2000, won praise from environmentalists for evironmental lobbying, and was a favorite on many social responsibility investment indexes. Their corporate values emphasized communication, integrity and respect. After Enron's fall, one of the hotter items on eBay was a sixty-four page paperback, the elegantly written Enron corporate code of ethics. "Never been opened," according to the former employee who was selling it.

On my desk now are three articles about Wal-Mart. One announces that on one day in 2002, Wal-Mart sales total exceeded the GNPs of thirty-six countries. It reports that a typical employee hourly wage is $8 and that half of Wal-Mart's US employees qualify for food stamps. Wal-Mart employees compose the largest single group in the state of Washington's low-income health program. While more than two-thirds of the employees are women, less than 10 percent hold management positions.[1]

A *Fortune* magazine article reports on how Wal-Mart flexed its massive distribution muscle to deliver supplies to victims of Hurricane Katrina. "If the federal government would have responded as quickly as

Wal-Mart, we could have saved more lives," claimed Jefferson Parish sheriff, Harry Lee. Wal-Mart trucks arrived with supplies and water days before the Red Cross and FEMA. The company set up a phone bank in Bentonville to take calls from displaced employees, and eventually non-employees, who needed assistance. They appealed to their army of truck drivers to haul food to the shelters in the flood zone. They gave bullets and holsters to local police and National Guardsmen. They gave $20 million in cash and supplies. Wal-Mart was there when no one else was.[2]

And as further testimony to our cultural divide, here are some findings from the American Demographics Perception Study, an online survey of 1,133 adults fielded by Aegis Group's Synovate. When consumers were asked to name the "most trustworthy company in America," Wal-Mart tied for second (with General Electric) behind Ford Motor Company. But more people picked Wal-Mart in a separate question as the "least trustworthy" company, putting it second on the rogue's list, just behind Enron, according to the report.

High school graduates ranked Wal-Mart tops in trust, believable ads, and service; yet in separate questions to pick the worst offenders in those areas, Wal-Mart also had the worst scores among high school graduates. Within the same age, income, education and regional demographic groups, the question of Wal-Mart's popularity sparks radically divergent views.[3]

Is one right and the other wrong? No. Is it worth getting in a heated battle over? No. Is there something to learn from this? Yes. That whatever the facts are, they can be spun to serve the needs of the spinner.

Paul Krugman, op-ed columnist for the *New York Times* and winner of the John Bates Clark medal for the best American economist under the age of forty, writes about George W. Bush and Harken Energy. He informs us that Mr. Bush acquired his position on the board of directors and audit committee when Harken paid $2 million for Spectrum 7, a tiny, money-losing energy company with large debts. Mr. Bush was CEO of Spectrum 7. Krugman writes, "Explaining what it was buying, Harken's founder said, 'His name is George Bush.'"[4]

Harken was also losing money, but in 1989 hid most of its losses with the profits it reported from selling a subsidiary, Aloha Petroleum, at a high price. As it turns out, Aloha was bought by a group of Harken insiders, who got most of the money for the purchase by borrowing from Harken itself. Eventually the Securities and Exchange Commission ruled that this was a phony transaction and forced the company to restate its 1989 earnings. "Only a few weeks before bad news that could not be concealed caused Harken's shares to tumble, Mr. Bush sold off two-thirds of his stake, for $848,000," writes Krugman. "Oddly, though the law requires prompt disclosure of insider sales, he neglected to inform the SEC about this transaction until thirty-four weeks had passed. An internal SEC memorandum concluded that he had broken the law, but no charges were filed. This, everyone insists, had nothing to do with the fact that his father was president."[5]

When Ann Coulter, UPS syndicated columnist and legal correspondent for *Human Events*, refers to these events in her book *How To Talk to a Liberal (If You Must)*, she writes: "The facts are: Bush sold his stock in Harken Energy to purchase the Rangers. The price of stock later went down...The imputation of criminality to Bush [and Cheney] is so ludicrous that even in the girly-girl, eye-poking attacks on the *New York Times* op-ed page it has been roundly admitted that there is no question of 'any criminality' (Frank Rich) and that 'Mr. Bush broke no laws' (Nicholas Kristof)."[6]

So there we have it. Half of us will believe Krugman. The other half will go with Coulter. And our adolescent war between the worlds will continue, until enough of us realize that Rome is burning and put down our fiddles. We don't need to conjure up evidence about who is wrong and who is right. We need to take a look at what needs fixing and get out our tool kits.

Our entire news industry is built on dramatizing our differences. Dozens of new television shows offer little but an hour's worth of conflict personified by competition, mean-spiritedness, and back-biting. The very worst of human nature is our prime time fare. And we've come to expect the same from politics. Many of us are weary of the whole thing, and are tempted toward apathy, but this will harm us immeasurably.

We will die in our Lazy-Boys from broken spirits and wasted muscles if we do not now speak our minds. We will forsake the very spirit that fuels our life if we do not wake up and remember that there's a reason for our aliveness, that we came here with a purpose. We are a perfectly

> The most interesting and highest-leverage action for leadership is to expand the way we think.
> BILL ISAACS

> If you look for the truth outside yourself, it gets farther and farther away.
> TUNG SHAN

> The most dangerous of our prejudices reign in ourselves against ourselves. To dissolve them is a creative act.
> HUGO VON HOFMANNSTHAL

embodied blend of spirit and matter, the most potent engines of creativity in the world, and the only thing that is required for our personal and planetary well-being is the conscious application of our creative power. We are healed by creation and by the creations of others. We are healed when we transform the events of our lives into other shapes that can be of use—into stories and poems, music and films. We are healed when we listen to the voice within and let it guide us to the work we were born to do.

Whether or not we consider ourselves artists, we are all in the business of creating our lives and co-creating the culture we live in. Each of us is here to bring to life that something that's unique to us. None of us is aiming for triteness, in pursuit of the shallow. It's greatness we're after—and not some hollow applause coming from somewhere beyond us, but the deep down thrill of knowing we went all out, put our soul into something, created a life that sparked something new, had an impact, made a difference.

In an essay circulating by e-mail, Clarissa Pinkola Estes, author of *Women Who Run With the Wolves*, writes: "Ours is not the task of fixing the entire world all at once, but of stretching out to mend the part of the world that is within our reach. Any small, calm thing that one soul can do to help another soul, to assist some portion of this poor suffering world, will help immensely. One of the most calming and powerful actions you can do to intervene in a stormy world is to stand up and show your soul."

Those who do original work in any field do so because they mine themselves deeply and bring up what is personal.

RALPH STEINER

It is this generous gift of our essence, this soul-sharing that attracts others to our light. It is our speaking out that calls forth the co-creators we are looking for. Just as the beauty of a rose summons the bee when it is time for pollination, so does the beauty of our soul summon our kindred spirits when we dare to bare it. There is nothing more luminous and alluring than the human soul, and nowhere does it shine as clearly as it shines in the process of self-revelation. We are relational beings and we come to understand ourselves precisely in the context of our relationships. We are

Whenever there is a conflict between the will and the imagination, the imagination always wins.

EMIL COUE

If an idea is important intellectually, it should be presented spiritually and emotionally if inspired action is to result.

JIM CHANNON

grist for each other's mill.

Poet Sheila Bender writes that "there are feelings and longings we understand and accept in ourselves only when we recognize them in someone else's words, words that have never been ours to speak until we saw them written out of someone else's life." When you share your fears with me, your joys or brokenness, you give me a way to better understand my own. Your speaking is a mirror in which I find myself. That is the gift of our self-expression. When we give shape to our interior world, put words to it, offer it to others, we are offering more than the eye can see.

In an interview in *Common Boundary* magazine, Alice Walker said:

> The process of the storytelling is itself a healing process, partly because you have someone there who is taking the time to tell you a story that has great meaning to them. They're taking the time to do this because your life could use some help, but they don't want to come over and just give advice. They want to give it to you in a form that becomes inseparable from your whole self. That's what stories do. Stories differ from advice in that, once you get them, they become a fabric of your whole soul. That is why they heal you.[7]

This is why our creative work is so essential. It is not pointless or fool-hardy. It is an act of faith, an act of kindness, crucial to our own healing and the healing of the planet. To create is to make something whole from the pieces of our lives, and in the process, to become more whole ourselves. It is a healing act, a leave-taking from the chaos as we move from the choppy surface toward the stillness of the center.

The creative journey is a heroic enterprise. It is a brave pilgrimage to the center of our lives where we mine our depths for what seeks to be released, transmuting one thing into another, turning tragedies and triumphs into new forms conjured in our private hours and offered to others like food for the soul, a wrap against the chill. It demands our stillness and rapt attention, calls for courage as we pass through the dark on the way to the light. And this is the journey that defines the new myth-maker. This is the journey home to ourselves, where we discover what we know and what to make of it. This is the journey where we humbly accept our role as a co-creator and commit to bringing our light into the world.

In a world as divided as ours, there is a great opening for voices that can unify, words that can weave our tattered pieces back into their original oneness. It is a creative endeavor that involves as much spirit as thought and calls for a most illuminated imagination, which exists right now in the center of each of us. It may be sluggish from disuse, or enshrouded in fear or doubt, but it is there, waiting to be rediscovered, dusted off, and deployed into service. And what is it that brings our imaginations back to life? What is it that lures our creativity out of its hibernating state? It is exposure to the imaginative work of others. It is the arts that wake us up, that shake us out of our numbness and reel us back into the circle of life. And I'm not referring to the high arts of opera, classical music, ballet—though these surely do the trick—but to the common arts of story-telling, music-making, singing, poetry.

The arts reflect us to ourselves. They are a mirror of our magnitude, evidence of our power as alchemists to transform the lead of our daily lives into stories and images that heal and nudge. In *The Grace of Great Things*, Robert Grudin writes:

> Art is a primal strength, a communal impulse. It is a language holding society together by stronger cords that the mere language of words. It lives in harmony not with the alien surfaces of things but with their inner spirit, their intimately familiar ideas. It bears these ideas into our awareness and makes us participate in them. It knows us not as individuals with names but as a single awareness, receptive and unified. And as the language of interior humanity, it is one of the very few available means to self-knowledge.[8]

Art returns us to a sense of relatedness, because true art, while it may be channeled through one artist, comes from the common soul. Its reference is universal. It points to the whole and is sourced from the whole. In *A Room of One's Own*, Virginia Woolf writes, "Masterpieces are not single and solitary births; they are the outcome of many years of thinking in common, of thinking by the body of the people, so that the experience of the mass is behind the single voice." This experience of the mass is what gives art its healing power, its prophetic strength and durability.

Artists are the ones who make the invisible visible, who give words and colors and sounds and shapes to the human adventure. They portray it in such a way that we understand more clearly who we are, how we are connected. Italian poet and Nobel Prize winner Salvatore Quasimodo said that "poetry is the revelation of a feeling that the poet believes to be interior and personal but which the reader recognizes as his own."

Poetry, like all the arts, helps us find ourselves. It directs us inward, points us to our essence. It is neither feminine nor masculine, but the perfect blending of the two. It is where the wild wooliness of our physical being joins with the deep holiness of our spiritual being, giving birth to a new entity that expands the magic and meaning of both. Poetry awakens the imagination, stimulates the intellect, stirs the deep waters of our intuition—opening new doors to originality in thought and action.

There is a host of gifted poets who maintained full-time careers in the business world and fulfilled themselves by writing poetry at night. T. S. Eliot worked in the international department of Lloyd's Bank of London; Wallace Stevens was vice-president of Hartford Accident and Indemnity, a corporate lawyer, and an expert on surety bonds; Archibald MacLeish was a lawyer who spent a decade as editor of *Fortune* magazine; A. R. Ammons was a salesman for a scientific glass manufacturer in New Jersey; Richard Hugo spent thirteen years working for the Boeing Company in Seattle; William Carlos Williams was an obstetrician when he wrote the words:

> It is difficult
> to get the news from poems
> yet men die miserably everyday
> for lack
> of what is found there.

Another executive poet, James Autry, used the workplace as grist for nearly all his poems. Before he retired in 1991, Autry was senior vice-president at Meredith Corporation and president of its Magazine Group, a $500 million operation with over nine hundred employees. In his book *Love and Profit: The Art of Caring Leadership*, he writes:

> Wherever did we get the notion that, in management, there is a reasonable and acceptable separation of the intellect and spirit—that, in our work-world terms, the intellect controls the rational work life and the spirit is relegated to the soft stuff of romance, family, and religion? Where did it come from, all this hiding of emotion, of the spirit, of passion, behind some cool mask of macho detachment? I wonder if it is that business is considered too important to be diluted by all those feelings, or is it that business is not considered important enough to deserve them? Either way is wrong.[9]

Autry did not draw a line between his creative persona and his business persona, but found a way to fuse the two. When he walked through his office doors, he did not leave his heart behind, or his spirit. He was aware that every moment, every meeting, every encounter was a moment of creation, and he brought the fullness of his entire being to the business at hand. His poem "Threads" illustrates this beautifully:

Threads
Sometimes you just connect,
like that,
no big thing maybe
but something beyond the usual business stuff
It comes and goes quickly
so you have to pay attention,
a change in the eyes
when you ask about the family,
a pain flickering behind the statistics
about a boy and a girl in school,
or about seeing them, every other Sunday.
An older guy talks about his bride,
a little affectation after twenty-five years.
A hot-eyed achiever laughs before you want him to.
Someone tells about his wife's job
or why she quit working to stay home.
An old joker needs another laugh on the way
to retirement.
A woman says she spends a lot of her salary
on an au pair
and a good one is hard to find
but worth it because there's nothing more important
than the baby.
Listen.
In every office you hear the threads
of love and joy and fear and guilt,
the cries for celebration and reassurance,
and somehow you know that connecting those
threads
is what you are supposed to do
and business takes care of itself.[10]

This is what the creative enterprise is all about. It's about connecting the threads—from our minds to our hearts, from our selves to others, from our souls to the world. It's a moment-by-moment transmutation of energy into matter, where we take the raw materials of our emotions, our ideas, our sensibilities, our experiences and convert them into stories and relationships, actions and creations that have an energy of their own, can make an impact, and cause a change.

James Autry paid attention to the lives of his employees. His heart was fully engaged and he noticed the nuances, tuned into the subtleties, and honored the emotional lives of the people he worked with. What he created, besides poetry, was a workplace of integrity and wholeness. He understood the power of intimacy and had the courage to initiate it, embrace it, and write about it. In the introduction to *Love and Profit*, he writes that "work can provide the opportunity for spiritual and personal, as well as financial, growth. If it doesn't, then we're wasting far too much of our lives on it."

Creativity is the energy that flows through us naturally when our emotional, spiritual, and mental channels are fully opened. We are creative by default. It's our nature, our natural destiny. The only thing we have to learn is how to keep our channels open. And this calls for practice on every level. We have to practice feeling our emotions; we have to practice our spirituality, however we experience it; and we have to practice thinking and speaking our own thoughts, arriving at our own conclusions, in the face of polarizing contradictions.

And when we have practiced enough that we wake up each day knowing it is ours to create as we choose, feeling confident enough to call ourselves creative, then we will be ready to help others clear their channels and offer the world the gift of their originality. It is this simple process that will restore us to wholeness, as individuals, as sisters and brothers, as co-creators and custodians of this beautiful planet.

TEN

Prophets and Profits: Capitalizing on Wisdom

The ignorant work for their own profit; the wise work for the welfare of the world, without thought for themselves.

BHAGAVAD GITA, 3:25 26

If you don't share your wealth with us, we will share our poverty with you.

NIGERIAN TRIBAL CHIEF

For centuries, our wise elders, the prophets, have been trying to talk sense into us. Every spiritual tradition encourages compassion and good works, inner awareness and outward generosity. The Talmud tells us that "whoever saves one life, saves the world entire." Muhammad said, "There is a key for everything, and the key to Paradise is love for the poor." Buddha said if we knew the results of giving and sharing, we would not eat without having given. A Hopi elder explains, "Almost everything we do is a religious act, from the time we get up to the time we go to sleep. How can the white man ever understand that?" The Qur'an states, "Wheresoever you turn, there is the face of God." James says in the New Testament that "faith, if it doesn't lead to action, is dead," and an Ethiopian wise woman reminds us that "when spiders unite, they can tie up a lion."

Here we are on planet Earth with one precious life to live and what are most of us caught up in? The quest for money. Living takes money. Business takes money. Growth takes money. So the question is how can we tend to the business at hand without living divided lives? How can we bring our spiritual values into workplaces driven by the bottom line? How can we live with the Hopi awareness that every act is a spiritual act and align our actions with our inner wisdom and social values?

Original thinking is ignited by the fusion of opposites, and the challenge of merging spiritual values with material realities is sparking creativity in every arena. A while ago, while carpooling to Santa Fe with two other women to a workshop I was facilitating on "Creativity and Transformation," one mentioned that she was an atheist. I asked her how it felt when people talked about God in her presence, and she said it was uncomfortable, but that she was getting used to it.

"You know, spiritual issues always come up when you're talking about creativity and transformation. It's the nature of the beast," I said, trying to prepare her for a weekend with a group of women who would likely be spiritually-inclined.

"Whatever," she shrugged her shoulders. "It won't be a big deal."

But it was for me. One of my commitments when facilitating groups is to be sure that everyone feels included, and I wracked my brain trying to think of ways to create a space that would feel right for everyone there. By the time Friday night rolled around and we were gathering as a group, I had a plan.

Before we did any of our introductions, I told them about the only rule we'd have to abide by for the entire weekend: No one could use the word "God." They could say whatever they wanted to say, but they would have to be creative and speak in such a way that they could be understood by a person who did not understand the concept "God." Two women from the Bible Belt had a little trouble at first, but by Sunday morning, we were well-practiced in the art of communicating our spirituality without the use of "religious" language.

Spirituality is like breath. It is our vital force, and it is communicated more in how we speak, than what we say. It shows up in how we listen, in how attentive we are, how present we are to others. Where religion is the word, spirituality is the meaning. It's in the choices we make, the values we embody, the stands we take. Little is gained from conversations about religion, but action rooted in love and compassion can move mountains.

The United States was founded on the principles of keeping church and state separate and we have all been trained to separate our spiritual lives and our work lives. But, in essence, spirituality is not about the church. It's about our relationships with each other. Religion is about our beliefs and what we think; spirituality is about our values and how we act. Traditionally, in the matter of business and economics, values have not figured into the equations for success. Business decisions have been made with one thing in mind—profit—and social costs, no matter how devastating, are "externalized" in a value-free context.

An example of this is when General Motors came out with their

Chevrolet Malibu in 1979. Prototype tests indicated that the fuel tank was too close to the rear bumper, significantly increasing the risk of fire in the event of a collision, but GM did nothing about it. As it turned out, two women and four children were severely burned after an accident in their Malibu, and during the trial two internal memos surfaced that explained GM's rationale. One stated that gas tanks should be placed no closer than fifteen inches to the rear bumper, and that the Malibu's gas tank was eleven inches from the bumper. It would cost the company $8.59 per car to fix this. But in a "value analysis" memo, a GM engineer calculated that deaths from such accidents would cost the company only $2.40 per automobile, so GM made a decision not to fix it.[1] Business as usual.

These are the kinds of decisions that are made when we draw a dividing line between our business and spiritual selves. When we fail to integrate our values into our everyday choices, we end up living divided lives, and the "whole"—our integral self—is shattered into fragments. An executive would never think of pouring chemicals into his child's sandbox, or filling her family's pool with polluted water, but somehow there is permission to poison the environment of others if it makes good business sense. This is a dangerous disconnect that is becoming apparent to many business leaders and several have been organizing to change things.

In 1999 the fourteenth Dalai Lama, Tenzin Gyatso, said during a conference in Amsterdam that "business is the only thing that will have an influence on the future of this planet." A few years later, Sander Tideman co-authored a book with the Dalai Lama called *Compassion or Competition: A Discussion on Human Values in Business and Economics,* which contains a rare exchange between the Dalai Lama and business and economics leaders from around the world. Tideman, after a career in law and banking, co-founded and currently chairs Spirit in Business (SiB), a fast-growing network organization promoting ethics and values in the business world. In a recent essay, he wrote: "Spiritual teachings tell us that we make up reality, so likewise it must be us who make up the economy. For better or for worse, economies and business don't function separately from our decisions, since without us they wouldn't exist. So if we want a better economy we have to look deeply at who we are and how we live."[2]

And Tideman has a lot of company. More than five hundred executives, consultants, entrepreneurs, and spiritual leaders attended a three-day conference to launch the Spirit in Business World Institute in

2002, and over four thousand individuals from thirty countries have been involved with SiB. Leading corporations such as American Express, Verizon, and *Forbes* have sponsored SiB events, and senior corporate leaders from Citigroup, Videophone, British Petroleum, Goldman Sachs, Hewlett-Packard, and Honeywell have stepped forward in support.

With offices in Greenfield, Massachusetts and the Netherlands, SiB facilitates a variety of events that allow business leaders to deepen their own wisdom and find ways to foster spiritual leadership in their organizations. Through involvement with SiB, companies are learning to develop mechanisms that measure the human and business impact of spirituality-based programs, apply learning modules on compassion and trust throughout their organization, and improve decision-making by focusing stakeholders in a common vision through a broad concept of spirituality.

Since 2001, the Association for Spirit at Work, the Spirit in Business Institute, the World Business Academy and the European Baha'i Business Forum have collaborated to honor organizations that explicitly include human spirit on their strategic agendas and find ways to nurture this asset in their policies, practices, and cultures. The nine 2005 award honorees represent approximately 100,000 employees in multiple industries in offices all over the world. "The award honors the recipients for their spiritual policies, programs or practices that explicitly nurture spirituality in their organizations. Their cultures strive for integrity, discipline, creativity, and effective growth. They honor all religious traditions. This dedication to wholeness and health creates increased financial value and a dynamic organization," according to Elisa Mallis, selection committee chairperson of the International Spirit at Work Award.

According to Sander Tideman, because of our mutual dependence in this increasingly smaller and interconnected world, we can understand the need for values such as compassion, but, in his opinion, spiritual traditions point to a more profound and personal dimension of compassion. "They advise us to make altruism the core of our practice, not only because it is the cheapest and most effective insurance policy for our future, but specifically because the *real* benefit of compassion is that it will bring about a transformation in the mind of the practitioner. It will make us happy."[3]

The *Course in Miracles* states clearly that "giving is receiving," but science is now proving it. With a generous grant from the John Templeton Foundation, the Institute for Research on Unlimited Love

(IRUL) was founded in 2001 and is now exploring the source, dimensions, and impact of altruism with the help of scientists from fifteen different disciplines. Bioethicist Stephen Post, a professor of bioethics at the Case Western School of Medicine, says that "with generous behavior, people have fuller lives, deeper self-esteem, and a more creative engagement of their capacities." It pays to be good.

IRUL grantees have discovered that volunteerism reduces the risk of depression in young people, and that those who volunteer do better in school and get into better colleges. In a five year study of 423 elderly people, researchers found that people who reported helping others were only about half as likely to die in the five years as those who did not. A study of 2000 Presbyterians showed that mental health improvements were more closely linked to giving help than receiving it. And in a ten-year study of nuns, neurologists who had reviewed essays the nuns had written back in the 1930s found that nuns whose essays expressed positive emotions outlived the others by an average of ten years and were slightly less likely to develop dementia.[4]

"When you live for others as much as for yourself, you're going with the grain of human nature, even the grain of the universe. It's all paradoxical. In the giving of self lies the unsought discovery of self," writes Post in his book *Unlimited Love: Altruism, Compassion and Service.*

We're also learning that mindfulness, with its offspring forgiveness and compassion, leads to improved health and increased wealth. Dr. Frederic Luskin, a researcher at Stanford University who specializes in the connection between spirituality and health, initiated the Stanford Forgiveness Project to look at the effectiveness of forgiveness intervention. In one study, thirteen American Express financial advisors and three vice presidents were given a one day training in emotional competence focusing on forgiveness. Each advisor was offered follow up through four conference calls over the subsequent year. At the end of the study, a reduction of 25 percent was seen in stress. Participants showed a gain of 20 percent in positive emotion and an increase of 18.3 percent in gross sales. The rest of their market group showed a corresponding gain of 10.4 percent in gross sales over the year.[5] With statistics like these, it's no wonder that companies and organizations with visionary leadership are introducing values-based programs into their corporate cultures.

Other discussions and projects at the Stanford Research Institute (SRI) led to the founding of the World Business Academy (WBA), a not-for-profit established to explore and clarify the fundamental paradigm shifts underway globally in business, government, academia, and the public. The Academy sponsors and disseminates leading-edge research by scholars, business leaders, and visionaries. Its goal is to enable its members to integrate this knowledge into their lives and business practices and to disseminate it into the world to rekindle the human spirit in business. The WBA maintains that since business has become the most powerful institution on the planet, it needs to adopt a new tradition of responsibility for the whole, which means that it needs to redefine its own interest in a wider perspective of society.

Philosopher, social scientist, and futurist Willis Harmann sensed the beginning of this evolution. In an article called, "Why a World Business Academy," WBA co-founder Harman wrote: "A respiritualization of society is taking place, but one more experiential and non-institutionalized, less fundamental and sacerdotal, than most of the historically familiar forms of religion. Science, in turn, is reassessing its foundation assumptions to better accommodate the human spirit and the conscious awareness that comprise our most direct link with reality. Such a change in basic assumptions must inevitably be accomplished by a long-term shift in value emphases and priorities."[6]

According to Harmann, the sociopolitical transformation we are now undergoing is actuated by the push of the global dilemmas and the pull of a vision of what could be. It is that very tension between *what is* and *what could be* that is causing an eruption of evolved thinking like we've never seen before. Old systems and institutions are self-destructing before our eyes and new ways of being and doing are rising like a phoenix from their ashes.

Built into the concept of capitalism and free enterprise from the beginning was the assumption that the actions of many units of individual enterprise, responding to market forces and guided by the "invisible hand" of Adam Smith, would somehow add up to desirable outcomes. "But it's becoming clear that this 'invisible hand' is faltering," writes Harmann, who suggests that the whole enterprise relies upon a consensus of overarching meanings and values that are not operative in our current system. Somewhere along the line we forgot that Adam Smith also wrote in *The Theory of Moral Sentiments* that markets could not function without ethics and morals.[7]

So, says Harmann, "Business has to adopt a tradition it has never had throughout the entire history of capitalism: to share responsibility for the whole. Every decision that is made, every action that is taken, must be viewed in the light of that kind of responsibility." And what this means, in the long run, is a total reworking of our key assumptions and a revolutionary rethinking about the part business plays in planetary well-being. The belief system that we have bought into may have been appropriate at one time in history, but now it is as fashionable as a horse and buggy. It simply doesn't fit anymore.

Just as technology has exponentially changed our ways of doing business, so has it altered our ways of perceiving reality. People are beginning to think and feel in non-linear ways. The World Wide Web is not just a place to visit for research and communication. It is a metaphor of our connectedness, the architecture of our engagement. We are in touch as we've never been in touch before and our enhanced accessibility to each other is causing a dramatic escalation not only in communication, but in human consciousness. "Out of sight, out of mind" is no longer plausible in a world where we have instant access to images and the imaginations of our sisters and brothers all over the planet. Our oneness is manifesting itself through our very technology. As a living organism, our planet is constantly evolving and adapting to the stresses it is undergoing. And we, having come from the earth, are part of that evolution.

As the Persian poet Rumi writes, "We began as mineral. We emerged into plant life, and into the animal state, and then into being human, and always we have forgotten our former states, except in early spring when we slightly recall being green again." We may have forgotten our former states, but from the moment our consciousness evolved, we have been active co-creators in the planetary enterprise. Evolution is not happening to us, but through us, and the fact that we have created a technology that connects us like cells in a neural network is a telling thing.

Universal intelligence is coursing through us as it courses through every atom in every cell. It is the source of our inspiration. As the writer Doris Lessing once said, "I didn't have a thought. There was a thought around." All of our inventions and creations come from this intelligence, which is the same force that causes the seed to burst through its husk and journey upward in search of the light. Constant change, constant progress, constant adaptation. It is the nature of being. And what we are undergoing in our own evolutionary cycle is the same natural process that amoebas undergo when their survival is threatened—they unite.

Einstein once wrote that "something deeply hidden had to be behind things." This deeply hidden thing—what some think of as God, or Brahman, or Yahweh, or Nature, or "electricity with a capital E" as my brother refers to it—this is the force that unites us, that compels us toward compassion and pulls on our consciousness like the moon on the waves. It causes us to think differently, to perceive more multi-dimensionally, to sense what is needed in times of crises, and to move decisively in the direction of life. Though we have not officially placed humankind on the endangered species list, the decisions we are making in the name of progress may put us there soon. We've given carte blanche to economic development and are just beginning to calculate the staggering toll it has taken on the very resources we need to live—the air, the waterways, the forests.

But the organism that is hosting us—our mother earth—is well aware, and the survival mechanisms are kicking in. Evolution is making a quantum leap and it is doing it through our consciousness. Just like in the fall, when the leaves start to change, each leaf changes in its own time, according to its nature and cellular composition. And we, like those leaves, are changing in our own time. Some of us have a complete and visceral sense of the "human community." Some comprehend what is happening and are actively and consciously reaching out, creating networks, building community. And for some, the change is more subtle: a heightened interest in spirituality, a hungering for more meaning, a disenchantment with materialism, and a longing for connectedness.

As the intelligence surges through us, we become motivated to express our higher natures, to care for each other, and to put systems in place that are healthy, holistic, and good for the whole. As agents of evolution, we are converting this intelligence into informed action, just as those leaves convert water and carbon dioxide into sugar and oxygen. Photosynthesis is the work of plants; info-synthesis is the work of humans. There is more information in the daily news than our ancestors were exposed to in their entire lives, and our job, as a human race, is to absorb it and use it for the benefit of the whole, as our bodies metabolize food for the benefit of every cell.

Part of this process, at this point in our survival, is a re-evaluation of the systems now in place. At no other time in history have we taken such a critical look at our own constructions—our businesses, our institutions, our politics, and public policies. In every milieu, evolving minds are dissecting the structures on which we've built our culture, re-pairing parts we have torn asunder, and calling attention to tears in the fabric we have wrapped ourselves in as American citizens. Everything is on trial in this evolutionary advance, and our concerns for the future are leading us inward. Like butterflies wrapped in the dark cocoon, we are saying goodbye to our caterpillar selves, and doing what we can to prepare our beings for the great transformation. This is what's known as spiritual work—this inner looking, this letting go—and it is calling us by name, one by one.

In every field, there are leaders emerging, challenging the old and creating the new. No institution is spared examination, and no assumptions remain unchallenged. As the visionary physicist David Bohm writes in his groundbreaking book *On Dialogue*, "Intelligence requires that you don't defend an assumption." The greatest leaders in any field are those who are challenging themselves and others to release their grip on "how it is" and explore the question of "how it might be better." Douglass North, winner of the 1993 Nobel Prize in Economics writes, "We live in an uncertain and ever-changing world that is continually evolving in new and novel ways. Standard theories are of little help in this context. Attempting to understand economic, political and social change requires a fundamental recasting of the way we think."[8]

A few assumptions that are being re-examined from a more holistic point of view are the notions that it is acceptable to have the economy be the dominant institution with more power than anything else, that the singular function of business is to provide rewards to investors, and that there is little relationship between material development and spiritual concerns. Research in all the sciences is proving that the cultivation of values such as insight, compassion, and generosity is what leads to true happiness and wholeness—not just for individuals, but for organizations and society as well.

For ages we have discounted such intangibles as spiritual values, seduced by tenets of economics that said it makes no sense to devote time, effort, or expense to maintaining values, if money can be made by ignoring them. And now, economics itself is under attack, beginning with a student rebellion against dogmatism in economics that began in France in June 2000. After spreading to Cambridge, England and reverberating around the world, the movement is erupting in universities across the US. Over seven hundred Harvard students and alumni have signed a petition addressed to the Harvard Economics Department asking it to approve a new introductory economics course that would cover a broader spectrum of views, examine the assumptions of economics, and challenge students to think critically.

The movement is referred to as *autisme-économie*, the post-autistic economics (PAE) movement, having been instigated by students who considered economics "autistic."[9] Like sufferers of autism, the students assert that the field of economics is intelligent but obsessive, narrowly focused, and cut off from the outside world. They demand reform within economics teaching, which they say has become enthralled with complex mathematical models that only operate in conditions that don't exist.

Students have not been alone in mounting increasing pressure on the status quo. Thousands of economists from dozens of countries have taken up the cause for "post-autistic economics" with the slogan "bringing sanity, humanity and science back to economics." André Orléan, a renowned French economist, supports this idea, and writes that "the economist must engage him or herself as a citizen with convictions regarding the public good and ways of treating it."

The PAE movement is intent on reopening economics for free scientific inquiry, and making it a pursuit where critical thinking rules instead of ideology. Though they don't use the word "spirituality" in their papers, they appear to be motivated by a sense of their connectedness and responsibility to others around the world who end up being victims of "good economics." What they are rallying for is a plurality of approaches and an economics with conscience.

By reinventing capitalism and injecting our own souls into the machine, you and I can raise the bar of human possibility.
HOWARD BLOOM

You can't have a world where 50 percent of the people are dieting and 50 percent of the people are starving if you want stability.
JOHN SHELBY SPONG

When your thinking rises above concern for your own welfare, wisdom independent of thought appears.
SEVENTEENTH-CENTURY SAMURAI TEXT

A memo signed by Lawrence Summers, current president of Harvard University, when he served as chief economist for the World Bank gives an idea of the kind of economics they are calling into question. The memo, cited in the Global Situation Report, addressed the subject of dumping the toxic wastes of the industrial world on the less developed world. It was written in December 1999 by World Bank economist Lant Pritchett, and signed by Summers. Phrases from the memo include:

"Just between you and me, shouldn't the World Bank be encouraging more migration of dirty industries to the LDCs [less developed countries]?"

"I think the economic logic behind dumping a load of toxic waste in the lowest wage country is impeccable and we should face up to it."[10]

Decisions of this nature may make economic sense on some level, but they are neither inspired nor inspiring. Economics, from this perspective, is cold, calculating, and brutal, and it is not surprising that students and academics are calling for a rethinking of the entire system. People are tuning in to the reality that we are ultimately interdependent, and when they realize this, a tectonic shift occurs in their being.

Old mindsets dissolve, opinions change, decisions become more spirit-derived and values-driven. Where before it was only the measurables and tangibles that mattered, now there is concern for the intangible and invisible. Now, one thinks of "the other." Now, the word "spirit" begins to make sense, and though it may never be uttered, it becomes the foundation for a new way of being. Such is the process of evolution. It's a growing awareness of our ultimate unity with every living thing. And once somebody shifts into this level of consciousness, all heaven breaks loose and there is no one and nothing on earth undeserving of our highest regard.

As we grow to embrace and understand our interrelatedness, the quality of our relationships begins to matter. People begin to respond to the energy in an organization, to distinguish between colleagues who drain them and colleagues who sustain them. The corporate culture becomes more important as people seek out meaning and authenticity in their workplace. More is expected. More is demanded. And when people feel enlivened on a spiritual level, more is given.

It's no surprise, then, that according to research, a company's performance is at least 30 percent attributable to the corporate culture, where these values play out.[11] When we feel *in-spired*, from the same root word as *spiritus*, then we are more creative, more imaginative, more productive. And we feel inspired when we are seen by other people—when they recognize our gifts and acknowledge our uniqueness. Spirituality in the workplace pertains to our relationships and our commitments to support our colleagues. If the culture itself fuels the employees with feedback, opportunities for sharing and networking, and a visible commitment to fostering community, then those employees

> *The place God calls you to is the place where your deep gladness and the world's deep hunger meet.*
> FREDERICK BUECHNER

> *I firmly believe that there is no single factor more critical in influencing whether or not we achieve a humanely, ecologically, and spiritually satisfying future for this society and for humanity, than a free, aware, responsible and vital private sector—profit and nonprofit.*
> WILLIS HARMANN

> *We cannot strive for what we do not believe in.*
> KAZUO INAMORI

will be propelled toward excellence by the very nature of the culture itself. Treating people honorably leads to honorable behavior. As Daniel Goleman points out in his book *Emotional Intelligence*, leadership success or failure is usually due to "qualities of the heart."

In a recent article, Warren Bennis, founding chairman of the Leadership Institute at the USC Marshall School of Business, cites a survey that found nearly two-thirds of companies believe they use less than half their employees' brainpower. Employees themselves were less optimistic. Only 16 percent said they use more than half their talents at work.[12] If less than half of a body's organs were working, the body would not be considered "well." Nor should an organization consider itself well if it is using less than half the brainpower of its people. So the question is: how can we as leaders inspire people to show up in their totality? How can we create a meaningful environment that excites people and stimulates them to fully engage their whole beings so they're not sailing through their workdays at half mast?

In their book, *A Spiritual Audit of Corporate America*, business professor Ian Mitroff and organizational consultant Elizabeth Denton provide a compelling case that companies that foster a spiritual environment tend to have employees who are more creative, loyal, productive, and adaptive to change than companies that stifle spirituality. Mitroff and Denton conducted in-depth interviews with over ninety high-level managers and executives, collecting both qualitative and quantitative data. What they found is that spirituality is one of the most important determinants of organizational performance. People who are more spiritually involved achieve better results. In fact, they suggest that spirituality may well be the ultimate competitive advantage.[13]

Participants of the study differentiated strongly between religion and spirituality, viewing religion as a highly inappropriate form of expression and spirituality as a highly appropriate subject for the workplace. Most believed strongly that organizations must "harness the immense spiritual energy within each person in order to produce world-class products and services." And their perception of spirituality was that it pertained to the process of becoming, that it involved the continuing unfolding of the human spirit. If the company is not invested in the whole person—body, mind and soul—then the person will not bring their whole being to the corporate enterprise.

According to Mitroff and Denton, meaning and purpose are the top items on a lot of people's agendas. When survey participants were asked how these were imparted in the workplace, they offered the following, ranking from highest to lowest in importance: (1) the ability to realize my full potential as a person; (2) being associated with a good organization or an ethical organization; (3) interesting work; (4) making money; (5) having good colleagues and serving humankind; (6) service to future generations; and (7) service to my immediate community. Beyond a certain threshold, the authors point out, pay ceases to be the most important factor in work life, and higher needs prevail; the desire for "self-actualization" becomes paramount.

Patricia Aburdene, author of *Megatrends 2010*, sees the rise of spirituality in the workplace as a trend that is about to become a megatrend. To Aburdene, the future will be one in which "the spiritual transformation of capitalism" will shift the American way of doing business "from greed to enlightened self-interest, from elitism to economic democracy, from the fundamentalist doctrine of 'profit at any cost' to the conscious ideology that espouses both money and morals."[14] The coming megatrend, Aburdene asserts, will not be driven by external, social, or technological forces so much as "the *internal* dimension of change" that will reinvent free enterprise. And she predicts this will happen by the year 2010. The precipitating conditions for this megatrend include the enormous stress people are under due to the economic and security crises of the past few years, the impact of the fifty to sixty million "cultural creatives" for whom values upstage money and other trappings of success, a convergence of the movements of social responsibility and spirituality, and the ripple effect of the transformative personal and spiritual work that thought leaders are engaging in and bringing into their institutions.

Dr. Roger Desmarais, president of Corporate Systematics, Inc. in Walnut Creek, California is one such thought leader whose spiritual path cuts right through his office suites. He writes that "the movement towards *corporate spirituality* is gaining momentum, and the goal of this spirituality is a greater personal awareness." Desmarais views spiritual intelligence as the most fundamental of the three intelligences, referring to it as "humanity's transformative intelligence."

For the most part, the word "spirituality" has not become part of the corporate vernacular. People are still trying to distinguish between "religion" and "spirituality" and most companies are making only tentative steps toward opening a dialogue on the subject. Sixty percent of the people polled for Mitroff and Denton's book said they "believe in the beneficial effects of spirituality in the workplace, so long as there's no bully-pulpit promotion of traditional religion." But while people may not be using the word "spirituality," many are attuned to the spiritual dynamics unfolding in their organizations. Spiritual intelligence, unlike mental and emotional intelligence, is a meta-intelligence—it's bound to the sacred, and its awareness goes beyond the physical and beyond the confines of the individual body.

Spiritual intelligence is transformative because it removes our limitations, dissolves our blinders and opens our eyes to the connecting threads that unite us all. The spiritually intelligent person understands that another's loss is his loss, another's gain is hers. The spiritually intelligent person makes decisions based on what's good for the whole, aware that we are intricately bound together like cells in an organ, each of us part of this living, breathing Earth. And more people everyday are coming into this new awareness—not necessarily able to articulate it, but able to feel it and delight in it. Spiritual intelligence is evolving through us as our DNA adapts to the stresses and complexities of the times. And there are choices we can make, actions we can take that actually cause our DNA strands to relax and unwind, allowing us to access deeper levels of creativity. It is creativity and originality that we need to be evoking these days as we search for solutions in every enterprise, and that process is a spiritual process, a journey inward. It is an exploration, not of the known, but of the unknown and yet-to-be-created.

Our creativity expands as we deepen our awareness and tap into our inner dimensions, for this is the place where we discover that we are not our bodies, but that which is *aware of* our bodies. This is the place where we learn that our essence is one with the essence of every living thing, and where we *feel* that oneness that every prophet refers to. This is where we access the universal consciousness and draw it into our beings. And as we open ourselves to the greater wisdom, it speaks to us, through us, its brilliance and light the perfect match to our deepest ponderings.

There is nothing anyone has to learn in order to go within. It is simply a matter of quieting down, setting aside time, committing to a practice of solitude and silence. There are no rules to follow, no creeds to learn, nothing to memorize. All that is needed is just the willingness to take some time out of every day and look inward to the greatest gold mine of all. Mindfulness practices are their own reward, and people who are engaging in them are experiencing unique and positive results.

An article in the *Asia Times* reports that Thomas L. Freese, engineer and vice president of Freese and Nichols, Inc. changed his approach to business management after a ten-day Vipassana retreat near Dallas, in one of the six Vipassana centers in the United States.[15] Vipassana, meaning "to see things as they are," is an ancient Indian self-observation technique that, according to Freese, "leads to clearer thinking and clear thinking is good for business." Following his retreat, Freese took on the task of blending compassion and ethics with bottom lines and profits in his daily work. Eighteen months later, the Fort-Worth based company won the "Best Engineering Firm to Work For" in Texas, an award sponsored by *CE News*, a trade publication for civil engineers. The contest was based on employee satisfaction surveys and *CE News* received 12,587 surveys. For Freese, and many others, the value of Vipassana has gone far beyond the spiritual.

Special Vipassana courses are being organized worldwide for leaders in every imaginable field, and senior staff members of companies including Microsoft, Citibank, IBM, Merrill Lynch, and Zee TV have experienced the practice as a powerful human-resources tool. Vipassana is a practical, universal tool to purify the mind, and it has nothing to do with any religion. It is an ancient technique that causes wisdom and compassion to rise to the surface. It was rediscovered by Gautama Buddha, who practiced it to reach enlightenment. Arun Toshniwal, managing director of the Instrument Society of India, has practiced Vipassana for twenty-five years. "My capacity for work and clarity of thinking have increased and I gain time," he reports, adding that his whole staff attends Vipassana courses with paid leave.

In India, the premiere business school, Symbiosis Institute of Business Management, sends entire classes of management trainees for Vipassana courses. The central government and some provincial governments offer paid leave for their staffs to learn the discipline, and courses are organized for prison inmates, students of technological powerhouses, and scientists at the Bhaba Atomic Research Center.

On the western front, business leaders across the country are coming out as spiritual practitioners, revealing a rising trend toward more conscious commerce. Ken Blanchard, coauthor of *The One Minute Manager®* and Chairman of Blanchard Training and Development, Inc. said in a recent interview that he starts his day by feeding his "inner Spiritual Self," with silence, spiritual reading, and often a walk. Bob Stiller, CEO of Green Mountain Coffee Roasters, is a certified meditation instructor who meditates twice a day for at least forty-five minutes. In 2001, Green Mountain Coffee was named one of America's fastest-growing small companies by *Forbes, Business Week,* and *Fortune.* In 2002, the company made the *Forbes* "200 Best Small Companies in America" list for the third consecutive year.

Retired Aetna International chairman Michael A. Stephen, author of *Spirituality in Business: The Hidden Success Factor*, extols the benefits of meditation, a practice he says has transformed his life since the mid-1970s, and was instrumental in building Aetna's foreign business and encouraging his employees to maximize their potential. "In Asia, I quickly discovered that personal integrity, family values and human experience are the critical business drivers—not just profit margins and performance metrics. Over time, you realize that nothing is more important than bringing your life values into your work."

Timberland CEO, Jeffrey B. Swartz, is one of the few orthodox Jews at the New Hampshire company, and because community service is an important part of Swartz' faith, every employee at Timberland gets forty paid hours a year off to volunteer at the charity of their choice. For their twenty-fifth company anniversary, Timberland closed down for one day in a "Serv-A-Palooza," where employees, customers, vendors, and others volunteered in an array of activities. Timberland has discovered its employee volunteer program, largely centered on environmental activities, helps with worker retention.

In the spring of 2005, Boston-area Babson College hosted a symposium on Spirituality and Business where CEOs and other leaders convened to discuss the importance of integrating spirituality in the workplace. "My idea of spirituality in the workplace is how I am when I'm in there. It's what motivates me to do what I do," said Julius Walls, CEO of Greyston Bakery. "We're not there practicing a religion, we're there practicing a personal spirituality." Greyston is owned by a national Buddhist foundation and Julius is Christian. They share a commitment to the value of working and the promotion of spirit-based principles. Almost all their employees are homeless people from Yonkers who learn how to work and how to value themselves as well at their Greyston jobs.[16]

"At Ben & Jerry's, we learned that there's a spiritual life to businesses as there is in the lives of individuals," said Ben Cohen, co-founder and former CEO of Ben & Jerry's Homemade Ice Cream in a recent interview with Frederica Saylor, health editor at *Science & Theology News*. "As you give, you receive. As you help others, you are helped in return. For people, for businesses, for nations—it's all the same." Cohen co-founded the company in 1978 on an initial investment of $8,000. By 1999 the enterprise had grown to an annual sales volume of over $250 million with seven hundred employees and Cohen had become a pioneer in the area of socially responsible business. The *Wall Street Journal* recognized Ben & Jerry's as having one of the top ten corporate reputations in the United States.

When accused of doing "nice things" to sell more ice cream—like only buying local milk and using sustainable rain forest products in their Rainforest Crunch ice cream—Cohen said they only did what they believed in and it just happened to have a positive effect on their sales. "Our actions are based on deeply held values," said Cohen. "We're all interconnected, and as we help others, we cannot help but help ourselves. Creating a consonance of values with employees and customers builds loyalty and even more value," he added.

According to a *Business Week* cover story on spirituality in the workplace, ever since Austaco, Inc., the sixth-largest Pizza Hut and Taco Bell franchisee in the US, began hiring chaplains through a nonprofit called Marketplace Ministries, the company has reduced its annual turnover from 300 percent to 125 percent. Now McDonald's and some Wal-Mart subsidiaries are getting in on the act, with studies showing that having chaplains on hand pays off in higher morale, less turnover, and increased productivity.[17]

As part of Xerox Corporation's commitment to revolutionize product development, over three hundred Xerox employees have participated in "vision quests" to stimulate their creative juices. From New Mexico's deserts to New York's Catskill mountains, workers have quested after visions, communed with nature, and sought inspiration for twenty-four hours with nothing more than sleeping bags and water jugs. On one quest, after envisioning a rotting computer polluting a stream, a group of engineers committed to creating a recyclable Xerox machine. Back from the desert and at their desks, they got to work and came up with 265dc, a 97 percent recyclable machine, which has become one of Xerox's best sellers.

George Zimmer, CEO of Men's Wearhouse, said in an online article that he constantly looks at his corporation as a place for the development of the human spirit. Thirteen years ago, when he decided to create a new corporate culture, he took one giant step in a new direction: he made employee fulfillment his company's first priority, followed by that of other stakeholders. After putting those values into operation, the $64 million business grew into a $1.4 billion international company with projections of $10 billion by 2010. For the past three years, it has made Fortune's list of "100 Best Companies to Work for in America." Says Zimmer, "I realized that our 'outer' relationships were driven by the quality of our 'inner' work environment, so our collective honesty, sincerity, integrity, responsiveness, authenticity, mutual good will, and caring for each other became my focus as CEO."[18]

Another organization that capitalized on their inner wisdom is Unitel, a Canadian telecommunications company. According to an article in the *Christian Science Monitor*, in 1995 the business was losing more than $1 million a day, with inferior products and a dire employee morale problem. When Bill Catucci came on board as new CEO, he led a dramatic turnaround by asking employees to define the company's corporate values and put in place whatever structures they needed to ensure that they lived by them. The values they chose were integrity, customer delight, respect for people, innovation, teamwork, and prudent risk-taking. By 1999, customer turnover had declined by 30 percent, revenues nearly doubled, and the company's value had quadrupled to $1 billion. The firm, which became AT&T Canada, was also among the top five in North America in employee morale.[19]

In San Diego, Kyocera Corporation, a multinational company with over 60,000 employees, believes that spirituality belongs not only in the home or places of worship, but also in the workplace. The motto of a modern Buddhist priest, "Respect the Divine and Love People," is taught at some 160 Kyocera subsidiaries circling the globe.

The priest's name is Dai-wa, but he is better known by his secular name, Dr. Kazuo Inamori, founder and chairman emeritus of the company. In 1959, Inamori founded Kyocera and brought it into a position of worldwide prominence, stressing that the practice of environmentalism is necessary to show proper respect. In 2004, Kyocera reported net sales of $10.96 billion, with profits up 65.4 percent from the previous year.[20] "What I learned was that we must first think we can make it happen," says Inamori. "If we keep telling ourselves 'I know this would be ideal, but in reality, it is impossible,' then nothing will happen."

Creating organizations that foster wholeness and tap into the magnitude of the human spirit *is* an ideal and it *is* possible. As leaders around the world share their experiences and reflect on the subject, bit by bit, ideas are surfacing. One group of senior managers attended a retreat at a Benedictine abbey to focus on the question of spirituality in the workplace. When they were asked to come up with job specs for recruiting a "soul-friendly" CEO, they arrived at the following:

> The ideal candidate will:
> - be able to demonstrate compassion which means showing mercy or judgment, as appropriate, to all
> - at all times operate with moderation and self-control,

showing maturity and awareness of self and taking
courageous action when needed
- be impartial, consistently treating employees according to
their needs
- be flexible, adaptable, and open to persuasion and debate
- use his/her serenity and wisdom to enable other people's
spirituality to flourish[21]

When I asked Sander Tideman of SiB what impact he felt this trend
toward spirituality was having on the global business community, he said
he is noticing an impact in three areas. He sees more organizations
investing in spiritually-based leadership development programs that
involve the whole of the human being, not just behaviors. "Business now
understands that ethics help in risk and reputation management and
there is a serious reconsideration of decision making and strategic
choices in business from an ethics and values viewpoint," he said.
"Corporate social responsibility (CSR) and sustainability concepts are
now part of the mainstream in European business, and most companies
have CSR officers. Some are risk management related, others more
PR/communication related—but all are unified in realizing that business is part of a larger eco-system and societal structure."

Progress is occurring, through us and in us, as we enfold ourselves
in the human community and unfold our gifts where they are needed. It
is our very connectedness that ignites and unleashes our creative powers,
and programs that foster awareness and relationships are the key to
unlocking the wealth inside the corporate body. When the inner and
outer, the spiritual and material, are brought together, a synthesis of a
higher order is born from the union of opposites. This is the art and
alchemy of transformation, and it is dependent on the fusion of what
once was separate.

As we learn from the Hindu Vedas, compiled in 3500 BCE, "What is
within is also without. What is without is also within. He who sees difference between what is within and what is without goes forevermore from
death to death." In a battery, when the electrons from the negative
terminal connect with the electrons from the positive terminal, power is
generated. In a woman's body, when the male sperm merges with the
female egg, a new life is conceived. When the negative energy in a storm
cloud makes contact with the positive earth surface, lightning occurs.
Power, life, energy—this is what comes with the merging of opposites. So
the consequence of bringing together our spiritual and material selves

would be more vitality, more creativity.

In the prophetic words of Jesus from the Gospel of Thomas, we read, "If you bring forth what is within you, what you bring forth will save you. If you do not bring forth what is within you, what you do not bring forth will destroy you." What does it profit us to gain the whole world and forfeit our lives? These are times to bring the inner outward, to engage our souls in every endeavor and express our meaning in the teeming marketplace. We are creation becoming conscious of itself, nature beholding nature, human beholding the Divine.

It has never been like this before, for evolution progresses moment by moment, and no other humans have stood where we stand today. This is *our* threshold and these are *our* times and only now has it become clear that our survival is dependent on our spiritual awakening. What is past is past, but the future that awaits us is in our hands, in our words, in every decision and choice we make. As the great prophet and paleontologist Teilhard de Chadin once said, "Humanity has reached the point where we must decide between suicide and adoration."

And Jonathan Schell, a modern day prophet, propels us forward with his compelling words, "Because everything we do and everything we are is in jeopardy, and because the peril is immediate and unremitting, every person is the right person to act and every moment is the right moment to begin." Wherever we are, whatever we're doing, there is always the chance to reveal the inner, to shed that light, to share our warmth with a shivering soul.

| Creating the Future |

Local Brain, Global Mind

Commerce with a Conscience

The Triple Bottom Line

Insight to Action

You Are the Help

| CHAPTER |

Local Brain, Global Mind

We assert our commonality through our capacity for empathy, for thinking and feeling our way into the minds of others.

ROBERT JAY LIFTON

The hardware for omniscience is installed in our brains.

JOAN BORYSENKO

I was eating dinner with friends at a small Italian restaurant when three men with guns walked through the door. "Get up!" they shouted as they approached our table. We were stunned and sat frozen in our seats, none of us moving. Two of them walked through the swinging doors into the kitchen and the other came closer with his gun pointing. "Keep your eyes down and get into the kitchen, now! And take your bags!" By now it had sunk in that this was really happening and we all stood up and headed into the kitchen, the gunman behind us.

"Don't anybody look," he warned. "Just lie down on the floor and keep your eyes shut." We did as he said, and took our places on the floor, along with the kitchen staff, who were already lying face down. He told the men to put their wallets on the floor, then instructed all of us to remove our jewelry and watches and put them on the floor next to us. "Keep your eyes shut," he kept shouting while his cohorts collected the wallets and jewelry.

They went into the office next, while one kept guard over us. I heard someone go through the swinging door, and then there was a long silence. I thought they had left, so I lifted up my head and looked toward the door, just as one pushed it open. He saw me looking and came at me with his gun pointed at my head, shouting "I told you to keep your eyes shut!"

"I can't see anything without my glasses," I said, burrowing my head under my arms, and at that point, the strangest thing happened. I saw the whole scene from above, as if I were suspended from the ceiling. As I viewed our bodies sprawled out on the greasy kitchen floor, powerless and terrified, I heard a voice in my head say "This is what we've come to." And out of my right eye, as I lie there on the floor, fell one large, mournful tear.

In this moment, my local brain and global mind became one. The local me was the victim, paralyzed with fear, worried for my life, grieving over an image seen by the global me—an image of my own tribe run amok. From that upper view, I was a witness, not a victim. I was the many, not the one—the "we," not the "I."

Years later, as I think back on this event, I find that it gave me a metaphor for understanding the distinction between global and local, and seeing that they are two sides of one coin. My reality is simultaneously local and global. I am at once the witness and the witnessed, the creator of experience and the one who experiences it. I am like the cell in the organism—offering my vitality to the whole and taking my vitality from it. A singular and unique entity, I bring to the whole what no one else can bring, and doing that, I find my place in the family of things.

It is at the intersection of local brain and global mind that our creative fire is ignited and fanned. It is here, when these poles are brought together, that original thoughts are conceived and born, that the future enters into us before it happens. It is the recognition of our oneness that causes the quantum leap to a higher level of thinking. Einstein wrote: "The world that we have made as a result of the level of thinking we have done thus far creates problems which cannot be solved by the same level of thinking in which they were created." Until we shift into global mind thinking we cannot solve the problems that we have created with local brain thoughts.

We have built a world based on our separation from each other and it is unsustainable. To create a world that is just and sustainable, we must design and build with our oneness in mind, asking ourselves at every point, *What is best for the whole?* And that is why visionaries are needed so desperately now—because they operate from this place, they dwell in the awareness of oneness, and this consciousness radiates from their very beings, affecting everyone in their midst. The French philosopher Henri Bergson speaks of this, comparing it to music, when he writes:

Let the music express joy or grief, pity or love, every moment we are what it expresses. Not only ourselves, but many others, nay, all the others, too. When music weeps, all humanity, all nature, weeps with it. In point of fact it does not introduce these feelings into us, it introduces us into them, as passers-by are forced into a street dance. Thus do pioneers in morality proceed. Life holds for them unsuspected tones of feeling like those of some new symphony, and they draw us after them into this music that we may express it in action.[1]

When I think of thought leaders, I think of those who draw us after them, whose energy field, like that of a magnet, extends beyond the body itself, attracting others to the brightness of their light. It is true for all of us, that our heart energy precedes us as we navigate through life, extending beyond us as an aura potent enough to affect those in our path—but there is something particularly uplifting about the energy of people who are aware of the threads that connect us all and whose work in the world reflects this knowing. We are strongly affected by each person's energy, as studies in this area are now confirming.

Research from the Institute of HeartMath®(IHM) in Boulder Creek, California, shows that our heart's field changes distinctly as we experience different emotions, and it is registered by the brains of people around us. On their website is an informal experiment with a boy, Josh, and his dog, Mabel, demonstrating how one heart field can calm another heart down. IHM researchers monitored the heart rhythms of both the dog and the boy, then had Mabel enter a room by herself. Her heart rhythms were jagged and erratic. Then Josh entered the room and greeted Mabel, petting her and emotionally bonding with her. At this point Mabel's heart rhythms made a significant shift, synchronizing with Josh's heart rhythms and staying close to his rhythms throughout their visit. When Josh got up and left the room, Mabel's heart rhythms clearly shifted again, becoming very spiked and jagged. Although the experiment was not a formal study, it appears that Josh's calm heart field connected with Mabel's heart, helping her to feel secure and relaxed.[2]

That we have an effect on others is a matter of fact; the *kind* of effect we have on others is a matter of consciousness. We can radiate blessings and light or negativity and darkness. It is in our best interests to be mindful of our energy as we scatter it about, because thoughts can produce effects only of the same nature. Kindness to others favors a nervous system that is kind to itself, says the *Bhagavad Gita*. And Joseph Chilton Pearce says it even more clearly in *The Biology of Transcendence*:

> Every negative thought I entertain in my head, which I think
> is my own secret place, actually strengthens the negative field
> that sweeps our world. Every time I bemoan the negative world
> out there that I must suffer, I have supported and contributed
> to it through my moaning. My secret place in my head is not
> so secret after all.[3]

This is global mind thinking. It is countercultural, for we have been trained to think otherwise, but it is the very essence of original thinking and a prerequisite for visionary leadership. Before we can manage anything or anyone in the outside world, we must first learn to manage our energy and thoughts, to synchronize our mind and our emotions for optimal performance. Then we will be ready to enter deeper levels of consciousness, increase our intuitive capacities, and tap into a creativity greater than we have ever known.

Geneticists are discovering "unused" sections of DNA, which are thought to contain the blueprint of the future. And research shows that we can influence our DNA. With the power of our mind, we can cause our own DNA to relax and unwind, allowing us to access more of its codes. In another study at the Institute of HeartMath, human placental DNA was placed in a container to measure changes; twenty-eight vials of it were given to twenty-eight researchers who were trained in generating and feeling feelings. Researchers found that the DNA changed shape according to the feelings of the researchers.

In yet another IHM study, leukocytes (white blood cells) were harvested for DNA and placed in chambers to be measured for electrical charges. The donor, who sat in another room, was subjected to emotional stimulation, such as war images, sexual erotica, and humor. When the donor exhibited emotional peaks and valleys, measured by electrical responses, so did the DNA *at same time*. This was also true when researchers separated the donor by fifty miles.

Another study showed that when people touch or are in close proximity, one person's heartbeat signal is registered in the other person's brain waves. More refined techniques have since been developed by IHM that indicate there is an energy exchange that occurs up to five feet away from the body even without touching.

The heart is a sophisticated information processing center with its own nervous system. It has the ability to sense, learn, remember, and make functional decisions independent of the brain. It sends messages to the brain and the rest of the body in four different languages—

neurological, bio-physical, hormonal, and electrical—and these messages cause our awareness to expand. Studies on the heart present compelling evidence that the body's perceptual apparatus is continuously scanning the future, leading to the heart's intuitive intelligence. Conclusions that the heart receives and responds to intuitive information were based on studies where a subject was exposed to both emotional stimuli and calm stimuli. The results showed that prior to future emotional stimuli, a significantly greater heart rate deceleration occurred, compared to calm stimuli. The results also show that pre-stimulus information from the heart is communicated to the brain.[4]

When I asked Howard Martin, co-author of *The HeartMath Solution* and the executive vice-president of HeartMath, what research has most excited him, he said, "The first would be the discovery that the heart influences how the brain functions and that its language is found in the heart's rhythms. It's exciting to know that by simply shifting our heart's rhythmic beating patterns from chaotic to coherent we can produce profound and beneficial changes in the brain. These changes open the brain up so we can see the big picture and build new neural pathways that allow us to more easily experience positive emotions."

With the power of our own consciousness, we can cause a change in the rate of our heartbeat and create new pathways in the brain that lead to expanded imagination, more creative solutions, and peak performance. The implications for heightened creativity and human performance have not been lost on the corporate world, and companies such as Hewlett-Packard, Shell, Sony, Boeing, and GlaxoSmithKline are using HeartMath training for stress management and enhanced productivity. Martin reported that in a group of 1,500 people from five different companies that went through a one-day HeartMath training program there was a drop in fatigue from 49 percent to 31 percent in just six weeks. Anxiousness dropped from 35 percent to 14 percent, sleeplessness from 29 percent to 14 percent and there were several more changes across twenty-three different constructs, measured over a six week period. Steve Stephenson, a Senior Manager at Boeing, reports that their work with HeartMath "gave our team the coherence we needed to come in under budget—on time—with productivity gains of up to 12 percent."

At the individual level, coherence is the synchronization of mind and heart—intellect and emotion—allowing us to find clarity in the midst of chaos. At the global level, coherence is the synthesis of all the parts into one harmonious whole. It is what enables us to choose wisely, to think strategically, to manage our feelings, to communicate effectively, to lead people, and to be more attuned to the needs of others. When our hearts and minds are in harmony, we have more power, more insight, more courage. As Joseph Chilton Pearce writes in *The Biology of Transcendence*, "an unconflicted person has dominion over a conflicted or divided person."

We are living in a moment of accelerated collective fear, and, according to Pearce, fear of any kind throws us into an ancient survival mentality that shuts down our higher modes of evolutionary awareness. "But evolution is always on the prowl looking for the opportunity to shift us into a higher mode of functioning," he writes. When we come into coherence and employ our heart's intelligence, we defuse the defensive circuit, enlist the creative forebrain, and shift our neural frequency. This breaks the bonds of ancient instinctual behavior and opens us to the possibility of transcendence.

> We are more than observers or even participants in nature. We are its conscious agents, responsible for choosing its forms.
> PETER MARIN

> The goal of discoverers is not to outdistance their peers, but to transcend themselves.
> ROBERT GRUDIN

> It is our business to become courageous enough to face the radical depth of our freedom, to accept it and to live with it creatively.
> BEATRICE BRUTEAU

"That we are shaped by the culture we create makes it difficult to see that our culture is what must be transcended, which means we must rise above our notions and techniques of survival itself, if we are to survive," writes Pearce. It means, first of all, that we must rise above our notions of separateness and powerlessness, and open our eyes to all the evidence that proves otherwise. It means we need to consider, as Matthew Fox once suggested, outlawing war as we once outlawed slavery. It means we need to achieve coherence within ourselves so we have the insight and intuition necessary to create new structures as the old ones crumble.

When the Nobel Prize winner, chemist Ilya Prigogine, spoke about systems evolving, he said that as long as a system is stable, you can't change it, but as it moves toward disequilibrium and falls into chaos, the slightest bit of coherent energy can bring it into a new structure. Referring to this in a recent radio interview, Joseph Chilton Pearce said, "We are islands of coherent energy which bring about the organized, entrained energy for a new situation." Only this time, what we are creating is not based on

Newtonian science which claimed that the universe is one of independent, separate entities, but on quantum science which sees the universe as a process: a changing, flowing, evolving, and intimately interconnected system of interactions.

Roger Nelson, Ph.D., is director of the Global Consciousness Project (GCP), an international collaboration of researchers studying indications of the subtle reach of human consciousness in the physical world on a global scale. To do this, they maintain a network of special instruments (random event generators, or REGs) designed to produce random data. Researchers are stationed at more than sixty-five sites, with locations from Alaska to Fiji, on all continents, and in nearly every time zone. They collect their data and send it over the Internet to a server in Princeton University. The hypothesis of the GCP is that the continuous streams of data from these instruments will show anomalous deviations associated with "global events." The overall statistics for the project, after six years of data accumulation, indicate a probability of less than one in 50,000 that the correlation of GCP data with global events is merely a chance fluctuation.

"We don't yet know how to explain the correlations between events of importance to humans and the GCP data, but they are quite clear," says Nelson. "They suggest something akin to the image held in almost all cultures of a unity or oneness, an interconnection that is fundamental to life. Our efforts to understand these complex and interesting data may contribute insight into the role of mind as a creative force in the physical world."

According to Nelson, the network, which they designed as a metaphoric EEG for the planet, responded on September 11th as if it were measuring reactions on a planetary scale. "We do not know if there is such a thing as a global consciousness, but if there is, it was moved by the events of September 11, 2001. It appears that the coherence and intensity of our common reaction created a sustained pulse of order in the random flow of numbers from our instruments. These

Our evolution—as individuals and that of humanity in general—depends upon our ability to see beyond the confines of ourselves as separate entities. We all interpret events and data according to who we think we are. We never simply "know" the world; we create worlds based on the meaning we invest in the information we choose to notice. Thus, everything we know is determined by who we think we are.
MARGARET WHEATLEY

It will do us little good to wire the world if we short-circuit our souls.
TOM BROKAW

patterns where there should be none look like reflections of our concentrated focus, as the riveting events drew us from our individual concerns and melded us into an extraordinary coherence. Maybe we became, briefly, a global consciousness."

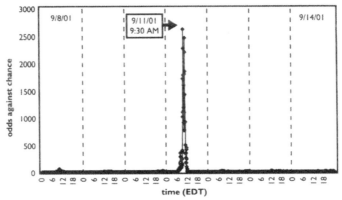

(Image by Dean Radin. www.noosphere.princeton.edu)

This picture shows a remarkable correlation between the behavior of the GCP's random event generators and an event that intensely focused mass attention worldwide. The graph plots the odds against chance associated with data generated by all thirty-six REGs running between September 8-14, 2001. This graph indicates that the GCP network—and by hypothesis, the collective psyche—responded to and possibly anticipated the attacks.[5]

While we can't scientifically prove there's such a thing as global consciousness, there is an abundance of research that confirms the power of collective consciousness. Many studies have found that just one percent of a population practicing transcendental meditation (TM) is sufficient to bring about a significant reduction in crime, sickness, and accidents, a phenomenon researchers call the "Maharishi Effect." An interest among sociologists and criminologists generated by those results led to a highly publicized "National Demonstration Project to Reduce Violent Crime and Improve Governmental Effectiveness" in Washington, D.C. from June 7 to July 30, 1993. According to quantum physicist John Hagelin, author of *Manual for a Perfect Government*, the $6 million scientific demonstration, which involved four thousand participants over a period of two months, was one of the largest and most rigorously designed sociological experiments in history.[6]

The prediction of a 20 percent drop in crime and the research methodology to be used was presented in advance to a twenty-seven member project review board consisting of scientists, government leaders, and the District of Columbia police department. The coherence-creating group consisted of one thousand meditators on June 7 and increased incrementally to four thousand by the end of the project on July 30. By the end of the demonstration project, violent crime dropped sharply by more than 23 percent. Later analysis determined that the drop in crime could not be attributed to temperature, precipitation, changes in police surveillance, weekend effects, or trends in the data. Consistent with the theory that coherence-creating groups reduce stress in collective consciousness, it was also predicted in the protocol that other indicators of social stress would show improvements during the project. A separate study found that other sociological variables such as accidental deaths, emergency room trauma cases, emergency psychiatric calls, and complaints against police all decreased significantly during the course of the project.

Hagelin reports on well-documented experiments in the Middle East of groups of TM meditators who were able to produce a 34 percent reduction in war intensity and a 76 percent reduction in war deaths during the Lebanon war. In 2003, the highly respected *Journal of Offender Rehabilitation* devoted all four quarterly issues entirely to studies demonstrating that the TM program is effective in treating and preventing criminal behavior, as well as reducing international conflicts and terrorism.

In another arena—"distance healing"—67 percent of 150 controlled studies have shown that individuals and groups can use intention, relaxation, enhanced concentration, visualization, and what is described as "a request to a healing force greater than themselves" to heal others to a statistically significant degree. Studies show that intercessory prayer on behalf of others who don't know they're being prayed for can reduce secondary infection rates and hospital stays among AIDS patients, reduce the risk of complications during heart surgery, and improve pregnancy rates for in vitro fertilization.

Biologist Rupert Sheldrake has also demonstrated in a number of studies that we can assist each other's learning across distances, without any external interaction or communication. In one study, for instance, a group of individuals completed a newly created crossword puzzle, and their average completion times were recorded. The same puzzle was then broadcast to millions via TV, for the viewers at home to complete.

Subsequently, a new group, who had not seen the puzzle at all, finished it significantly faster than the original group, suggesting that as a result of so many individuals having done the puzzle, knowledge of the puzzle was somehow etched into the field of collective consciousness, making it increasingly easier for others to solve.

Peter Tompkins and Christopher Bird offer fascinating accounts of the consciousness in matter in their book, *The Secret Life of Plants*. One experiment performed by a medical director and chemist involved a male subject who had brought a philodendron he had nursed from a seedling and cared for tenderly. The two scientists attached a polygraph to the plant and asked the owner a series of questions, instructing him to give false answers to some of them. The plant had no trouble indicating through the galvanometer which questions were answered falsely.

To see if a plant could display memory, six blindfolded polygraph students drew folded strips of paper from a hat. One of them contained instructions to root up, stamp on, and thoroughly destroy one of the two plants in a room. The "criminal" was to commit the crime in secret. No one knew his identity, and only the second plant would be a witness. When the surviving plant was attached to a polygraph, the students paraded before it one by one. The plant gave no reaction to five of them, but when the actual culprit approached, the meter went wild.

Even robots have been documented responding to the power of thought. Eighty different groups were tested in one experiment involving a robot and baby chicks. A robot was sent into a room full of baby chicks in bright daylight, and its movements were all observed to be random in nature. Knowing that the chicks prefer well-lit rooms, the researchers then devised an experiment where they turned off all the lights, leaving the chicks in the dark. They then sent in a robot carrying a lighted candle. In 71 percent of the cases, the robot spent excessive time in the vicinity of the chicks. Its former random movement were now affected by the desire of the chicks for its light.[7] There is mind in all matter.

Physicist Max Planck wrote, "All matter originates and exists only by virtue of a force which brings the particles of an atom to vibration and holds this most minute solar system of the atom together...We must assume behind this force the existence of a conscious and intelligent mind. This mind is the matrix of all matter." The *who* that we are is one with this very matrix. We are the vessels through which it operates, as the light bulb is a vessel for electricity. The force comes through us, taking whatever shape we give it. Whether one is a terrorist or a piano tuner, a murderer or a mystic, the very same force is behind each individual, holding the atoms and cells together, unifying us in the web of existence. As the poet Dylan Thomas put it:

> The force that through the green fuse drives the flower
> Drives my green age...

When Einstein reached the conclusion that "something deeply hidden had to be behind things," it is this force he was talking about. When the Indian mystic Sri Aurobindo wrote, "That within us which seeks to know and to progress is not in the mind but something behind it which makes use of it," he, too, was referring to the Great Consciousness of which we are a part and to whom we belong.

In his book *The Great Work*, cultural historian and visionary ecologist Thomas Berry writes: "We must consciously will the further stages of evolutionary process. Our responsibility is to be present to the Earth in its next sequence of transformations. While we were unknowingly carried through the evolutionary process in former centuries, the time has come when we must in some sense guide and energize the process ourselves."[8]

We are evolving into beings who understand the necessity of whole-ness and the urgency of balance. In order to reach our spiritual maturity, as individuals and as a human family, we must root ourselves as deeply in the heart as the mind, becoming as fluent in feelings as we are in facts. Our lives stem from our beliefs, and if our beliefs are not informed by affection, if they lack the heft of emotion, the grace of passion, they are nothing but a barren field of brainwaves.

Emotion helps neuron networks get stronger and become larger and more complex, according to Case Western biology professor James Zull. "We can't get inside and rewire a brain, but we can arrange things so that it gets rewired," he writes in *The Art of Changing the Brain*. Changes in networks can be generated by triggering neurons to dump "emotion chemicals" on the firing networks, which happens when a particular experience triggers emotion as well as cognition. "Thus, if we know what things trigger emotion, we can consciously incorporate those things into an experience, and make that experience much more likely to be remembered and learned. The concomitant frequent firing and expo-sure to the chemicals of emotion lead to great change in neuronal networks," writes Zull.

Neuroscientist Candace Pert writes about this very experience in her book *Molecules of Emotion*. Pert was in the midst of a stressful time when a colleague, a psychotherapist, thought she could benefit from an increase in her endorphin levels. The therapist, through guided imagery, directed Pert to her pituitary gland where the most powerful endorphins reside. The therapist then counted backward from ten, and when she got to one, Pert was supposed to release the endorphins out of her pituitary into her bloodstream. "I did exactly as she directed and felt an instantaneous rush, a feeling that accompanied what I knew was the outpouring of endorphins from my pituitary as they began swimming and binding receptors all over my body and brain to work their magical effects," writes Pert, who claims that the emotions are a key element in self-care because they allow us to enter into the bodymind's conversation.[9]

Emotions are what unite the mind and the body, and all honest emotions are positive emotions, according to Pert. "Every second, a massive information exchange is occurring in your body. Imagine each of these messenger systems possessing a specific tone, humming a signature tune...if we could hear this body music with our ears, the sum of the sounds would be the music we call the emotions. They are cellular signals that are involved in the process of translating information into physical reality, literally transforming mind into matter," she writes.

When the biochemicals of our emotions are flowing freely through our bodies, what we feel is happiness. Bliss is our default mode. To sustain it, what we have to do is allow the flow, all the while knowing we're conditioned not to do so. Until we get in the habit, it feels as if we're going against the grain, and we *are*. We're taking back authority over our own lives. We're forging an identity that's integrated, dynamic, energetically charged. We're unfolding and liberating our creative imagination, firing more neurons, sparking more ideas.

To live imaginative and inspired lives doesn't take genius, money, or luck. It takes time, the courage to go within, and the commitment to a practice of silence so we can quiet the voices of the small and petty and preserve our magnitude amid waves of mediocrity. It takes verve and stamina and rebellious originality. The poet Mary Oliver says, "In order to be the person I want to be, I must strive hourly against the drag of others."

That's why we need time alone, every day, to re-root ourselves in the fertile soil of our imagination. In *The Pregnant Virgin*, Jungian therapist Marion Woodman writes: "When society deliberately programs itself to a set of norms that has very little to do with instincts, love or privacy, then people who set out to become individuals, trusting in the dignity of their own soul and the creativity of their own imagination, have good reason to be afraid. They are outcasts." Any of us who are trying to live creatively, simply, compassionately are at risk of being outcasts. Any of us with a vision for a better way, any of us who are saying, "Enough!" and any of us who are bonding with others as the first in many steps toward building a new community, we are at risk of being outcasts—and so let it be.

Robert Grudin in his book, *The Grace of Great Things*, reminds us: "Creativity is dangerous. We cannot open ourselves to new insight without endangering the security of our prior assumptions. We cannot propose new ideas without risking disapproval and rejection. Creative achievement is the boldest initiative of mind, an adventure that takes its hero simultaneously to the rim of knowledge and the limits of propriety. Its pleasure is not the comfort of the safe harbor, but the thrill of the reaching sail."

Thought leaders *become* thought leaders by endangering the security of their prior assumptions. It is the only pathway out of our conditioned thought patterns which limit us immensely and lead more often to chaos than coherence. Thought leaders are bridge-builders who connect the local and the global, the past and the future, the heart and the mind. They know the power of emotion and they employ it confidently and courageously. They do not separate the metrics from the meanings, the figures from the feelings. They see themselves as a whole that is a part of a larger whole—and it is to this larger whole that they dedicate their lives. And if one wonders where meaning comes from, where joy and passion and purpose come from, it is from this one grand gesture of service to the whole.

The other day, I was photographing tide pools at the ocean's edge. The waves crashed onto the shore, ruffled their way across the rocks, and swirled and bubbled into the shallow, sandstone pools beneath my feet. I hovered over a patch of moss-covered rock and photographed a piece of the action. When the photos were developed, I was stunned. Every single tiny bubble I caught in my lens reflected back an image of myself. *Everything I looked at looked back at me and contained me.* This is the marriage of local and global. It is all one. As we are. All we have to do is remember, and live in that awareness.

TWELVE

Commerce with a Conscience

When we dream alone it is just a dream, but when we dream together it is the beginning of reality.

MIGUEL DE CERVANTES

Innovation is necessarily an aggressive act, not only because it enlarges human liberty and power, but also because it is the product of a bold individual assertion, a new word breaking the silence of history.

ROBERT GRUDIN

I drove by a cement truck the other day and the mixer was churning away as it rattled down the road. The logo on its side read, "Find a hole and fill it." This may become the mantra of the millennium as companies and cultural creatives continue to find ways to blend profit with purpose. When CBS MarketWatch's lead reporter Bambi Francisco asked venture capitalist Michael Moritz what it would take to become the next Google, Yahoo!, or Cisco, Moritz's response had a "find a hole and fill it" ring to it. And Moritz, referred to as "the hottest VC in the world," is no neophyte. Through Sequoia Capital, he has helped finance companies that now make up more than 10 percent of the market cap of NASDAQ.

"We try to anticipate a need that customers have—whether they're consumers or enterprise customers. We try to anticipate making an investment in a company that seems to be solving a problem that's brewing. Not a problem that's well recognized, but a problem that's brewing and that's only going to get bigger," said Moritz in the MarketWatch interview.[1]

Lucky for us, the United Nations has identified the world's most pressing problems and established the Millennium Development Goals to help us solve them—a perfect match for creative entrepreneurs

141

looking for holes to fill. Some of the most brilliant solutions of the day are coming out of thinkers who have the whole world in their view and are making bedfellows of purpose and profitability, commerce and social conscience. Studies of Gen-Xers and Gen-Yers published in *Workforce Management* magazine showed that more than 90 percent of them believe that helping others is more important than helping oneself. The workforce coming up is altruistic, collaborative, and community-minded.[2] They're looking for balance in their own lives and aspiring to create more balance in the world.

In an article in *Worthwhile* magazine, Kevin Salwen quotes from a letter written by Andrew Youn, an MBA student at Northwestern's Kellogg School:

> I am a second-year MBA student at Kellogg. I am one of growing numbers of MBAs that have a career focus on doing good in the world. We are learning not how to make millions of dollars, but how to change the lives of millions of people. The tools of business appeal to me because they are the tools of mobilizing and organizing large amounts of resources. In my lifetime, I hope to end poverty for as many people as possible.
>
> There are 850 million people in the world, mostly children, who are so poor that they are chronically malnourished. The best answer the world has come up with is $10 billion dollars in annual food and medicine donations. Despite decades of pouring aid into Africa, there are still more hungry people than ever.
>
> The paradox is that the majority of these hungry people are actually farmers, capable of growing food for themselves. They are just using ancient agricultural techniques, which are not very productive. I am very interested in finding ways to intelligently provide fertilizer and commercial seed to these farmers, which has the potential to increase their crop yields by at least 400 percent. I am interested in a permanent solution to their poverty problem, not just in repeatedly band-aiding their hunger and health problems. I will be starting a demonstration project in Kenya in December with about 20 families, to prove that their crop yields can be dramatically increased, and that this one-time intervention can result in a permanent path out of poverty.[3]

Andrew Youn is going to the root of the problem, which is the only sane and useful approach. And so do the Millennium Development Goals (MDGs), which address the very origins of the crises we face as a global community. These goals, adopted by 189 nations in 2000, are an invitation for original thinking on a global scale. Despite whatever criticisms one might have about the United Nations, this plan has galvanized people to work together, creating partnerships in government, industry, and civic society. Its objectives are simple enough to be understood and reasonable enough to be supported by people from Calcutta to Chicago, Brussels to Bucharest. It's as if the UN were a doctor saying to a person with a life-threatening disease, "Here is an eight-point plan. If you follow these directions, you can heal yourself." The question to the patient is: do you have the will to live? And the question to the global community is the same.

The Millennium Development Goals are based on a global partnership, calling for developing countries to get their own houses in order, with the support of developed nations. These goals are measurable, achievable, and time-bound, projected to be met by 2015. Progress toward these goals has already been significant, and once the business community recognizes the opportunity to profit through service to these goals, once it applies its ingenuity and results-driven expertise to the problems, we may enter into a new phase of commerce that is people-focused *and* profit driven, cost effective *and* compassionate. We made one giant step from win to win-win, and are about to make another, to win-win-win. It's good for me, it's good for you, it's good for our children.

The Millennium Development Goals(www.un.org/milleniumgoals) and their targets offer us the greatest creative challenge of our times. They are as follows:

1. Eradicate extreme poverty and hunger, reducing by half the number of people living on less than $1 a day. Global poverty rates are falling, thanks to Asia's progress in the matter. The number of people living on less than $1 a day dropped by nearly a quarter of a billion from 1990 to 2001—a period of rapid economic growth. In more than thirty countries, hunger was reduced by at least 25 percent during the last decade, but millions more people have sunk into poverty in sub-Saharan Africa. What's needed is an increase in agricultural output. Innovative approaches to fertilization and irrigation in places like Bangladesh are yielding tremendous results and helping small farmers grow more food and climb out of poverty.

2. Achieve universal primary education. Five regions are already close to universal enrollment in primary education, though in sub-Saharan Africa, fewer than two-thirds of children are enrolled in primary school. And two-thirds of the 130 million children currently not in school are girls. Kinandu Muragu, of the Nairobi-based Forum for African Women Educationalists (FAWE), says the participation of girls in the education system in Africa is critical to economic development, improved community health, and national welfare. In Sub-Saharan Africa, the social return on girls' education is estimated at 24.3 percent for basic education and 18.2 percent for secondary education, the highest rates in the world, according to FAWE. Primary and lower secondary education helps reduce poverty by increasing the productivity of the poor, by reducing unplanned pregnancies and improving health, and by equipping people with the skills they need to participate fully in the economy.

Oxfam estimates that for Africa to achieve universal primary education, some three billion US dollars per year would be needed. IKEA is one business that stepped up to the plate and donated one euro for each soft toy sold in its two hundred stores from November through December 2005 to support UNICEF and Save the Children programs, contributing more than $2.3 million worldwide. In July 2003, IKEA launched a similar campaign and generated more than $2.8 million for children in Angola, Uganda, Russia, and China.

3. Promote gender equality and empower women. In countries where resources and school facilities are lacking, a choice must often be made in families between sending a girl or a boy to school. Girls tend to lose out, but the gender gap is closing in primary school enrollment in the developing world. Targeted interventions can go a long way towards getting girls into school, and encouraging them to stay there. These include providing safe transportation to and from school, separate toilets for girls and boys, and removing gender stereotyping from the classroom. Education for girls is a crucial step in ensuring women's partnership in local and global decision-making, and although women's representation in national parliaments has been steadily increasing since 1990, women still occupy only 16 percent of seats worldwide.

4. Reduce child mortality by two thirds for children under five. Eleven million children a year—thirty-thousand a day—die from preventable or treatable causes. Most of these lives could be saved by expanding existing programs that promote simple, low-cost solutions. Almost half of all deaths among children under age five occur in sub-Saharan Africa, where progress has slowed owing to weak health systems, conflicts, and AIDS.

Most of these lives could be saved by expanding low-cost prevention and treatment measures. These include exclusive breastfeeding of infants, antibiotics for acute respiratory infections, oral rehydration for diarrhea, immunization, and the use of insecticide-treated mosquito nets and appropriate drugs for malaria. Among the diseases that can be eradicated by immunization, measles is the leading cause of child deaths. A safe, effective, and relatively inexpensive vaccine has been available for over forty years. Still, measles strikes thirty million children a year. Global coverage of measles immunization has risen slowly, but about a third of all children are still unprotected in the sub-Sahara and Asia.

5. Improve maternal health, reducing by three-quarters the maternal mortality ratio. More than half a million women die each year during pregnancy or childbirth. Twenty times that number suffer serious injury or disability. Some progress has been made in reducing maternal deaths in developing regions, but not in the countries where giving birth is most risky. Countries with already low levels of maternal mortality have made further progress. Reductions in the worst-affected countries will require additional resources to ensure that the majority of births are attended by doctors, nurses, or midwives who are able to prevent, detect, and manage obstetric complications. Universal access to reproductive health care, including family planning, is the starting point for maternal health. It is particularly important for addressing the needs of the 1.3 billion young people about to begin their reproductive lives. Currently, 200 million women have an unmet need for safe and effective contraceptive services.

6. Halt and begin to reverse the spread of HIV/AIDS, malaria, and other diseases. AIDS has become the fourth largest killer world-wide, leaving fifteen million AIDS orphans in Africa. It's estimated that by the end of the decade, one out of every five children in Namibia will be an orphan. In India there are four to eight million people infected with HIV and that figure is expected to rise to fifteen million in the coming decade. Surveys in sub-Saharan Africa have found that only 21 percent of young women and 30 percent of young men know the basics about how to avoid infection. Surveys of young women in Southeastern Asia show even lower levels of knowledge.

By the time you finish reading this paragraph, one hundred people will have died of a preventable infectious disease and half of them will be children under five. Malaria and tuberculosis together kill nearly as many people each year as AIDS, and represent a severe drain on national economies. A staggering 90 percent of malaria deaths occur in sub-Saharan Africa, where prevention and treatment efforts are being scaled up. Thailand and Uganda have shown that infection rates can be reversed with vision and leadership. All three of these diseases can be largely controlled through education, prevention, and treatment.

7. Ensure environmental sustainability, including reducing by half the people without access to clean drinking water, reversing the loss of environmental resources, and achieving significant improvement in the lives of 100 million slum dwellers. Access to safe drinking water has increased, but half the developing world still lacks toilets or other forms of basic sanitation. Nearly one billion people worldwide live in urban slums because the growth of the urban population is outpacing improvements in housing and the availability of productive jobs. The proportion of population using safe sources of drinking water in the developing world rose from 71 percent in 1990 to 79 percent in 2002.

8. Develop a global partnership for development. In an interdependent world economy, open avenues for trade, an accelerated transfer of technology, and improved employment opportunities for young people in the developing world are needed for poor countries to evolve in sustainable ways. Microcredit loans are proving to be a successful means to promoting self-sufficiency, financial skills, personal responsibility, and financial independence, particularly for women in developing countries. In past decades, according to the World Bank, microfinance has evolved from the provision of small loans to help start businesses to a vision of creating financial systems where none exist. Currently, it is estimated that only about 3 percent of the seventy-five million poor households in India who need access to credit receive financial services from the formal financial institutions and the microfinance sector put together. The potential for the microfinance industry throughout the world is vast. Close to 96 percent of Grameen Bank's microfinance loans have gone to women, and the repayment rate is over 90 percent.

On the home front, according to the latest census figures, 35.9

million Americans now live below the poverty threshold, a 1.3 million increase over last year's number.

In a recent study conducted by International Communications Research, 1,004 people were asked the question, "How much annual income would you say a family of four living in the United States needs to cover their basic needs?"

Although the mean level cited was over $44,000, there was a significant increase in those saying that a family of four needed more than $75,000. The Boston Foundation (www.tbf.org) recently reported that it now costs a family of four $64,656 to pay for basic necessities for a year in Greater Boston. As a point of comparison, the Federal poverty income threshold for a family of four is $19,350. Now, let's do the math: in America, a family of four making $19,000 a year will spend on average $6000 annually for the most basic of shelter. That, deducted from $19,000 leaves $13,000. Then let's subtract $2350 a year for utilities. That brings us to $10,650. Next we lose $4852 to transportation costs and $4815 to food. Now we have $983. If we calculate the annual costs of health care ($793) and child care ($2030) we're now $1840 in the hole. So say you're the parent here. You're almost $2000 over budget. What do you leave out? School supplies, birthday presents, life insurance, entertainment, shoes and clothing?

On average, one out of every three Americans—34.2 percent of all people in the United States— are officially classified as living in poverty at least two months out of the year.[4] Since 2000, the number of poor Americans has grown by more than four million. When using family budget measures, which embody the higher cost of living in cities, one finds that 42 percent of families living in cities and 30 percent of families residing in rural areas fall short of basic family budget thresholds.[5] The percent of survey respondents who indicated that poverty is a problem in the United States has remained between 87 percent and 90 percent since 2000.[6]

If we look at how the US compares with twenty-six participating Organization for Economic Cooperation and Development (OECD) countries, Denmark and Finland led with child poverty rates below 3 percent last year. Mexico and the United States were at the other end of the spectrum, both with child poverty rates of more than 20 percent.[7]

All economies face the trade-off between how much money should be spent and what level of childhood poverty is acceptable. The data used in the figure below compare social economic expenditures and child poverty rates of the United States to that of sixteen other rich, industrialized countries that, like the United States, belong to the OECD. The United States and these other countries face similar global conditions with respect to trade, investment, technology, the environment, and other factors that shape economic opportunities. Thus, this comparison provides a yardstick for gauging the commitment of the US government to reducing child poverty and its lifelong effects.

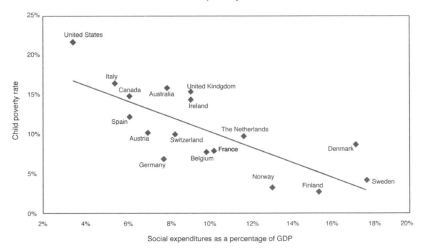

Social Expenditures as a percentage of GDP and child poverty in the OECD

This figure clearly illustrates that those countries with higher social expenditures—as a percentage of gross domestic product, or GDP—have dramatically lower poverty rates among children. The line in the figure shows the correlation between expenditures and child poverty rates for all countries. Individually, the Nordic countries—Sweden, Norway, and Finland—stand out, with child poverty rates between 2.8 percent and 4.2 percent. The United States stands out as the country with the lowest expenditures and the highest child poverty rate—five times as much as the Nordics.[8]

The paucity of social expenditures addressing high poverty rates in the United States is not due to a lack of resources—high per capita income and high productivity make it possible for the United States to afford much greater social welfare spending. Moreover, other OECD countries that spend more on both poverty reduction and family-friendly policies have done so while maintaining competitive rates of productivity and income growth.

In November 2005, the House of Representatives narrowly approved a budget reconciliation bill that makes cuts in a number of programs. Information from the Congressional Budget Office (CBO) shows that many of the cuts will hit low-income people directly and hard. CBO estimates that the provisions that will cause many low-income Medicaid beneficiaries to be required to pay more out-of-pocket for health care, and will reduce the health care services for which these beneficiaries are covered, represent cuts of nearly $30 billion over ten years. Its estimate of nearly $30 billion in savings in this area "reflect[s] CBO's expectation of reduced utilization of services due to higher cost-sharing requirements and decreased participation in Medicaid by individuals who would be required to pay premiums," according to the Center on Budget and Policy Priorities (www.cbpp.org).[9] The poor will not seek health care services because they will not be able to afford them. In addition, under the House bill, states would no longer be required to provide low-income children just above the poverty line with comprehensive preventive care and treatment. Substantial numbers of near-poor children could lose coverage for such services as eyeglasses, hearing aids, dental care, speech therapy, and crutches.

CBO estimates that the deep cuts in funding for child support enforcement included in the House bill would result in $24 billion in child support that would otherwise have been collected *going unpaid instead*. What message does this send to you, that we will no longer insist on neglectful fathers contributing to the support of their children? And how does it make you feel to know that child care subsidies will be eliminated for 330,000 children in low-income working families? No matter what your opinions are about the parents of these children, does it feel acceptable that we are punishing the *children* here? CBO estimates indicate that more than 220,000 people a month would lose food stamps, and the large majority of these are people in low-income working families. This number includes at least 150,000 low-income working people with children who now receive food stamps because they have substantial work and housing expenses that drop their net incomes below the poverty line. In addition, 70,000 *legal* immigrants who have been in the United States between five and seven years, primarily working-poor parents and poor elderly individuals, would be cut off food stamps by 2008.

According to the Center of Budget and Policy Priorities, the savings just from canceling the two new cuts, which will provide *no* benefit to middle-class households but confer an average tax cut of an *additional $19,000 a year* to people making over $1 million a year, would be more than enough to replace all of the House bill's cuts in assistance programs for low-income families and individuals. The Urban Institute-Brookings Institution Tax Policy Center reports that 97 percent of the benefits from these tax cuts will go to the 4 percent of households that have incomes of more than $200,000. The Tax Policy Center also found that when these two tax cuts are fully in effect, 54 percent of their benefits will go to households with income of over $1 million a year, which will receive $19,200 each year on average from these two measures alone.

While some of these statistics are unsettling, the good news is that we know what's wrong, and for the most part, what is needed to fix things. More than anything, what we have to stretch is our imagination. First, reflect on the fact that helping the poor is actually helping everyone. If you think for a moment about *real* worldwide security, what do you think would be most likely to contribute to it: better weapons and a stronger army, or decent jobs and working wages for the millions of young people maturing to working age? If you think about the best ways to build your company's reputation, consider the flurry of media attention Hyperion got when it launched its "Drive Clean to Drive Change" program and gave employees $5000 toward the purchase of hybrid car. That kind of positive press you can't buy.

What if companies encouraged their employees to brainstorm on how the company can positively impact just one of the eight MDGs? How would employees feel about being part of an organization that decided to be part of a grand solution? Think of the energy and creativity that could be stimulated out of an

> If the misery of the poor be caused not by the laws of nature, but by our institutions, great is our sin.
>
> CHARLES DICKENS

> Life on Earth was not biologically, but informationally seeded.
>
> ERVIN LAZLO

> What we thought of as isolated pathologies, scarcities of work or hope or security or satisfaction, are not isolated at all. In fact they're intimately related, they're all caused by the same thing, namely the interlocking waste of resources, of money, and of people.
>
> AMORY LOVINS

inquiry into the question: how can we profit from doing good in this world? All the research shows that people are looking for meaning and value in the workplace, and here's an opportunity to provide it.

The field of microcredit finance alone is offering a plethora of ideas for ways businesses and people can get involved on a personal level. When Deborah Lindholm wanted to inspire people in her San Diego community to support the financial independence of impoverished women, she started the Foundation for Women (FFW) in 1997. Women joined the organization because it offered a sense of community, and as they began to network, several programs were created that offered assistance to youth, to women with life-threatening diseases, and to homeless women. FFW raised money through a variety of creative programs, and, since its inception, has facilitated the opening of a microcredit bank every year. "To date we have opened five banks to service the poorest of the poor in Tamil Nadu, India," said Lindholm in a recent interview. "We reached our first goal by funding two banks (a $35,000 commitment) in just sixteen months by December 1999 and have gone on each year to expand the work. Each bank is servicing 2500 women and their families." Realizing the connection between education and the eradication of poverty, FFW expanded their reach and built a school for five hundred children of the microcredit borrowers. On the day of its dedication, over ten thousand women arrived to celebrate. FFW is now collaborating with two medical programs in Niger, Africa to provide microcredit access to women there, and they have also initiated two local microcredit projects in San Diego County.

Universities are also getting involved in microcredit, giving students a chance to support entrepreneurship in developing countries. At the University of Pennsylvania, a few students started a microfinance club and spent the summer in India learning how technology could improve small, local businesses. Their funds helped entrepreneurs in southern India set up Internet kiosks in Thiruvallur. According to student Sam Rosen

The trouble with trying to change the world is that weeks can go by and nothing happens.
REV. CAROL CARNES

There are a few billion people out there looking through the window from the outside in, seeing what we have, and they have nothing to lose. We're not going to solve this problem by trying to keep them out.
DEAN KAMEN

Deep down the consciousness of mankind is one.
DAVID BOHM

who helped found the club, the Indian internships were invaluable. "There are so many microfinance organizations that have more work than they can handle, and we're looking for people who want to take an active role," he said in a recent interview for the *Daily Pennsylvanian*. "We know that it works, we know that it's a source of wealth for both investors and entrepreneurs in the developing world. It's all about changing the world and leveraging the power of college students."

In November 2005, another college got in on the act when eBay founder Pierre Omidyar and his wife, Pamela, presented Tufts University with a $100 million gift specifically earmarked for microfinance organizations. The strings attached require that Tufts use only half the income from the investments for itself. The rest must be reinvested in microfinance. "Business can be a force for good, and you can earn profit for doing good," he said in a New York Times article. "That view is really informed by my experience with eBay, and its social impact."[10] Omidyar proudly acknowledged that the company was providing a source of "individual self-empowerment" for three-quarters of a million people who make a living on it.

Investment groups around the country are also providing people with ways to invest in microcredit and make a profit while making a difference. ACCION Investment Funds and the Calvert Foundation have socially responsible investment programs that support community development organizations, affordable housing, microcredit, and social enterprise programs across the country and around the world.

Community Development Financial Institutions (CDFIs) provide financing programs for microenterprise lending and microcredit development work. Nationwide, over one thousand CDFIs serve economically-distressed communities by providing credit, capital, and financial services that are often unavailable from mainstream financial institutions. CDFI loans and investments have leveraged billions of dollars from the private sector for development activities in low wealth communities across the nation.

The Council of Microfinance Equity Funds (CMEF) is the first membership organization that has brought together the leading private entities that make equity investments in microfinance institutions in the developing world. The Council's members seek both social and financial returns from their investments in these institutions, all of which provide a range of financial services to poor households in developing countries.

And according to Tom Easton, *The Economist's* New York Bureau Chief, even big banks are cashing in on the idea. "Local banking giants that used to ignore the poor, such as Ecuador's Bank Pichincha and India's ICICI, are now entering the market. Even more strikingly, some of the world's biggest and wealthiest banks, including Citigroup, Deutsche Bank, Commerzbank, HSBC, ING, and ABN Amro, are dipping their toes into the water," said Easton in a recent interview about microcredit.[11]

All over the globe, socially-aware entrepreneurs are applying invention and technology to the benefit of society. When an outbreak of a new strain of cholera began in India and killed up to ten thousand people, Ashok Gadgil, an Indian-born scientist working at the Lawrence Berkeley National Laboratory in California, decided to look for a new way to purify drinking water. From his experiences in India, Gadgil knew that any system would have to require little maintenance and not take for granted basic infrastructure like electricity and water pressure. The system he built, later named UV Waterworks, is remarkably simple. A UV lamp is suspended above a shallow pan in a compact, enclosed box. Water runs into the pan under the force of gravity, where it is exposed to the UV light, then into a holding tank. The only power that is needed is about forty watts to power the light, and this can come from a car battery. The system can disinfect four gallons of water a minute, killing 99.999 percent of bacteria and viruses. This produces enough clean water to serve more than 1,000 people.[12]

Another way to lift people out of poverty in Asia, Africa, and Latin America is to help provide cheap, individual irrigation systems to small farmers. When American agricultural researcher Norman Borlaug was asked what wealthy countries should do to reduce hunger, he said the long range solution would be in revolutionizing agricultural production among subsistence farmers—to increase food supply, create jobs, and generate new income from selling excess grain. One simple device that has helped farmers become more efficient is the human-powered treadle pump, which can irrigate half an acre of vegetables and costs only $25, according to according to an article by Paul Polak in the *Scientific American*.[13]

Paul Polak is the seventy-one-year-old founder of International Development Enterprises (IDE) and has spoken with thousands of small farmers in the developing world and spent many years designing inexpensive tools that would meet their needs. Polak's first big success was bringing the treadle pump to Bangladesh. It works like a StairMaster®, allowing farmers to pump shallow groundwater directly onto the crops using the energy of their legs. Over 1,500,000 Bangladeshi farmers have purchased these pumps and have netted an additional $100-500 more a year from their crops, a huge gain in a country where the per capita income is $300.

An MD and former psychiatrist, Polak put together a $3 million portfolio in 1981, vowed never to take a job only for money, cashed out and started IDE to develop and market low-cost, low-tech irrigation devices for small farmers. The litmus test for IDE products was that the farmer could recover the cost of the device within one season, according to Polak, who believes that the problem of rural poverty in the developing world boils down to what happens on quarter-acre plots. "So much development work is focused on macroeconomics and increasing GDP per capita," he said in a recent *Forbes* magazine interview. "Until the development community realizes that the solution to poverty lies in increasing the wealth of small-plot farmers, it will continue to fail."

Polak's IDE operates on a $10 million annual budget, raised through individual donations and grants from organizations like USAID and the Swiss Agency for Development & Cooperation. He hires people from the countries he's working in who recruit manufacturers to build the irrigation devices, then he creates an ingenious guerilla marketing program to get the word out. In one state, IDE hired troubadours to travel to rural villages singing the pump's praises. They also produced a Bollywood-style movie featuring a family whose fortunes were turned around by the pump. To Polak, the key is affordable design. According to him, 90 percent of the people who design things work on the problems of the world's richest 5 percent, and there is an enormous need to design things that will create a market for the poorest 4 billion people.[14]

Ashoka is one organization that is working on that idea. Founded by Bill Drayton, a former McKinsey & Company consultant and assistant administrator at the Environmental Protection Agency, Ashoka's mission is to shape an entrepreneurial citizen sector by investing in social entrepreneurs who have innovative ideas for change in their communities. "Learning to serve the poor through market-based approaches involves an acute learning curve for most companies, particularly large multinationals, as well as for many citizen sector organizations (CSOs). Succeeding requires inventing a new form of doing business and an unprecedented level of business-social congruence," writes Valeria Budinich, Ashoka's Vice-President for Full Economic Citizenship.

There are millions of CSOs around the world who have more experience than businesses in delivering products and services to low-income consumers and they have a huge array of social networks already in place. "These social networks constitute the early stages of an infrastructure that specializes in serving the poor, one that could also be leveraged by businesses as they enter this new market," writes Budinich, a supporter of commercial collaborations that leverage the core competencies of both sectors. In her opinion, CSOs can help businesses enter low-income market segments more effectively because of their deeply rooted community connections. And by leveraging the infrastructure and experience of business, the CSOs can broaden their reach and increase their impact.

Ashoka's *Changemakers* and *Full Economic Citizenship Initiative* have designed a framework for collaboration to help market-based models achieve both social impact and profits. They are challenging businesses to design products and services that tap into the wealth of the poor, radically change the logic behind their business model, and leverage the power of communities as both consumers and producers.

Traditionally, what's made it difficult for businesses and CSOs to serve low-income markets is the limited purchasing power of individual clients, the new niche of high-volume businesses based on small transactions, and a lack of awareness about the unique human and social capital that low-income communities possess. Although the purchasing power of individuals in these communities may be low, their collective purchasing power represents a significant market opportunity, as long as the cost of items is not prohibitive. A few examples of successful social entrepreneurs and Ashoka Fellows include Rebeca Villalobos of Costa Rica who developed a multi-million dollar operation that delivers vision care services to hundreds of thousands of consumers, irrespective of their income levels. By using a "multi-tiered" pricing system that allows consumers to pay according to their ability, Villalobos avoids discriminating against consumers on the basis of price.

David Green is another entrepreneur who is making medical technology and health care accessible to millions of low-income citizens. In collaboration with Seva Foundation and Aravind Eye Hospital, Green established Aurolab in India, the first nonprofit manufacturing facility in a developing country to produce affordable intraocular lenses (IOLs) to ameliorate cataracts, the main cause of blindness. Aurolab is now one of the largest manufacturers of IOLs in the world, with sales of more than 700,000 units per year (8 percent of the world market share) to eighty-six countries. Aurolab's selling price is $4 per lens, compared to over $100 in the US. They have also reduced the selling price of ophthalmic suture from $200 per box to $30. And while hearing aids usually sell for

$1500 per unit, theirs are sold for prices ranging from $0 to $200. The manufacturing cost is $50. Aurolab is financially sustainable from sales revenues, and Green is in the process of taking his concept global through a combination of business and social partnerships.

Ashoka Fellow Fabio Rosa is working on the issue of electricity for the poor. With no credit option available, millions of families living in rural areas go without electricity in spite of the fact that an appropriate technology exists. When Rosa decided to explore new business models for bringing power to these families, he began with a market research study that showed almost 70 percent of the families were spending at least $11 a month on non-renewable energy sources such as kerosene, candles, batteries and liquid petroleum gas to bring light and power into their homes. Rosa's plan was to lease his solar energy service for close to the same cost as people were spending on these inferior, non-renewable energy sources. He developed a basic photovoltaic solar home system that could be rented for $10 a month plus an initial installation fee, a little more than what people were already spending on nonrenewable forms of energy. Started in 2004, his company, called "The Sun Shines for All" (TSSFA), estimates that it will reach a break even point at the end of year four with six thousand customers.

Let's look at the water situation for a minute. As it stands today, half of us do not have access to clean water. Five thousand children die every day from waterborne illnesses. That's equivalent to twelve full jumbo jets crashing every day. How can it be that we have a dozen jets crashing every day and we're not doing anything about it? How does it happen that we let five thousand of our children die when we have everything it takes—but human will—to fix the problem?

In an article in *Technology Review,* writer Kevin Bullis interviews Segway inventor Dean Kamen about his latest product, an energy-efficient electrical generator and water purifier that could put power and clean water in the hands of rural villagers in poor countries. A few years ago, when Kamen was working on an electric generator for underdeveloped villages, he noticed that it produced about one thousand watts of waste heat. Kamen adapted his device to use that extra heat to distill the water by boiling and condensing it.

The results were a low-power, low-maintenance device that costs around $1,000 to manufacture and makes ten gallons of drinkable water an hour. Tests in Bangladesh showed that the generator, fueled by gas produced by local cows' dung, can produce enough power to run the purifier.[15] Imagine the opportunities here for a business to mass produce this at a much lower cost, for a local CSO to get involved with the marketing, for village entrepreneurs to profit from gathering the fuel, and for communities to end up with safe water and power.

These are the kinds of connections thought leaders are envisioning and creating, and these are the kinds of problems they are committed to solving. Dean Kamen knows his invention works. The trouble is, he is not as clear on how to market it or get it to the people who need it. But as David Green found out, through Ashoka and the Seva Foundation, there are plenty of networks being created now that are looking for global solutions and finding ways to apply them.

The business world itself is undergoing profound and dynamic changes, reshaping its contours to match the mindsets of an evolving public. As more and more people wake up to the fact that we're all in this together—all cells of this one living, breathing planet—more are insisting on across-the-board behaviors that protect and preserve it. As the 50-60 million American "cultural creatives" identified by Paul Ray and Sherry Anderson seek out more natural lifestyles, natural foods, natural remedies, so are they calling for a more natural capitalism—a system of wealth creation built less on destruction and more on respect for the earth and its people.

Thought leaders Amory B. Lovins and L. Hunter Lovins, who co-authored *Natural Capitalism* with Paul Hawken, are co-founders of the Rocky Mountain Institute, an entrepreneurial nonprofit with a focus on efficiency. As consultants and advisers to many of the world's largest corporations, they have helped shape the futures of the electricity, oil, real-estate, automobile and semiconductor sectors—showing businesses how to profit by doing what they do more efficiently.[16]

Their 4,000 square foot house in Snowmass, Colorado—which is also home to the Rocky Mountain Institute—has no conventional heating system, though winter temperatures there dip to forty degrees below zero. It was designed so efficiently that it consumes barely more electricity than a single 100-watt bulb. Solar cells generate five to six times that much electricity which the Lovins' sell back to the utility.[17]

In an article called "Harnessing Corporate Power to Heal the Planet," the Lovins share the principles of natural capitalism and offer several examples of how today's environmental challenges hold many profit-enhancing opportunities for pioneering companies. The first principle of natural capitalism is to radically increase resource efficiency, which not only increases profits, but solves most of the environmental dilemmas facing the world today. The others are: to eliminate the concept of waste by closing the loops of materials flows, to shift the focus of the economy from processing materials and making things to creating service and flow, and to reverse the destruction of the planet by instituting programs of restoration that invest in natural capital.

The article mentions that Southwire Corporation—an energy-intensive maker of cable, rod, and wire—halved its energy per pound of product in six years, and accumulated savings that roughly equaled the company's profits during that period. Company officials estimated that the energy-efficiency effort probably secured four thousand jobs at ten plants in six states that were jeopardized by competitive market forces.[18]

Dow Louisiana Operations implemented over nine hundred worker-suggested energy-saving projects during the period 1981 to 1993, with average annual returns on investment of over 200 percent. Both returns and savings rose in later years, even after the accumulated annual savings from the projects had passed $100 million. Practicing commerce with a conscience has its upside, though it still seems counter-intuitive to those who haven't tried it.

According to Lovins, it's whole systems thinking that lights the bulb. For example, in the world of real estate, typical tract home developments drain storm water in expensive underground sewers. Village Homes, an early solar housing development in Davis, California, instead installed natural drainage swales which saved $800 per house and provided more green space. The company then used the saved money to pay for edible landscaping that provided shade, nutrition, beauty, community focus, and crop revenues that paid the homeowners' assessments and a community center.

The development includes 220 single family homes, twenty apartments and a cooperative house, most incorporating solar design features and solar hot water. Business space is included in the community center and an inn was recently completed. The primary focus of the development plan was on community building. Shared ownership of common areas, shared laundry space for some units, shared and community gardens, community fruit and nut trees and vineyards, and bicycling and walking orientation were all important.

In a study comparing Village Homes to surrounding contemporary developments, the residents of Village Homes knew forty-two people in their neighborhood, compared to seventeen in other areas. The average resident identifies four of their best friends in the community, compared to 0.4 for people in the conventional development. The people-centered site planning (narrower, tree-lined streets, with the housing fronting on the greenways) saved land and money. It also cooled off the microclimate, yielding better comfort at lower cost, and created safe and child-friendly neighborhoods that cut crime 90 percent compared with neighboring subdivisions. Village Homes, once perceived as an oddity, is now the most desirable real estate in town, with market values $10-15 per square foot over average.

One of the most evolutionary principles of natural capitalism calls for a quantum leap in our thinking about business. We have to let go of an old idea and make space for a new possibility. This is a conscious evolutionary act. We've known for a long time that brain cells that fire together, wire together. Our thought patterns become habituated. Neurons fire in the same way over and over again, and our ideas eventually lose their plasticity and congeal into ideologies that soon need defending. To think originally is to connect the dots that have not been connected before and blaze new trails through the meadows of the mind. It is opening up to the future that is pulling us forward just as certainly as gravity pulls us downward. Original thinking calls for release of a certain kind—for we must let go of what we thought was true—but it leads us to a wiser way, a clearer path, and to choices that are good for all living things.

When the Lovins speak of natural capital, they talk about shifting our focus of the economy from processing materials and making things to creating service and flow. But it's a new concept and there is no neural pathway for it. We need to see images of it in our mind, we need to hear stories about it. We need to be able to imagine what it would look like and feel like to be "creating service and flow." It's an idea to be entered into, explored, and examined for rightness and fit.

When CEMEX, the second-largest cement manufacturer in the world, decided to move from selling materials to selling solutions they sent a team to live in a slum for several months. The point was to gain insight into the community and to explore the decision-making process of low-income families interested in building or upgrading their home. As a result, CEMEX created "Patrimonio Hoy," (meaning "Property Today"), one of the most successful housing programs in the world.

Would-be homebuilders pay about $14 a week, for seventy weeks. What the roughly $1,000 buys is consultations and inspections by CEMEX staff architects, and scheduled deliveries of materials divided into building phases that cover the seventy weeks. CEMEX is basically putting building materials in customers' hands, on terms tailored to the way they work and build. In return, the company saw its low-income partners deconstruct the myth of the irresponsible poor: 99.2 percent of the $42 million worth of materials that CEMEX has distributed is being paid for on time, according to the company. Since its inception, Patrimonio Hoy has sponsored the building of ten thousand homes in Mexico and launched a similar project in Colombia.

CEMEX involved itself in the community to discern how it could best deliver solutions and services to the people most in need. By making its building materials easier to buy, the company opened up a market segment it once believed was impenetrable and not profitable enough to pursue. Now the company predicts that within five years of the program's 2002 inception, over one million Mexican families will benefit from this new way of doing business. Along with some of the world's forward-thinking multinational corporations, CEMEX is discovering that the poorest of the poor represent the next major frontier for companies struggling to maintain rapid growth. Even with the current pause in growth, it is adding new families at the rate of two thousand per month, and sales are growing by 15 percent monthly.

Patrimonio Hoy has helped the CEMEX bottom line by tripling the rate of cement consumed by its low-income, do-it-yourself homebuilders. The amount of cement that used to be consumed in four years is now being consumed in fifteen months. Although the average value of a sale to a low-income customer is miniscule, their numbers are enormous compared to CEMEX's more affluent customers. Low-income communities end up being a more stable market that is less affected by the cyclical fluctuations of the economy. Sales to the poor could offset losses during economic downturns, offer the possibility of sustained growth, and offset the erosion of CEMEX's overall market share by international competitors. All this while providing housing solutions to people in desperate need. This is original thinking at is best. It's an indicator of how we can evolve the very concept of capitalism by pursuing the question "how can we profit *with* our customers, not just *from* them?"

Adam Smith used the term "the invisible hand" to demonstrate how self-interest guides the most efficient use of resources in a nation's economy, with public welfare coming as a by-product. But, having evolved some two hundred and thirty years since his *Wealth of Nations*, we're discovering that the most original and profitable solutions emerge when we take a more holistic approach and ask at once: what is best for us, what is best for the public, and what is best for the planet? Corporations that are asking these questions—that have adopted the notion that "waste is food"—are gaining immensely, and not just profits, but credibility in the eyes of a watchful public. They're building good corporate karma and it's paying off.

The concept of restructuring business relationships so that the provider and customer both profit by finding efficient and mutually beneficial solutions is a quantum leap away from older business models. But it is the wave of the future. In the old model, the company wants to provide more products more often, which leads to higher cost and higher wastes and is exactly the opposite of what the customer wants. In the new model, customers get the value and service they desire at a lesser cost and with no waste.

For example, Carrier, the world's largest manufacturer of air conditioners, is shifting its focus from selling air conditioners to leasing comfort. They are making more efficient and durable equipment, giving Carrier greater profits while its customers get better comfort at lower cost. Plus, they are also aware that in more efficient buildings, less cooling yields the same comfort. So they are collaborating with other firms that can improve lighting, glazings, and other building systems for higher energy efficiency. This is like watching evolution in action.

And Interface Carpet is doing something similar. They are shifting their focus from selling carpet to leasing floor-covering services. "People want to walk on and look at carpet, not own it. They can obtain these services at much lower cost if Interface owns the carpet and remains responsible for keeping it clean and fresh," writes Lovins. "For a monthly fee, Interface will visit regularly and replace the 10-20 percent of the carpet tiles that show 80-90 percent of the wear. This reduces the mass flow of carpet to landfills by about 80 percent and provides better service at lower cost. It also increases net employment, eliminates the disruption (worn tiles are seldom under furniture), and turns a capital expenditure into an operating lease."

Interface's new Solenium product provides floor covering that is almost completely re-manufacturable into identical carpet, cutting their net flow of needed materials and energy by 97 percent. It is also nontoxic, virtually stain-proof, easy to clean with water, four times as durable, one-third less materials-intensive, and renewably produced.

And what rewards has this higher level thinking reaped? In their four-year quest to turn waste into profit, Interface has doubled their revenues, tripled their operating profits, and nearly doubled employment. Its latest $250 million revenue came from mining internal waste, with no increase in energy or materials inputs. This is natural capitalism at its best.

CREATING THE FUTURE

We are getting there, slow but sure, like those cement trucks determined to "find a hole and fill it." We know from these stories that we are not alone, and that evolution is sweeping us forward in its own time, on its own terms. The best that we can do—any of us—is to remember the karmic truth that *we reap what we sow*. Abundance out, abundance in. Compassion out, compassion in. Great urgencies are upon us, and opportunities for service abound. The Millennium Development Goals are the hugest imagining humankind has ever undergone—the most profound and honorable of all our collective thoughts. And we can succeed. We *are* succeeding. There are thousands more stories just like these that we never hear. But they are happening, in accordance with our vision, in accordance with our will. We are the earth, repairing itself, and we will not fail.

| CHAPTER |

The Triple Bottom Line

Business is the only mechanism on the planet today powerful enough to produce the changes necessary to reverse global environmental and social degradation.

PAUL HAWKEN

Freedom is actually a bigger game than power. Power is about what you can control. Freedom is about what you can unleash.

HARRIET RUBIN

I was trying out a new hair stylist, and loving the extra head massage Allen delivered along with my shampoo.

"Nice touch," I said, as he squirted conditioner into his hand.

"Isn't this scent fabulous?" he said, rubbing it into my scalp. "I just *love* these products."

"Mmm," I replied, breathing in the fresh scent of rosemary and mint. "Dreamy."

By the time he started cutting, his contagious vitality had aroused my curiosity.

"You seem pretty chirpy today. I must be your last customer," I said, noticing it was after five.

"Yes, but I'm driving up to L.A. to teach a class this weekend," he said, stretching for a portfolio of photographs he'd been collecting from his classes. "I teach people how to work with the new colors. They're magnificent, and 97 percent natural. Everything Aveda has is plant derived. I just love this company. They're so triple bottom line."

"Triple bottom line?" I repeated.

"Yeah, you know. They don't just care about profit. They care about the people they do business with and the environment. People, planet, profits—triple bottom line."

As it turns out, he learned the term from his partner who is

163

studying for an MBA.

"Here's the greatest thing," he said. "Aveda is totally committed to environmental sustainability, and many of the ingredients we use are organically grown by tribes in the Brazilian Amazon. We're helping them save their rainforests. As long as we buy what they harvest from their trees, they don't have to sell the land to ranchers. So, their communities stay intact, the rainforests are protected, and we end up with the greatest products in the world. Win, win, win," he said triumphantly.

I checked out Aveda when I got home and found out that, according to Estee Lauder, who bought the high-end organic-cosmetics brand in 1997, Aveda is now one of its top-selling brands, its annual sales having almost doubled since 2002. And along with doubling their profits, Aveda is doing a good job at saving the rainforests as well. "There are rainforests still standing in Peru that probably would not be if not for Aveda." says Glenn Prickett, executive director of the Center for Environmental Leadership in Business in a recent *Fast Company* article.[1] For those skeptics thinking consciousness doesn't pay, Aveda is one of many companies coming up with evidence to the contrary, thanks to the originality and leadership of its founder, Horst Rechelbacher, and current president Dominique Conseil.

Rechelbacher, who founded Aveda in 1978, is a businessman with a global-sized mission. Born in Austria, the son of an herbalist and naturalist, Horst began a three-year apprenticeship in the beauty and salon industry at the age of fourteen. Since the mid-1960s, he has specialized in analyzing the chemical constitution of plants while pioneering the practical use of flowers, functional foods, and nutraceuticals for the benefit of personal health and well-being. In his effort to study plant-based medicine, he has collaborated with physicians, chemists, and pharmacognosists throughout the world, as well as traditional healers and tribespeople in the Brazilian rainforest and Australia. According to Rechelbacher, the mission at Aveda is "to care for the world we live in, from the products we make to the ways in which we give back to society. We strive to set an example for environmental leadership and responsibility, not just in the world of beauty, but around the world."

His concern for the rainforest is well-rooted. The Amazonian rainforest covers over a billion acres, and one-fifth of the world's fresh water is in the Amazon basin. If Amazonia were a country, it would be the ninth largest in the world. The Amazon rainforest has been described as the "lungs of our planet" because it provides the essential environmental world service of continuously recycling carbon dioxide into oxygen.

More than 20 percent of the world's oxygen is produced in the Amazon rainforest.

According to the National Cancer Institute, tropical rainforest plants provide one-quarter of today's pharmaceuticals and 70 percent of the plants useful in the treatment of cancer. In an article published in *Economic Botany*, Dr. Robert Mendelsohn, an economist at Yale University, and Dr. Michael J. Balick, director of the Institute of Economic Botany at the New York Botanical Gardens, estimate that there are at least 328 new drugs that still await discovery in the rainforest, with a potential value of $3 to $4 billion to a private pharmaceutical company and as much as $147 billion to society as a whole.

Despite the fact that rainforests are an integral part of our own personal ecosystem, they are being treated by some businesses as a third-world commodity and, as a result, are disappearing faster than any other natural community on Earth. According to the United States National Academy of Sciences, more than fifty million acres of rainforest, an area the size of England, Scotland, and Wales, are destroyed or seriously degraded each year. In 1950, about 15 percent of the Earth's land surface was covered by rainforest. Today, more than half has already gone up in smoke, and if deforestation continues at current rates, scientists estimate nearly 80 to 90 percent of tropical rainforest ecosystems will be destroyed by the year 2020.

Every day about ninety acres of rainforest land is deforested for timber, paper products, and cattle grazing. For every quarter-pound fast-food hamburger that comes from the rainforest, fifty-five square feet of rainforest is destroyed. That's about the size of a small kitchen for one hamburger, hardly a good return on investment. The latest statistics show that rainforest land converted to cattle operations yields the landowner $60 per acre; if timber is harvested, the land is worth $400 per acre. However, if medicinal plants, fruits, nuts, rubber, chocolate, and other renewable and sustainable resources are harvested, the land will yield the landowner $2,400 per acre. And this is where Aveda comes in. Recognizing that it is the sustainable resources, not the trees, that are the true wealth of the rainforest, they are working with the native people on developing projects that are sustainable and income-producing.

Aveda is indeed a triple bottom line business, and it is a stunning example of how concern for people and the planet pays off in the long run. In partnership with Conservation International (CI), a nonprofit environmental organization, Aveda is helping local communities in Peru's Madre de Dios territory develop businesses that conserve their natural resources. The Incan dialect called Quechua refers to their lush rainforest as *vilcabamba*—the sacred valley. The region is home to stands of vast Brazil nut trees which act as a buffer zone protecting conservation reserves to the south from logging concessions to the north. Because the nut trees are critical to the health of the rainforest, a new Peruvian forest law grants concessions to traditional nut-collectors (*castañeros*) of the region—such as the indigenous Ese'eja peoples—to gather the edible nuts for personal use and to sell them for income. Without earnings from Brazil nuts, indigenous people would be pressured to earn their livelihood from logging or other practices that result in deforestation.

Local workers gather fallen Brazil nuts from the forest and extract oil from the nuts. The leftover meal is combined with wheat protein to create morikue™ protein complex, a pure plant-derived protein, ideal for use in Aveda hair care products. According to Conservation International, Aveda's project funding, training, and market support provide critical enabling conditions for viable sustainable enterprises in tropical Peru. "This support is leading to lasting conservation in one of the world's richest ecosystems," says Roberto Roca, CI's vice-president and executive director for the Andean Regional Program.

In the eastern Amazonian region of Brazil, women gather to collect nuts from lush, new-growth babassu palms, then sit under shade trees and break the hard shells with a stick over ax blades adjusted to their legs. The women have occupied the Maranhão region of Brazil for over four centuries and are among 600,000 peasants who have developed a livelihood consisting of garden agriculture (corn, beans, and small livestock) and the rudimentary processing of babassu nut oil for cooking and cleansing. They call themselves *quebradeiras de coco*–"coconut breakers."

Twenty years ago, when many people were forced from the land while vast sections of forest were burned and cleared for cattle ranching, these women fiercely resisted, standing up to clear-cutters, tractors, and guns to protect their palm forests. Now they are partnering with Aveda, learning to process babassu organically into a richly foaming cleansing ingredient known as babassu betaine. Aveda has financed the construction of a babassu processing facility, a soap-making facility, and a paper press for processing babassu fibers. They have also funded training in processing and management.

With Aveda support, the *quebradeiras de coco* have begun a living pharmacy project to produce plant-based medicines, and one collective is becoming a certifying agency in organic agriculture. In this way, the native communities are not reliant on Aveda alone for financial wellness, as they pursue environmentally sustainable means of economic development.

There are hundreds of businesses around the world devoting resources to sustainability and profiting as they do it, but the execution of sustainable practices has a long way to go in the corporate world. In their book, *Our Ecological Footprint,* Mathis Wackernagel and William Rees state that if the developed world's model of commerce and consumerism were to become the standard everywhere, it would require the equivalent of four earths to supply the raw materials, fossil fuels, and waste sinks that would be needed.[2]

In the United States, companies are notoriously resource-intensive, and this is borne out by statistics revealing that US companies use twice the energy of Japan and Germany; produce thirty-two truckloads of waste for every truckload of goods we make; use twice the energy to produce one dollar worth of goods as other industrialized nations; and extract, move, waste, and burn four million pounds of material to feed the demands of the average, middle-class American family.[3]

Evolutionary biologist Elisabet Sahtouris reminds us that global co-operation is occurring everyday in the arts, in travel, in money exchange, in sciences and communications—but when it comes to economics, there's a problem. She writes: "Suppose our bodies' northern industrial organs could exploit the bone marrow all over the body for its raw-material blood cells. They are then swept up into the heart-lung system where the blood is purified, and oxygen is added. Suppose, now, that the heart distribution center demands a price for blood, and some organs cannot afford it. Could our bodies stay healthy in such a system?"[4]

Metaphors like these help us understand the cost of our failure to think inclusively, globally, originally. They are a visual stimulant to our creativity, giving us a look at the whole instead of our tiny personal fragment. In the larger scheme of things, each of us is a cell making up this entity known as Earth, just as your trillions of cells make up the entity known as you. Your cells are in constant communication twenty-four hours a day, seeing to it that the whole they are part of works as efficiently as it can.

And each one of us, in one way or another, is affecting the well-being of the earth, for better or worse. Every choice we make has a planetary impact—what we eat, what we drive, where we travel, where we shop. Hundreds of new businesses have cropped up to help individuals and corporations make choices that are socially responsible, from driving to dating, eating to cleaning. A fact-filled website, Newdream.org, makes it easy to buy environmentally responsible versions of everyday items, and Concernedsingles.com is making it fun and simple for socially-conscious singles to find each other. In just two months, more than 12,000 subscribers turned to Idealbite.com for free advice on saving money and finding environmentally friendly products and services. Simultaneously, Ideal Bite has created a community where companies can directly access a niche market of consumers. The company is currently conducting a brand awareness study for a top global food company looking to learn more about how to market its organic line.

We've come a long way since the first Earth Day in April, 1970, and it is not just environmentalists who are speaking out and taking a stand. CEOs of many large corporations are taking their concerns to their boards, their fellow executives, and their stakeholders. Michael Sauvante, president and CEO of Rolltronics speaks of the universe as a "living, evolving mechanism and our responsibility is to endeavor to relate in a constructive, positive sense to all that is around us."

Rolltronics is a high-tech company that uses a roll-to-roll process, similar to the way newspapers are printed, to produce devices such as ultra-high-density memory, ultra-light batteries, and integrated circuits on thin plastic films, including "electronic paper" and wearable computers. Compared with the current approach, in which chips are produced in billion-dollar fabrication facilities using millions of gallons of water and toxic chemicals, the process they use is modular and clean. Lower capital costs make it possible to locate smaller production facilities closer to end markets, enabling them to bridge the digital divide between technology-poor and technology-rich countries. The company uses triple bottom line reporting and defines sustainability as "meeting the needs of the present without compromising the ability of future generations to meet their own needs."

Triple bottom line reporting was devised in 1994 by SustainAbility, a London think tank. The idea behind it is that companies that want to be successful in the long term should be able to meet society's demand for goods and services without destroying natural and social capital. The assumption is that there are three forms of capital that contribute to the success of a business and, in turn, should receive a return on investment. Other than cash capital, there is natural capital and social capital.

In their white paper on sustainability, Rolltronics asserts that natural capital is represented by all the raw materials provided by the planet. Treating these resources as if they were limitless is an unsustainable practice, akin to living off a fixed savings account that is drawn down faster than interest can accumulate. In time, the natural resources will be exhausted, just as one's cash supply would be—so the next step is to rethink our actions and devise new approaches to our required resources. "It is well known that waste reduction, either in the production of the product or the product itself at the end of its useful life, represents direct cost savings to corporations. What is less well recognized is that waste represents a resource that should be recycled and reused instead of discarded. This approach is often called 'cradle-to-cradle' to represent a closed loop. Every company that has adopted the cradle-to-cradle philosophy in conducting their business has discovered significant gains on their financial bottom lines."[5]

Many companies have already discovered that waste reduction leads to direct and significant cost savings, but those who treat waste as natural capital that should receive a return on investment are thinking more originally and profiting more significantly. The United States Postal Service earned revenues of $6.6 million in one year from the sales of recyclable materials. Bell Atlantic recovered 30,000 tons of material from obsolete equipment and sold it for $25 million. Quad/Graphics recycled 146,000 tons of paper in one year, saving $12.5 million in disposal fees.

The public utility company Exelon generated nearly $4 million in operational savings through material recycling in 2004. Not only are they reducing greenhouse gas emissions by converting landfill gas to energy, they are also recycling 100 percent of the by-products of coal combustion at their fossil generating stations. IKEA requires all of its stores to reuse, recycle, or produce energy from 75 percent of their waste. In 1975, 3M began running its Pollution Prevention Pays (3P) program, which has generated over $750 million in first-year savings over the last two decades. Greenbiz.com reports that Procter and Gamble saved $1 million with a variety of nationwide energy efficient plans, working with their partner, Cinergy Solutions, a company that works with businesses on turning their energy challenges into cost-saving opportunities.

Baxter International, the global medical products and services company that produced the first portable kidney dialysis machine and the first commercially manufactured intravenous (IV) solutions has been on the Dow Jones Sustainability World Index (DJSI World) and the Dow Jones Sustainability North America Index (DJSI North America) for seven consecutive years. The Dow Jones Sustainability indices are the world's first benchmarks tracking the financial performance of leading companies in terms of sustainability. The DJSI World tracks the financial performance of the top 10 percent of the 2,500 biggest companies in the Dow Jones Global Index in terms of social, economic, and environmental performance. The DJSI North America—a new addition to the DJSI family as of September 2005—includes the top 20 percent in each sector out of the biggest six hundred North American companies.

Baxter International has sixty-seven manufacturing facilities located in twenty-eight countries. In an address made to the Science Committee of the House of Representatives on June 8, 2005 about the business benefits of climate change initiatives, Ron Meissen, Baxter's Senior Director for Environment, Health and Safety Engineering, affirmed that reasonable improvements in energy conservation and emissions reductions are possible without huge investment. According to Meissen, a key driver for the proactive initiatives at Baxter has been the realization that sound environmental practices can contribute to and, in some cases, drive competitive advantage.

In his opinion, companies that have been forward-looking on this issue are in the best position to build upon the momentum they have created and better compete on a global basis. He reported that by driving greater operating efficiencies, by piloting and adopting new technologies, and by sharing ideas and best practices within the company and through collaborations and voluntary programs sponsored by the EPA and others, Baxter has achieved a 35 percent reduction in greenhouse gas emissions, a 22 percent improvement in energy efficiency, and savings and cost avoidance totaling several millions of dollars each year. In 2004 alone, he estimated their energy savings and cost avoidance exceeded $9 million.

"We learned of the Green Suppliers Network and the impact it was having in other industries, like the automotive industry, and we were immediately attracted to the program," said Meissen. "As a result of these changes, the facility estimates it has saved in excess of $100,000 per year in utility costs. While $100,000 a year may not seem like a big number, when you consider that we have 67 manufacturing facilities alone, these kinds of projects and incremental savings quickly add up to much larger numbers and do make a difference."[6]

Besides the Green Suppliers Network, there are hundreds of nonprofits and non-governmental organizations (NGOs) building alliances with corporations on sustainability issues, in effect marrying the operating efficiency of business with the public purpose of nonprofits. The World Wildlife Fund (WWF) and the Center for Energy and Climate Solutions are looking for companies willing to lead the way in environmental solutions. WWF and the Center support companies in developing strategic energy management plans and help to communicate these efforts to the public, to policymakers, and to the wider business community.

WWF's goal is to reverse the rising trend in carbon dioxide emissions from industrialized countries. They do this by helping companies adopt a portfolio of energy management strategies that include a mix of immediate and long-term actions. In a customized Climate Savers agreement, companies commit to greenhouse gas reduction goals and work with WWF and the Center to outline key action areas for achieving measurable reductions in carbon dioxide emissions.

Companies that join WWF's Climate Savers Program measure their progress against other companies internationally, participate in annual events with like-minded businesses, and gain public recognition for environmental achievements through WWF's communication outlets. Businesses that have already joined the Climate Savers Program include International Business Machines (IBM), Johnson & Johnson, Polaroid Corporation, Nike, Lafarge, the Collins Companies, Sagawa Express, and Xanterra. There's a potent PR advantage to joining since WWF has nearly five million members, and the Climate Change program has staff working in over thirty countries on different aspects of the issue. Companies in Climate Savers are highlighted in WWF's *FOCUS* publication, sent six times per year to 1.2 million homes in the US and staffs at both WWF and the Center for Energy and Climate Solutions consistently draw attention to the commitments undertaken by companies in Climate Savers while speaking to the media and at conferences. It's a continuation of the doing well by doing good theory.

Another organization that's bringing together businesses at the vanguard of environmental consciousness is the World Business Council for Sustainable Development. (WBCSD), a coalition of 175 international companies united by a shared commitment to sustainable development via economic growth, ecological balance, and social progress. Their members come from more than thirty-five countries and twenty major industrial sectors, and their global network of national and regional business councils and partner organizations involve some one thousand business leaders globally. Almost one-third of the companies listed on the *Global 100 Most Sustainable Corporations in the World* are WBCSD member companies, and they're making smart choices according to the Dow Jones Sustainability Index, which notes that companies seen as leaders in sustainable development consistently outperform conventional market indices.

WBCSD member companies have combined annual sales of more than $5 trillion, and their products and services touch the lives of about 2.5 billion people every day. As businesses are discovering that it pays to be concerned about society, a growing number of companies are investing in ideas that have clear development benefits, especially in terms of creating opportunities for people. These ideas include designing products and services that address specific needs of the poor, increasing sourcing from local suppliers and involving low-income communities in the delivery of innovative products and services. SC Johnson in Kenya, GrupoNueva in Guatemala, Rabobank and Unilever in Indonesia are all working to boost the competitiveness of local low-income farmers, significantly improving their livelihoods. France's electricity utility, EDF, is providing affordable solar energy to villagers in Morocco, too remote to be connected to the national grid. Procter & Gamble has developed a low-cost product that purifies drinking water where no source is available.

Business and development are two sides of the same coin, claims WBCSD President Björn Stigson. "Companies are an integral part of the societies and communities in which they operate, and they cannot succeed if the society around them fails. The companies that do not manage their social issues in the same way they manage other strategic business issues will not stay in business long-term." [7]

Geoffrey Colvin, in a an article for *Fortune* magazine, writes that companies today are doing more of what the activists want than they ever have done before, but it's not because they're being socially responsible. It's because they're listening to the markets. He claims that as the world has become more virulently capitalist, it has also become more concerned about the environment, child labor, and human rights, with more consumers basing their buying decisions on "who made their Nike shoes or where Exxon Mobil got its gasoline or what McDonald's does with its paper waste." Another thing he mentions is that more and more employees want to know that what they do at work is good and right in some large sense. "Consumers care and employees care. That means equity markets care. And that means CEOs care. Thus, for example, we see Ford and British Petroleum (BP), formerly monsters in the view of social-responsibility types, working hard to greenify themselves. Some of what they've done is real and some is window dressing, but the fact is that Ford Chairman William Clay Ford got a standing ovation from the Coalition for Environmentally Responsible Economies, and BP CEO

John Browne gets plenty of media calls seeking his comment on all kinds of enviro-matters. That would have been unimaginable a few years ago."[8]

Even DuPont, once considered one of America's worst polluters, has seen the light. While it set out a decade ago to curb pollution and reduce waste, it now has a new mission: to own a collection of businesses that can go on forever without depleting natural resources. "The company spun off its massive Conoco oil-and-gas unit five years ago and used the proceeds to buy Pioneer Hi-Bred International, whose seeds produce not only food for people and livestock but renewable materials for commercial uses—turning corn into stretch T-shirts, for example," writes Marc Gunther in a *Fortune* magazine article.[9]

When I spoke with Dawn Rittenhouse, DuPont's Director of Sustainable Development, she said that it was Ed Woolard, DuPont's former CEO, who started the sustainable ball rolling in 1989. "Ed Woolard believed that it wasn't enough to be in compliance. We had been in compliance for years and were still known as the number one polluter in the world. Nothing we were doing was illegal, but it was still hurting the environment. Woolard said that in order for the company to be successful in the mind of the public, we had to go beyond compliance, and that's when we committed to sustainable growth." Rittenhouse, who's worked at the company for twenty-five years, says that being a sustainable company means that every corporate decision is based on how it adds value in the economic, social, and environmental arenas. "We see them as all one thing now, and we have a large technical and development department always looking ahead at greener alternatives."

When it comes to triple bottom line reporting, DuPont supports the Global Reporting Initiative (GRI) as the best format for reporting data on economic, environmental and social performance. "Once we committed to sustainability, we started hearing from socially-responsible investment communities who were interested in our progress," said Rittenhouse. "In the mid-90s, as part of the conversation on sustainable growth, we were asked if DuPont was willing to support a standardization in reporting. Joining GRI was part of that process."

Started in 1997, GRI became independent in 2002, and is an official collaborating center of the United Nations Environment Program (UNEP). GRI was established in response to the growing need for common standards to report against and international agreement in this area. "It is fast becoming the de facto standard defining the triple bottom line," according to Allan Fels, Dean of the Australia and New

Zealand School of Government. In its September 2003 Quarterly Report, Henderson Asset Management reported that "the Global Reporting Initiative (GRI) is increasingly regarded as the 'best available' model for corporate disclosure on social, environmental and ethical issues."

On its website, (www.globalreporting.org), GRI defines itself as "a multi-stakeholder process and independent institution whose mission is to develop and disseminate globally applicable Sustainability Reporting Guidelines." Within eighteen months of its founding, GRI had 380 members. A look at its website today (in November 2005) shows a membership of 728 members, including some of the world's top countries and a number of national governments. These are telling figures, given that as recently as seven years ago, the concept of sustainability reporting did not even exist.

The Accountability Rating, which rates sustainability reports from the *Fortune Global 100*, finds significant growth in sustainability reporting. Almost three-quarters (72 percent) of G-100 companies issued sustainability reports by 2004, whereas less than half (48 percent) had done so by 2003. The escalation trend is most conspicuous in the USA, where the percentage of companies involved in GRI reporting rose from 18 percent to a remarkable 49 percent in one year. Also conspicuous was the dearth of US companies in the top sustainability report ratings: Hewlett-Packard was the sole US-based company in the top ten, which included BP, Shell, Toyota, and Unilever, among others.

The GRI points out that the Socially Responsible Investment (SRI) community has grown remarkably over the last twenty-four months. For the SRI community, the GRI reporting framework is increasingly seen as a key tool to progress in many of the areas and sectors of interest to this group. SRI funds such as Barclays, Calvert, Henderson, Hermes, and Insight are all requesting companies to report on GRI Guidelines.

It seems that we're reaching a tipping point in the matter of sustainability reporting, as more and more CEOs step out as thought leaders, writers and speakers on the subject. DuPont CEO Edgar Woolard helped to instigate things when he wrote in 1990: "The green economies and lifestyles of the twenty-first century may be conceptualized by environmental thinkers, but they can only be actualized by industrial corporations. Industry has a next-century vision of integrated environmental performance. Not every company is there yet, but most are trying. Those that aren't trying won't be a problem long-term, simply because they won't be around long-term. That is the new competitive reality."[10]

Woolard was quoted in the book *Eco-Efficiency: The Business Link to Sustainable Development,* written by two other CEOs who are committed to conscious commerce, Livio D. DeSimone, CEO and chair of 3M, and Frank Popoff, chair of Dow Chemical. And DuPont's current CEO, Charles O. Holliday Jr., has recently co-authored the eco-wise *Walking the Talk: The Business Case for Sustainable Development.* These authors all speak to the role of business in initiating practices that are environmentally sound, stressing the benefit of partnerships with government, associations, and nonprofits in designing more sustainable systems and applications.

One organization that's doing just this is Redefining Progress, an Oakland, California-based think tank that works with a broad variety of partners to shift the economy and public policy toward sustainability. In October 2004 they released a ground-breaking state-by-state analysis of the job creation potential of a smart energy policy, which is viewable on their website, www.redefiningprogress.org. The "Smarter, Cleaner, Stronger" report provides a comprehensive new policy package that would stimulate the creation of new jobs—approximately 1.4 million more new jobs by 2025—while lowering energy bills that will save US consumers an astounding $170 billion per year.[11]

Emphasizing that American ingenuity will lead the way to energy security and a strong economy, the imaginative and clear-thinking proposal writers assert that, if the policies outlined in this package were adopted, the US would reduce its dependence on foreign oil by 1.7 billion barrels per year, cut in half the amount of greenhouse gases that would be emitted into the atmosphere under a "business as usual" approach, and increase the annual GDP by $123 billion in 2025.

Another development that has emerged to support sustainable farming practices around the world is Fairtrade labeling. It was created in the Netherlands in the late 1980s when Max Havelaar launched the first Fairtrade consumer guarantee label in 1986 on coffee sourced from Mexico. The United States consumes one-fifth of all of the world's coffee, making it the largest consumer in the world, but few Americans have an idea of the hardships coffee growers regularly endure. Many small coffee farmers receive prices for their coffee that are less than the costs of production. Coffee prices have plummeted and are currently around $.60-$.70 per pound, making it nearly impossible for farmers to maintain their land and their families, while coffee companies are free to decide whether to lower consumer prices or pocket the difference.

CREATING THE FUTURE

Fairtrade is a viable solution to this crisis, assuring consumers that the coffee we drink was purchased under fair conditions. To become Fairtrade certified, an importer must meet stringent international criteria: paying a minimum price per pound of $1.26, providing much needed credit to farmers, and providing technical assistance such as help transitioning to organic farming. Fairtrade for coffee farmers means community development, health, education, and environmental stewardship. Since 1999, the market for Fairtrade Certified™ coffee has grown by an average of over 70 percent each year, a sign that consumers are making their voices heard.

Even McDonald's is getting in on the act. Franchise owners in the Northeast have formed a partnership with the Fairtrade-certified Green Mountain Coffee Roasters to create an exclusive coffee blend under the Newman's Own Organics brand. They rolled it out in Fall 2005 and are filling cups with the socially-responsible java in 650 McDonald's restaurants in Connecticut, Maine, Massachusetts, New Hampshire, Rhode Island, Vermont, and Albany, New York. New coffee cups prominently feature the Green Mountain Coffee and Newman's Own Organics logos and carry only a small version of McDonald's Golden Arches logo at the bottom. Tabletop promotions proclaim: "Good for you...Good for the environment...Good for the world."[12]

No matter how many people complain about the ubiquitous Starbucks, you have to give them credit for being a stand-up corporation. This year, Starbucks will purchase ten million pounds of Fairtrade certified coffee, making it North America's largest purchaser of Fairtrade certified coffee. Next year, the company plans to purchase twelve million pounds. In 2004, Starbucks paid an average price of $1.20 per pound for all of its green (unroasted) coffee, a price 74 percent higher than the average New York "C" commodity market price.

A $400,000 loan to Sidama Coffee Farmers Cooperative Union is part of a $5 million coffee producer financing arrangement Starbucks has developed with EcoLogic Finance, a Cambridge, Massachusetts-based nonprofit organization that offers affordable financial services to community-based businesses operating in environmentally sensitive areas. The loan to Sidama represents the first time a coffee cooperative in Ethiopia has been able to access affordable credit. Coffee farmers often face a shortage of cash before harvest, which may force them to sell their crops early to local buyers for prices lower than what they might otherwise earn, or may cause them to forsake investments in improved farming techniques, structures, and equipment. Access to affordable financing helps ensure coffee quality and long-term economic sustainability in Ethiopia and throughout the world.

Starbucks has a long history of integrating a social conscience into all aspects of its business. Recently the company announced a contribution goal of $10 million over the next five years, through Ethos™ Water, to help children and their communities around the world get clean drinking water. Ethos™ Water, founded in 2002 by Peter Thum and Jonathan Greenblatt as a means to raise funds to bring clean water to children around the world, was acquired by Starbucks in April 2005. Five cents from the sale of each bottle of Ethos™ Water will support Starbucks goal of donating $10 million over the next five years to nonprofit organizations that are helping to alleviate the world water crisis.

In addressing the social capital aspect of the triple bottom line, Starbucks is setting a sterling example in the health benefits department. They spend $200 million a year on insurance for their 80,000 US employees—more than they do on all the raw materials needed to brew their coffee, according to chairman Howard Schultz. Schultz was part of a group that included CEOs from Verizon, Costco, Honeywell, and Pitney Bowes who went to Congress in October 2005 to spark some interest in controlling health care costs. Each of the companies offers health insurance to virtually all of its employees, despite the skyrocketing costs.

"We want to tell the story in a way that other companies can see that you can make money and do the right thing by taking care of your people," Schultz said during a meeting with Senator Patty Murray from Washington. Schultz's main argument is that companies can be profitable *while* being morally responsible. He credited their benefits policy as a key reason for high productivity and low employee turnover, which has led to extraordinary profitability. According to Schultz, Starbucks' stock is up almost 4,000 percent in thirteen years, and surged 80 percent in 2004.

Companies around the country are learning that they can get a higher return on their social capital if they value and respond to the needs of the people they employ. A story in *Worthwhile* magazine by David Batstone, author of *Saving the Creative Soul*, and Caralee Adams highlights some of these companies' creative approaches. At Triage Consulting, a health care consulting firm in San Francisco, their consultants typically work Monday through Thursday out of town for four months at a stretch. As a reward, the company picks up the tab for one of three options on the weekend: the employees can fly home, fly to another city, or have a family member or friend flown into their location for the weekend. And for every month consultants spend out of town, they bank one day toward a sabbatical to take at the end of their fourth year.

At Green Mountain Coffee Roasters in Waterbury, Vermont, employees can take lunchtime yoga classes in the company meditation center, and in Berkeley, California at Clif Bar, they can improve their rock-climbing skills on the indoor climbing wall hovering over their cubicles. Discovery Communications in Silver Spring, Maryland opened an on-site health and wellness center complete with a nurse practitioner and physician. On opening day, one hundred employees signed up for physicals. The center also provides routine prescriptions during flu season and sponsors a skin screening day and special wellness programs for men and pregnant women. Last year one thousand employees took part in their annual healthy living competition and lost a total of five thousand pounds. According to the article, the center has shown a good return on investment— a savings of $600,000 in direct and indirect costs.

At SAS headquarters in Cary, North Carolina, the 4,100 employees are offered child care, dry cleaning, and health care. They can also get their car detailed, and a massage or a hair cut at the company salon. For eight weeks in the summer, SAS sponsors Camp Awesome Adventure on their nine-hundred-acre campus. Employees can bring their kids ages nine through fourteen to play soccer, softball, or swim in the huge pool. Or they can learn to cook, sign up for Hooray for Hollywood to perform plays, or join the Mad Scientist Club and conduct scientific experiments.

Hyperion, a software company in Santa Clara, California has initiated a "Drive Clean to Drive Change" program and gives employees $5000 toward the purchase of hybrid or other fuel efficient car. Hyperion promises to distribute the bonuses to as many as two hundred employees annually on a first-come, first-serve basis, and anyone who has worked at

None of my books or ideas mean anything to me in the long run. What are theories? Nothing. The only thing that matters is how you touch people. Have I given anyone insight? That's what I want to have done. Insight lasts; theories don't.

PETER DRUCKER
TO HARRIET RUBIN

The time is coming when people will be astonished that mankind needed so long a time to regard thoughtless injury to life as compatible with ethics.

ALBERT SCHWEITZER,
PHYSICIAN/NOBEL LAUREATE

The two-word definition of sustainability is "one planet."

MATHIS WACKERNAGEL

Hyperion for at least a year is eligible. They have fifty slots each quarter, at a total of $1 million a year, and all their employees are either driving a green car or on a waiting list to get one. Hyperion has set up a how-to guide on its website for other companies looking to launch fuel-friendly initiatives.

A *Wall Street Journal* article quotes Godfrey Sullivan, Hyperion president and CEO, who says that he aims to help the environment as well as distinguish Hyperion's profile as an employer: "If the economy is improving and now the options for where you work are a little bit more diverse, some of the soft touches are as important as the compensation," says Mr. Sullivan. "One of the factors in where you want to work is how proud are you to work there." And is this thinking paying off? Absolutely, according to Jeffrey Rodek, Hyperion's executive chairman who announced record revenues and operating margins in both the fourth quarter and 2004 fiscal year.

Triple bottom line reporting is an idea that can, and probably will, be debated for years. Some skeptics say these social responsibility measures are little more than public-relations tactics to divert attention from corporate corruption. Detractors say it's an unworkable concept, that nobody has actually proposed a way to use the data on social performance to calculate some kind of net social bottom line. Their issue is with metrics and measurability, and with the difficulty of achieving global agreement. There is also the view that organizations contribute most to the welfare of society when they focus on what they do best. Let business do business, they say, and do not divert attention away from its core competency.

On the other hand, proponents of triple bottom line reporting argue that Earth's carrying capacity is at risk and they see a need for comprehensive reform in global financial institutions in order to avoid planetary catastrophes. The primary benefit of measuring social and environmental deficits would be first to see what needs to be addressed, then to design ways and means to

> The first day or so we all pointed to our countries. The third or fourth day we were pointing to our continents. By the fifth day we were aware of only one Earth.
> SULTAN BIN SALMAN AL SAUD, ASTRONAUT

> It is the absence of broad-based business activity, not its presence, that condemns much of humanity to suffering. Indeed, what is utopian is the notion that poverty can be overcome without the active engagement of business.
> KOFI ANNAN, UN SECRETARY-GENERAL

address them. With the emergence of green economics and agreement on definitions of terms such as full-cost accounting, natural capital, and social capital, the prospect of coming up with formal metrics for ecological and social loss or risk is growing closer every day.

As usual, both sides are right, but only partly so. And there is no point in arguing. The invitation here is to take this idea into your heart and see how it feels. How would it feel to run a business, or work for a business, that cared as much about people and the earth as it did about profit? How would that change your life, your commitments at work, your relationship to your family? How would it feel to be part of an organization or group that took a stand for the environment or for a particular social issue and actually created a partnership with a business to make something happen that was good for the world?

Nothing will ever come of arguments over triple bottom line accounting, but whole new vistas can open up when we ponder it in our imagination. The threshold we're at right now is a precious one. The whole world *is* in our hands, and every one of us has the power to act on that or not. If we do, what will change is us, what we'll save is *ourselves*— and what will happen in turn is a deepening of our joy, our sensibilities, and our relationships to our families, our friends, our Earth.

The issues of poverty, global warming, species extinction—all the things related to human and natural capital—will never be solved by our talking, our coursework, our panels and commissions. They are emotional issues and solutions will never occur to us until we open our emotions and feel their impact—until we are struck by a grace that helps us see the real meaning behind *what you do for the least of them, you do for me.*

We will not change the minds of anyone with our thoughts and statistics. Think of the last time you changed your mind about something, or were moved to action, or brought to tears. What was the cause of that? If you have gained authority in any matter—personal, undeniable, undaunted authority—think about how that happened, what you had to release, what you had to claim, what you had to suffer to come into your own power in that matter. Transformation happens when our hearts break open, when we surrender and reach out. And it is this final act, this reaching out, this opening of our very souls to others, or the Other, that opens the door to healing and change. In nature, every seed must die as a seed in order to become the greater thing it was destined for. It is only when the seed cracks open that its real essence is nurtured, fed, and called into being by the earth, the waters, and the sun.

As a people, we are being broken open by the tragedies and travesties of these times. We are individually and collectively confronting the brokenness of every American institution—from education to politics, health care to home-buying. If we take a look at how our country is treating its own human capital, the news is heartbreaking. Holly Sklar, author of *Raise the Floor: Wages and Policies that Work for All of Us*, reports that if Americans without health insurance were a nation, the population would be bigger than Canada, plus Michigan, Montana, New Hampshire, and Vermont. We number twenty-nine in the World Health Organization's healthy life expectancy ranking and do worse than thirty-six countries in child mortality under age five. The National Coalition on Health Care has offered four different scenarios for universal health coverage. The first three scenarios would net $320-$370 billion in savings over the first ten years, and the fourth would save $1.1 trillion, but these scenarios have gone nowhere.

Although worker productivity rose 78 percent between 1973 and 2004, full-time worker pay averaged 11 percent less that 1973's average worker pay. Today's $5.15 minimum wage is 41 percent less than 1968's inflation-adjusted minimum wage of $8.78. The *Multinational Monitor* reports that if the minimum wage had increased as quickly as CEO pay since 1990, it would be at $15.76 an hour. *Business Week* reported in a 2004 cover story that more than twenty-eight million people, about a quarter of the workforce between the ages of eighteen and sixty-four, earn less than $9.04 an hour, which translates into a full-time salary of $18,800 a year—which is below the federal poverty line for a family of four. Overall, 63 percent of US families below the federal poverty line have one or more workers, according to the Census Bureau, and the majority possess high school diplomas and even attended some college.

According to the US Conference of Mayors Hunger and Homelessness Survey, 17 percent of the homeless were employed, as were 34 percent of adults requesting emergency food service. Though one out of eight Americans lives below the meager poverty level, Congress has had seven pay raises since 1997, increasing their yearly salary from $133,600 to $162,100. The richest 1 percent of households owns more wealth than the bottom 90 percent combined, and tax cuts for them will cost more than $120 billion, about the same amount budgeted for the Environmental Protection Agency, Education, Housing and Urban Development, and Veterans Affairs combined for 2006.

If the United States were a company using triple bottom line reporting, things would have to change drastically to ensure its total profitability. The signs point to serious unsustainability, an erosion at the very foundations. But did anything *happen* to you when you read all these statistics? Did you feel inspired to do anything? Did you feel like talking about it with anyone? Were you angry? Sad? Was it exhausting or energizing?

And what about when you read this conversation that happens in the year 2050 between a boy and his grandfather:

Grandpa, did you know it was happening?
Well, sort of. There was news about it, but it didn't seem too real.

How did it feel when you couldn't eat the fish anymore?
Well that was hard. We never thought that would happen.

Didn't they warn you?
Not really. I guess some tried to, but not in a big way. Not like on television, or even much in the newspapers. You had to really want to know, I guess. People just didn't care that much. We were pretty busy then. Pretty caught up in our own lives.

What about the forests? Didn't you know how much we needed them, just to breathe?
People never thought about that connection, son. We needed that timber. Companies needed it for their business. That's what was important back then. Business.

But why would you let them take away everything we needed? Why did you let them make all those stupid things out of plastic? Why didn't you save some of the oil for us?
I swear, we never thought we'd use it up. We weren't trained to think about the future. No one taught us how to think. We did the best we could do, day by day.

I thought you were smart. You had your own business, didn't you?
Yes.

If you were so smart, why didn't you stop them from ruining

all the water? Didn't you ever think I might want to swim like you used to?
It's not like that.

Oh yes it is. If you were so smart you would have known what was happening. But you didn't care. It's your fault.
It's not my fault, son. There were millions of us here. Everyone was to blame.

Then why didn't they stop it? Why did they ruin things for us? Why didn't you care enough to *do* something? Why? Why? WHY?

That question, "WHY?" is coming at us from the future even now, from everyone of our descendants who will wonder what their ancestors did to keep the world safe for them. And just as we are preparing for our own personal futures, so should we prepare for theirs. Triple bottom line reporting was one person's suggestion, the culmination of one person's reflection on how we might standardize a level of corporate accountability. It is a beginning, not an ending, but it is doing the job of stirring up interest in different ways of doing business. Google hits for the term "triple bottom line" numbered 15,600 in August 2002. Today, they are up to 5,040,000.

In the long run, TBL will most likely morph into another form that is more evolved and acceptable to the whole, but for now, it is a good place to start, for it guides our thinking beyond the present and beyond the confines of or own selfish ambitions. It is a community-minded approach, and nothing less than that will move us collectively, as one country and one world, from these dire conditions we have created.

Our solutions live in the body politic and they are waiting to be unfolded in our honest and heartfelt conversations with each other. It is not more research that we need, but more relating. Like seeds in the deep soil, when we break open and acknowledge our need for each other, when we look around and see that our life depends on the earth, the water, and the purest of air, then we will naturally evolve to the next step. But we cannot fulfill our destiny in private. We are part and parcel of this planetary organism, each of us a cell in the great Mother Earth, and like the cells in our own bodies, we must be in constant, conscious communication to remain viable.

The poet and philosopher Wendell Berry reminds us, "It may be that when we no longer know what to do, we have come to our real work, and that when we no longer know which way to go, we have begun our real journey. The mind that is not baffled is not employed. The impeded stream is the one that sings." These are indeed baffling times, and we have come at last to the real work: to collectively create new systems, new businesses, and new partnerships that will result in a world that is healthy and whole.

FOURTEEN

| CHAPTER |

Insight to Action

The need and interest of soul consciousness is not how to draw things to itself from the environment, but how to draw out from itself the qualities and energies from which a greater environment can emerge.

DAVID SPANGLER

There's someone out there who needs you. Live your life so that person can find you.

COKORDA TSTRI RATIH TRYANI, BALINESE DANCER

In 1981, I was working as a picture framer in a mall in Syracuse, New York. I had been involved in the peace movement, which was quite active then due to an escalating global buildup of nuclear weapons. As a photographer and concerned citizen, I attended and photographed demonstrations for peace throughout the US and Canada. Then I assembled my images into a slideshow, put them to music, and showed them in every venue that welcomed me. In many ways, it was a healing thing to do. For one, I was actively taking a stand for something I believed in, so I felt like an agent of change rather than a victim of circumstances. And then there was the sense of being part of a community, a diverse and daring group of people who operated with the belief that their voices mattered. It was democracy in action, and I felt proud to be a part of every demonstration, rallying for a world with fewer arms.

One day, someone inadvertently left a copy of *The Hundredth Monkey* on my workbench and I read it on my lunch hour. It was about a series of experiments done with monkeys off the coast of Japan in the 1950s, but this paragraph is what caught my attention:

> When a certain critical number achieves an awareness, this new awareness may be communicated from mind to mind...When only a limited number of people know of a new way, it may remain the consciousness property of these people. But there is a point at which if only one more person tunes into a new awareness, a field is strengthened so that this awareness reaches almost everyone. Individuals can communicate private information to each other even though located in different places. The strength of this extrasensory communication can be amplified to a powerfully effective level when the consciousness of the "hundredth person" is added.

Something lit up like a light bulb in my mind. Maybe I could be the "hundredth person." Maybe I could take my slides and my music and show them to people around the world. I didn't know any other languages, but a picture is worth a thousand words and music opens people's hearts, so maybe my just being there—creating an occasion for people to come together—would strengthen the field for world peace. I went right across the street to the nearest bank and opened a savings account. "I'm going around the world," I said to the teller. "I'm making a peace pilgrimage, as soon as I get $5000."

It took a year and a half to save it, working two jobs, but I left for Japan in 1983 with $5000 in my pocket and two hundred rolls of film in my backpack. I figured out how to do it as I went along, because I was inspired. That one little book caused me to think differently, to see how I fit into the whole picture. It opened up the world to me, literally. And as a result, I met with thousands of people in fifteen countries, in schools, office buildings, churches, living rooms, and board rooms.

When people saw the images and heard the music, *they* were inspired, because that's what art does. It opens us up to our own greatness. It thaws our frozenness and dissolves the barriers that keep us separate. And my being out there, alone on this quest, determined and committed as I was, that, too, inspired people, because it is our nature to be moved by each other's loving acts. When we see someone else turn an insight into action, it stirs a memory within us of our own power to do the same. We think, "if she can, I can," and our own creative gears start grinding away.

And that, perhaps, is the most splendid result of our work, subliminal as it is—the fact that our very action, when it is inspired and purposeful, has a contagiousness about it. It causes others to look differently at their own lives and actions. When I encounter a person with a mission, a person whose intention is focused and unwavering, I become clearer myself. I've heard it said that you play better golf when you're playing with someone who's better than you. So maybe it's like that. We become more purposeful if we align ourselves with people who are true to their purpose.

Each of us is a teacher to someone and a student of someone. Who is teaching you these days, and what are you learning? And who is learning from you, and what are you teaching? Someone sent me a videotape today of Orrin Hudson, who grew up in public housing in Birmingham, Alabama, the seventh of thirteen children. After working many years as an Alabama State Trooper, Hudson, a champion chess player, is now teaching youth at risk how to play chess, delivering life skills disguised as chess tools. "By teaching them chess, I get to teach them critical thinking skills and good decision-making skills. I teach them how to make every move count, and if they do that in their lives, they can end up winners," says Hudson. His chess students are learning winning formulas, and as a result, many are watching their grades go from Cs to As. Hudson tells them, "If you're the smartest one on your team, then you need a new team," encouraging them to align themselves with the right influences and the right people. Through his nonprofit, Be Someone, Inc. (www.besomeone.org), Hudson is contributing to the lives of hundreds of disadvantaged kids doing what he loves.

And that's the key: taking what we love to do and figuring out how to do it in the service of others. That's part one. Part two is figuring out how to have the whole thing be sustainable. The formula for original thinking is wisdom plus intelligence, heart plus brain. We get an impulse from the heart zone—an insight, an intuitive feeling, a desire to be useful—and we have to mesh that with a multi-dimensional intelligence that takes the insight to its next level. This is the alchemy of creation, this transformation of a thought into a physical reality.

Some of the questions we could benefit from asking ourselves are: what is the gift I have to offer? What do I know that can be leveraged so as to add value to someone else? Who might benefit from the experience and knowledge I have? What might I learn from them? What is the best vehicle to share what I know? What do I want to get back in return? How can this be a self-sustaining enterprise? Who could I partner or collaborate with to expand the reach of this idea? What arena do I want to work in—local, statewide, national, or global? What communities have a stake in this issue and how shall I engage with them? When this idea is fully realized, what will be the impact?

When Wendy Kopp was a senior at Princeton University, she had an idea. She wanted to teach in an inner-city school, but there was no system in place to pave the way. So she created one. In 1990, she founded Teach For America, a national corps of recent college graduates who commit two years to teach in rural and urban public schools in low-income communities. It began with five hundred teachers in six regions. Today, nearly 3,600 Teach For America corps members are reaching more than a quarter of a million students in twenty-two urban and rural regions nationwide, from South Central Los Angeles to the Bronx and Harlem and Washington Heights in New York to remote, rural areas in southern Louisiana and the Mississippi Delta.

Since its inception, Teach For America has directly impacted the lives of more than two million students. Corps members work throughout their two-year commitment to move their students ahead academically, many achieving gains equivalent to two grade levels in a single school year. Following that, most corps alumni work throughout their lives on the systemic changes required to put children growing up in low-income communities on a level playing field with children from more affluent areas.

Kopp, the author of *One Day, All Children,* talked about the genesis of her idea in a radio interview with Gwen Ifill. It showed the meshing of mind and heart. "We were the generation of kids who supposedly just wanted to make a lot of money and work for investment banks and management consulting firms. And I found myself searching for something that I wasn't finding. And I started getting the sense that I wasn't alone and that there were thousands of other graduating seniors out there searching for the same thing. And one day that *thought came together with my concern* [italics added] about issues of educational inequity that I had explored as public policy major and such, and I just thought of this idea. You know, why doesn't this country have a national teacher corps?"[1]

So now she's inspired. She has an insight, which now has to be converted into action. In the interview, Kopp stated that her intention "was not to start as a little nonprofit organization. This was about creating a movement among some of our nation's most promising future leaders to effect change in education. And it magnetized so many thousands of people, everyone from graduating college seniors, to people in the philanthropic community, to people in the education community...And what I learned along the way was that the big idea wasn't enough, that it would only fulfill its potential if we complemented that with the kind of management and organization-building skills that it takes to be successful in any sector."

This is where she addresses sustainability. *The big idea wasn't enough.* She had to consider management and organization. Now the brain comes in to join the heart. She has to think like a business person. What would have to happen for this idea to thrive in the business sector? She met with people in a variety of fields and got their attention. She also discovered it wasn't all about what *she* knew. "I think what we have all learned is that it's important to approach these environments with tremendous humility and respect, because there is *so much to be learned*," she said.

And even though Kopp decided to work on a national basis and kept her focus on that, her idea jumped across the ocean. So now what we see is the evolution of an idea adapting in another shape, this time to meet the concerns of a business community. In autumn 2001, two London business membership organizations dedicated to community involvement, engaged management consultants, McKinsey and Company, to investigate how businesses could help improve pupil performance in London. Though many factors were considered, the McKinsey team found that the number of excellent teachers in a school was one of the strongest predictors of improved pupil performance, especially in inner city schools. Inspired by the highly successful Teach For America program, they recommended a program based on its principles, and a team consisting of business people and educators worked to make the recommendation a reality.

They gained the support of the business community, the academic community, the government and opposition parties, the Teacher Training Agency and other policy makers, and with their help, an innovative business training program emerged that would develop leadership qualities among its participants and at the same time bring the excellence and enthusiasm of top graduates into schools. The Teach First program became a reality in London, and everyone stood to profit. After the Teach First participants completed their two year commitment, the businesses would hire these corps members, knowing their capacity for leadership and their willingness to serve. They would also be more well-rounded citizens, having taught in schools that would open their eyes to many new experiences and insights.

Over five hundred graduates have been recruited over the last three years and placed in London secondary schools. Recruiting is underway for the fourth cohort of graduates who will be placed not just in London, but in schools throughout Britain in need of help. The first group graduated in summer 2005 and have already embarked on the next stage of their Teach First journey as ambassadors of the program. The teaching profession and worlds of business, nonprofit, and industry have received an influx of Teach First graduates, a cadre of young leaders equipped and strategically positioned to become a force for good in the world.

Teach First ranked number nineteen in the UK *Times'* "Top 100 Graduate Employers" survey for 2005, voted for by over 16,000 undergraduates. For the third year running, this makes Teach First the highest ranked nonprofit in the survey. Deloitte and Touche is funding the cost of leadership training and support for eight Teach First participants throughout the two year teaching program, as well as offering three-week internships over the summer break and the support of a Deloitte coach for the two years. Other businesses that have sponsored and supported the work of Teach First—Capital & Provident Management, Canary Wharf Group, Capital One, Citigroup, Microsoft, Unilever, and McKinsey and Company—are good indicators that the international business community may be ready to sign on as supporters of change if approached in the right way with a smart idea.

When Wendy Kopp sat in her senior dorm room wondering what she could do to help balance out the inequities in our public school system, she was gifted with a beautiful insight, as many of us are when we turn our thoughts to service. If we really mean to be of use, there is not usually much of a gap between our question "how" and a workable solution. What Wendy did was act on her insight. She made a full-bore commitment and was enthusiastic enough to drum up support from people who could help her turn it into something real. Millions of students have gotten a fair shake who wouldn't have if it weren't for Wendy Kopp's determination and thousands of young teachers have benefited from working with those students who have a lot to teach about the constraints of poverty.

In her book *Finding Our Way: Leadership for an Uncertain Time,* Margaret Wheatley writes, "When people understand the forces creating the adverse conditions of their life and how they might change those forces, they become eager and rapid learners. They are capable of learning sophisticated skills that far surpass traditional assumptions about their intellectual capacity."[2]

When the Brazilian educator Paulo Freire worked among the poor in Brazil, he found that people who were illiterate could quickly learn skills in reading and complex reasoning if those skills would help them improve conditions in their communities. Once they learned to think critically about the forces contributing to their own poverty, they learned just as quickly the skills and analytic tools to help them get out of it.

When community organizer Michael Eichler started working with displaced blue-collar workers in Pennsylvania's Monongahela Valley, he encountered a widespread public opinion. "These were steelworkers. People thought of them as strong, but not smart—you know, a good back, but no brain kind of thing. But when people saw them take a lead in their own economic redevelopment strategy, they had a good reason to drop that stereotype," said Eichler, who is now a professor of social work at San Diego State University.

In 1985, Eichler was called upon to evaluate the situation in the Mon Valley communities after US Steel, Westinghouse Electric, WABCO, Union Switch and Signal, and Wheeling-Pittsburgh Steel had all closed major manufacturing plants in the area. These facilities provided a major portion of the employment base of not just the Mon Valley, but of Western Pennsylvania. Particularly affected were the skilled blue-collar jobs that defined and often dominated the Pittsburgh regional work force. The industrial sites occupied hundreds of acres of land, and as landowners the corporations were major taxpayers.

Things did not look good for Mon Valley, and Eichler's job was to come up with an action plan. His strategy was to facilitate the formation of grassroots community organizations using the Local Initiatives Support Corporation (LISC) model (www.lisc.org). This meant that projects would have an economic rationale to attract local partners and investors and would have to provide both a social benefit and financial return to the community. The style of organizing that Eichler developed to pull all this off was called consensus organizing and it focused on dialogue, relationship-building, and the dismantling of stereotypes that obstructed progress.

By April 1988, the Mon Valley Development Team was formed and nine community development corporations (CDCs) were organized. Representatives of these CDCs began to discuss forming a regional coalition, and eight months later the Mon Valley Initiative (MVI) was incorporated to provide a staff to assist the all-volunteer CDC boards in identifying and implementing development strategies, to raise funds to support development projects, and to collaborate in regional action and advocacy. The organizational structure had three focus areas: business loan fund, workforce development, and housing. These laid off steelworkers have accomplished much. Since 1988, the MVI and its CDCs have created more than 220 units of affordable housing throughout the Mon Valley region, with 70 new units in various stages of construction. MVI believes that homeownership permits people to build assets and increases the vibrancy and stability of communities. They put their muscle behind this program because homeowners build stronger neighborhoods, and stronger neighborhoods lead to community empowerment.

They invited Verizon to contribute to their successful Workforce Development program, and Verizon responded by providing a state-of-the-art Technology and Skills Center where people go to learn computer skills. They have also expanded the program to provide working skills to ex-prisoners. And the MVI Small Business Loan Fund has made twenty loans totaling more than $954,000, which has led to the creation or retention of over one hundred jobs. This year, thanks to support from Citizens Bank, the loan fund will be increased by $500,000.

This community of laid off workers has created an organization that is self-sustaining and life-changing. "They're recognized for their political clout, people know they're smart and capable, and they even managed to get the governor to speak at their annual meeting this year," said Eichler in a recent phone interview. "People need a reason to change their negative stereotype of the poor. This group gives people a good reason."

Continuing his work in facilitating healthy community dialogue and action, Eichler founded the Consensus Organizing Center (www.rohan.sdsu.edu/~consensu) at San Diego State University, which trains grassroots community leaders to build relationships with business leaders, government agencies, churches, and other organizations to collaborate in solving urban community problems. Involving youth in consensus organizing work gives them a chance to use their creative talents to build something lasting from the ground up. According to Eichler, "Their energy and resourcefulness dramatize the most positive of human traits:

Creating a positive future begins in human conversation. The simplest and most powerful investment any member of a community or an organization may make in renewal is to begin talking with other people as though the answers mattered.
WILLIAM GREIDER

No great improvements in the lot of mankind are possible, until a great change takes place in the fundamental constitution of their modes of thought.
JOHN STUART MILL

Reality is not something bequeathed to us but rather something we create, whole cloth, by communicating it into existence.
JEREMY RIFKIN

concern, dedication, honesty, and integrity. The one constant is their desire to succeed, with success defined in different ways by all the partners, but always benefiting the poor and the place where they live, and always sharing power to gain power."

Another instigator of citizen action is author Thom Hartmann, who brings his "radical middle" viewpoint to the public airwaves on his nationally-syndicated radio program (www.thomhartmann.com). Hartmann believes that cultural change begins with new insights propagating through enough people to reach a critical mass—the hundredth monkey theory. "When we change our stories, then we change the world. That's what inspires us—the stories we tell each other," Hartmann said in a recent phone interview. And indeed, his stories have inspired others. His book *The Prophet's Way* led to an invitation to a private audience with Pope John Paul II in 1998. His book *The Last Hours of Ancient Sunlight* led to an invitation to spend a week with the Dalai Lama at his home in Dharamsala, India, and inspired a web-based movie written and produced by Leonardo DiCaprio.

A historian at heart, Hartmann hit the mother lode when he decided to research the evolution of "corporate personhood" which was supposedly granted to corporations in the 1886 Supreme Court case *Santa Clara v. Southern Pacific Railroad.* When he looked at the actual case documents, Hartmann discovered that this was never stated by the court, and the chief justice ruled that matter out in consideration of the case. The claim that corporations are persons was added by the court reporter who wrote the introduction to the decision, known as "headnotes" which have no legal standing.[3]

It appears that corporations may have acquired personhood through some crafty persuasion. As it turns out, both the Supreme Court judge, Justice Stephen J. Field, and the court reporter, J. C. Bancroft Davis, were well-connected to the railroads. Davis had served as president of the board for a railroad company, and Justice Field had ruled repeatedly in favor of

A capacity for new ideas is built over a lifetime of exploration but the capacity for thought leadership is built as a result of social forces and sensitivities, which marry the revolutionary impulse with tact, diplomacy, and compassion. A novel thinker can easily just be an iconoclast rather than someone who leaves an enduring legacy. A true thought leader is thus attuned to the more intricate dimensions of social evolution.

STEPHEN DINAN

When you move into an energetic frequency of authenticity, nothing around you can stay the same.

DEBORAH JONES

his patrons, the railroad companies, in previous lower court cases. "The language used in the Santa Clara case headnotes even matched the language Field used in earlier cases," said Hartmann, who has in his personal library twelve books by Davis, mostly original editions. The books display Davis's close alliance with the railroad industry, and they support the argument that Davis injected the personhood statement deliberately, to achieve rights for the corporations who had failed to achieve them in litigation.

So it appears that the fourteenth amendment, drafted to protect the rights of African Americans after the Civil War, which was passed by Congress, voted on and ratified by the states, and signed into law by the president, was reinterpreted in 1886 for the benefit of corporations. "The notion that corporations are persons has never been voted into law by the people or by Congress, and all the court decisions endorsing it derive from the precedent of the 1886 case—from Davis' error," said Hartmann.

Simultaneously, a concern is rising up in the public consciousness over the potential damage these corporations can cause if they are solely profit-driven and not accountable to the commons. Groups of people are coming together across the country and organizing databanks, resource materials, curricula for teachers, and networks for citizens who want to become more active in shaping the culture that will be our legacy. A brilliant demonstration of collective genius is underway, providing unlimited portals for participation and platforms for thought leaders who can articulate a vision for America that works for the children, for the poor, for the earth, *and* for business. I'll mention a few of the organizations whose work specifically addresses corporate accountability, but a visit to any of their websites will lead to a plethora of other resources and networks.

The New Rules Project, Center for Corporate Policy, The Women's International League for Peace and Freedom, Citizen Works, Alliance for Democracy, The Aurora Institute, Program on Corporations, Law and Democracy (POCLAD), and Reclaim Democracy all have extensive and helpful websites. Reclaim Democracy has developed a critical thinking curriculum which helps teachers nurture critical thinking skills in students of all ages, beginning with media literacy.

According to visionary and social scientist Duane Elgin, author of several books including the best selling *Voluntary Simplicity*, the media is having a massive impact on our "social brain" and most of us are unaware of its effect. On his website (www.simpleliving.net/awakeningearth)

Elgin writes that it is the citizens who literally own the airwaves, and if programming goes through the public airwaves, the public has the right to take an active role in choosing the programming. "Unlike cable and public television, television broadcasters (primarily CBS, ABC, NBC, and FOX) in local communities in the US have a unique contract with the people of each community. Based on legislation dating back to 1927, TV broadcasters have an overriding obligation to 'serve the public interest, convenience, and necessity.' This duty to serve the public before their own pocketbooks has been affirmed by more than a half-century of law in the US Supreme Court, Congress, and the FCC."

Elgin encourages citizens to develop tools of mass communication—television viewer feedback forms—that would provide a democratic means for the public to express its collective interests with regard to how its "social brain" is to be programmed. He predicts that an extraordinary cultural shift will occur when we begin using the public airwaves to communicate to broadcasters about their legal responsibility to serve the public interest. "If the public does not assert its overriding rights and responsibilities as mature citizen-viewers, then the mass media will continue to program the mindset of our society for commercial success and evolutionary failure," he writes. The 25,000 commercials we see every year are contributing to a schizophrenic state that has a deadly potential. On the one hand, we're constantly exposed to ads that say we need more of everything. On the other hand, if we continue down the slippery slope of unbridled consumerism, we will devour the very resources that more rightfully belong to our grandchildren.

A recent article in *Ad Age* illustrates just how insidious this industry is. Journalist Alice Z. Cuneo writes, "Tonight, in what is being touted as a branded entertainment and mobile media first, a new cell phone ring tone will be integrated into a TV show, and then sold in the next commercial break directly to cell phones through a short code text message." When a phone rings on the show *CSI: New York,* the characters will discuss the tone from the media website *Cold Play.* "This is the biggest growth opportunity in this market—this is the next generation," said Cyriac Roeding, VP-wireless, CBS Broadcasting digital media. When he was challenged about the possibility of the ring-tone plug being perceived as overstepping bounds, Roeding said "There is no reason for a phone in the show to beep with a boring ring, which would be inauthentic and not true to character."[4] In another example, the Turkey-based Aerodeon, won the award for best use of mobile marketing for a project done in collaboration with Frito-Lay's Doritos. They staged a contest in which they asked consumers which they preferred, love or money. Of just under one million participants, 86 percent said they preferred money. The marketer used information on the time of day the text messages arrived to plan media for TV and other outlets. You can hardly help but feel duped or somehow invaded by these kinds of schemes that *do* seem to be overstepping some privacy boundaries, but for the industry, it's simply business as usual—a casual strip mining of the consumers' imaginations.

Educator Joseph Chilton Pearce speaks often of the entrepreneurs in the marketplace selling programs that show how to best exploit the child mind. In a radio interview, he reported that when Ralph Nader approached Bob Pittman, who invented MTV, and asked him if he realized the profound influence they were having on fourteen year olds, the guy leaned back and said, "Ralph, we don't influence fourteen-year-olds, we own them."[5]

"Every advertiser knows that before you can convince anyone of anything, you shatter their existing mental set and then restructure an awareness along lines which are useful to you. You do this with a few very simple techniques like fast-moving images, jumping among attention focuses, and switching moods," says former San Francisco advertising executive Jerry Mander. "Why do you think they call it *programming?*"[6]

Mander pointed out in his book *Four Arguments for the Elimination of Television*, that when television was first introduced it was advertised as a wonderful, democratic technology that would make everybody's life better and serve as an educational tool, available free of charge to everyone. And everyone believed it. But since those carefree days of *I Love Lucy* and *The Lone Ranger,* we've "come a long way, baby" and the brink we're at demands our full attention. A 1966 US Court of Appeals ruling states: "Nor need the public feel that in taking a hand in broadcasting they are unduly interfering in the private business affairs of others. On the contrary, their interest in television programming is direct and their responsibilities important. Under our system, the interests of the public are dominant. They are the owners of the channels of television—indeed of all broadcasting. And in a Supreme Court decision in 1969 the court states, "It is the right of the viewers and listeners, not the right of the broadcasters, which is paramount."[7]

This being the case, then it's our responsibility to hold broadcasters accountable for providing programming that serves our best interests. Toward this effort, Helen Grieco and Kim Weichel founded Our Media Voice: Campaign for Accountability (www.ourmediavoice.org), which gives people everything they need to know to work with their local stations, and a national community coalition to be part of for sustained support. Grieco and Weichel have worked extensively on citizen feedback forums, which are a thrilling use of the airwaves, since they enable the public to express its collective interests on an ongoing basis. A Citizen Feedback Forum is a democratic way for citizens in local communities to communicate directly with television broadcasters and tell them what kinds of programming will best serve their public interest. Because television broadcasters have a strict legal obligation to serve the public interest before they serve their own profits, this feedback can be extremely important for guiding broadcasters toward a more positive media.

The non-partisan, participatory democratic process provides a vehicle for articulating each community's voice, and the forums can employ live polling of a random sample of citizens to get a more accurate sense of public views. According to Grieco and Weichel, all the technology required for successful feedback forums already exists. All that's needed now is a public that wants to be informed and involved in co-creating a healthy, democratic, and sustainable world.

And it looks like that public is rising to the occasion. In an article in *The Nation*, media expert and communications professor Robert McChesney writes that local media watch groups are surfacing all across the nation. And on the advocacy front, Citizens for Independent Public Broadcasting and People for Better TV are pushing to improve public broadcasting and to tighten regulation of commercial broadcasting. Commercial Alert organizes campaigns against the commercialization of culture, from sports and museums to literature and media. The Center for Digital Democracy and the Media Access Project are both working the corridors of power in Washington to win recognition of public-interest values.

"Citizens' organizations do battle to limit billboards in public places and to combat the rise of advertising in schools, fighting often successfully to keep Channel One ads, corporate-sponsored texts and fast-food promotions out of classrooms and cafeterias. Innovative lawsuits challenging the worst excesses of media monopoly are being developed by regional groups such as Rocky Mountain Media Watch and a national consortium of civic organizations, lawyers and academics that has drawn support from Unitarian Universalist organizations," writes McChesney.[8] Hundreds of thousands of citizens are putting their insights to action and vast networks are being created in every social arena, so when a person is ready to act, there is somewhere to plug in. And prior to action, for many individuals, is the slow and courageous act of finding one's voice, clarifying one's thoughts, communicating one's feelings. Very few of us were trained to step out publicly, to speak out for others, or even ourselves. Few of us have role models for this in our own families, so the act of self-revelation is a painstaking and profound gesture. For many of us our conditioning, for the most part, has been *not* to talk about ourselves, so even the act of personal sharing is a giant step. But it is the first step, and the most important step, since it is from our very depths that we want to proceed when we come to the table as a co-creator.

What you bring to the table, no one else has—they have not had your experiences, they have not suffered your losses, they have not learned your lessons. You are a wellspring of originality. You are a mine full of jewels that others can use, as others are to you, rich with treasures only waiting to be found. And no matter how different we appear to be, on the inside we're all exactly the same—wanting to be loved, wanting to love, and wanting to be seen through the lens of compassion. To take this step toward public discourse, to reveal ourselves honestly and emotionally to others—this is, in itself, a generous gift. As Ramana Maharshi writes, "Your own self-realization is the greatest service you can render the world."

While some people can find their own treasures, unearth their unique insights independently in the quiet hours of solitude and grace, others only find it in the act of communion—for there our companions hold a mirror to our mysteries, and their listening calls forth words that reveal us to ourselves. The very creative gesture of our lives is bringing the inner outward, transforming feeling to thought, thought to word, word to deed. "How can I know what I think unless I see what I write?" asks Erica Jong, "How can I know what I think till I see what I say?" writes E. M. Forster. And May Sarton says, "I suppose I have written novels to find out what I thought about something, and poems to find out what I felt about something."

These writers found themselves by making the private public. And in the process of meaningful, intentional and communal self-disclosure, so can we find ourselves, our meanings, our personal and collective wisdom. As Henri Bergson wrote in *Creative Evolution,* "A new system of philosophy will only be built up by the collective and progressive effort of many thinkers, of many observers also, completing, correcting and improving one another." It may very well be that the answers to our most burning questions will surface in the context of our simple and honest conversations with each other.

And to that end, there is a whole movement afoot in this country. In the early 1990s when the editors of *Utne* magazine suggested that readers form Salons to share their ideas about issues that really matter to them, over eight thousand readers responded and asked to be matched up with other *Utne* readers in their community, marking the beginning of the neighborhood Salon movement.

At its peak in 1995, *Utne*'s Neighborhood Salon Association had 25,000 members in 600 groups meeting monthly across the nation and in several foreign countries. Leif Utne, founder of the magazine, has been working with a number of partners—including the National Coalition for Dialogue and Deliberation, the Conversation Cafés, and the World Café—to convene a national conversation about people's hopes and dreams for the future, and they're calling it "Let's Talk America."

Let's Talk America (www.letstalkamerica.org) is a nationwide movement that is bringing Americans from all points on the political spectrum together in cafes, bookstores, churches, and living rooms for lively, open-hearted dialogue to consider questions essential to our lives. Let's Talk America reconnects with the "town hall" meeting spirit that's the lifeblood of our democracy, and provides a meeting ground for amicable and animated conversations. They offer telephone training for people wanting to become hosts of the conversations and have an array of support materials on their website.

Another great magazine, *The Sun*, is linking people around the country who are interested in meeting with others for stimulating conversations. They have a map of the United States on their website (www.thesunmagazine.org) listing all the Salons in the country where Sun readers are converging for conversations of consequence. And several local libraries are sponsoring Salons. In Youngstown, Ohio, the Conversation Salons at the Library series was established as a partnership between Youngstown State University and the Public Library of Youngstown and Mahoning County in 2004. Describing their Salons, they write: "The Conversation Salons are not book or journal clubs, or political action groups, or classes or therapy groups, or gossip circles, or debating societies with winners and losers. The goals of a Conversation Salon are to have good conversation among the members and to engage in the exploration of new ideas in an open discussion with others who share your interests rather than to passively absorb editorials, news and talk radio and television."

And there's no need to wait for a Salon to surface in your neighborhood. You can create your own. In 1998, when Kathy Hamill and Robin Slater read an article on Salons in *Utne*, they put an ad in the local newspaper to see if they could spark any interest in their community. The ad, listed under "Seeking Friends," solicited "suburban unconventional thinkers starving for imaginative, intelligent conversation."

Twenty people from all over the suburbs showed up for the first Salon at their home in a rural subdivision southwest of Elgin, Illinois. Five months later, the couple was hosting two Saturday night Salons each month to accommodate the growing interest. They now have more than one hundred people on their mailing list. Some of the questions the group has explored include: What events, if any, in your childhood significantly influenced who you are now? What does "America" mean to you? What do you think it means to everyone else? What does "Un-American" mean? What is the millennium version of "The American Dream"? What is the role of the sacred in contemporary and individual lives? Are Americans becoming more, or less, spiritual? What is the role of emotion in spiritual experience? When I say, "This is me," what am I referring to? If you live in the area, and want to join their Salon, go to www.elginsalon.org.

The World Café (www.theworldcafe.com) originated by Juanita Brown and David Isaacs, is an innovative methodology that enhances the capacity for collaborative thinking about critical issues by linking small-group and large-group conversations. Groups as small as twelve and as large as twelve hundred from around the world have engaged in Café learning conversations, and they are changing the ways many companies do business. Brown and Isaacs believe that the future is born in webs of human conversation, and that compelling questions encourage collective learning. Their methodology is based on the assumption that intelligence emerges as a system and connects to itself in diverse and creative ways. It is their belief that we collectively have all the wisdom we need, and that this wisdom is best surfaced in public conversations.

I had the opportunity to participate in a World Café conversation at a recent conference and the results were fascinating. There were about fifteen tables set up in the room with four chairs at each table. We all took our seats and the facilitator announced that we would have fifteen minutes of conversation on the subject, then three of the four participants would go to other tables, leaving behind one "host" at each table to welcome the three new individuals. The question he posed to the group was "What have you learned in your life about compassion?"

Given the time limitation and the fact that none of us could talk more than four minutes each if we were going to give everyone a chance

sations in the workplace."

Supporting conversation as a core business practice will be a re-learning process in itself, given business' traditional "stop talking and get back to work" mentality. Learning to ask essential questions is a significant part of the process, as is creating aesthetic spaces that lend themselves to conversation. Brown and Isaacs offer examples of two companies that have intentionally designed workspaces conducive to conversation. Executives from Steelcase Corporation in Grand Rapids, Michigan, met with space planners and a social psychologist for input in designing a workplace that fostered dialogue and team activities. They now have office areas designed as "neighborhoods" and "community commons" where teams can work together in close proximity and interact as a community. Their website contains many photographs of their new interior, and one, referred to as "an interactive, decision-making environment for top management" shows several café-type tables with three and four chairs around them.

European offices are also getting in on the act. In the center of its corporate headquarters in Stockholm, Sweden, SAS Airlines has a "central plaza" containing shops and a café where people from all levels intermingle and share their ideas. Making the right space for conversations to occur is the first step in making it happen. Then comes the work of framing the questions that will inspire the strategic dialogue businesses are hoping to foster. This, say Brown and Isaacs, will require a critical leadership skill.

"Strategic questions create dissonance between current experiences and beliefs while evoking new possibilities for collective discovery. But they also serve as the glue that holds together overlapping webs of conversations in which diverse resources combine and recombine to create innovative solutions and business values...Strengthening personal relationships through networks of collaborative conversations will be essential for building intellectual capital," they write.[11]

Dissonance is a phenomenon we are witnessing more and more as our culture polarizes itself and the media trains its lens on the drama of our distancing. When therapist Laura Chasin was watching an abortion debate on Boston public television, she realized that the debaters were acting like a dysfunctional family. It occurred to her that she wouldn't put up with that if they were in her office, and neither would any of her colleagues. They know how to intervene in a family that's torn apart, and they know how to help make something more constructive happen, she thought, and it was at that moment a light bulb went off in Chasin's head. "My family therapy head and my citizen head connected," said Chasin, and she decided to act on the insight that what she did with couples and families could be adapted to people embroiled in civic and political conflict.

Chasin recruited six of her coworkers and started the Public Conversations Project (www.publicconversations.org) inviting people who wanted to dialogue about reproductive freedom to come talk to each other. PCP was not striving for common ground, but rather focused on getting participants to just listen to each other with respect. In an interview for *Utne* magazine, Chasin said, "It may seem counter-intuitive, but after three hours of dialogue, at least the outline of what some would call common ground begins to emerge. The people involved in the private process started behaving differently in the public process. Instead of attacking each other in the press, they would call each other on the phone."[12] Although PCP dialogues are not intended to push pubic policy or move disputing parties toward collaboration, that surprisingly happens in the process. "The more you push for an agreement on outcomes, the less you tend to get it," said Chasin. "But if you shift the relationships, often they will move spontaneously toward collaboration on solutions."

Communication and relationship are the building blocks of original thinking. They spark the fire, fan the flames, spread the warmth, transmit the light. It is through dialogue and intimacy with others that we experience the gift of communion consciousness and the subtle dissolution of barriers that once seemed to separate us. It is in the safe company of trusted companions and colleagues that we can unfold our brilliant potential, unshackle our wild imaginations, and release our newfound energy and insights into the world. It is in solitude that we incubate our creativity, but it is in community that we express it.

Thought leaders traverse constantly between the private and the public, deepening themselves in silence and study, then reaching outward with awareness gained on the inner journey, merging with others to synthesize and share, collaborate and create. Their energy, then, is whole and integral; their intelligence is embodied; and in their words and every action is a power that others identify as a force for good. It is this integration of inner and outer, self and other, insight and action that fuels the mind of original thinkers and fosters the potential for thought leadership.

For every person mentioned in this chapter, there are millions of others equally committed, equally creative, spreading their ideas like seeds across the fertile landscape, some never knowing if they've taken root or not. Nor did I know on that journey around the world, how it mattered or what difference it made, for it is only the future that can measure our gains. But I took comfort that day in November 1989, when I first heard they were dismantling the Berlin Wall. I remembered being there, showing my slides, talking with people about the possibility of peace, driven by that notion in *The Hundredth Monkey* that just one person could strengthen the field and have an impact on global consciousness. As all those bricks came tumbling down, I took personal credit for at least one.

FIFTEEN

You Are the Help

Whatever it is that's awakening us is much more intelligent than who we become when we are awakened.

RICHARD MOSS, M.D.

Things behave in alignment with how the observer expects them to behave, so as we change our collective story about the state of the world, the state of the world also changes.

ARJUNA ARDAGH

I pulled my car into the breakdown lane and grabbed my video camera. There was a flock of birds above Highway 194 that I couldn't keep my eyes off. There were hundreds of them performing a sky ballet that took my breath away. When I first looked, they were all white. Then they swooped down en masse, rolled over, and suddenly turned silver. When I looked again, they flew off in a new direction, and this time they all looked black.

Leaning up against my car hood, I turned on the camera and zoomed in on the flock. I had just focused in when I heard the sound of metal crashing into metal. Then everything became silent. I had one brief image of three things: my camera, my car, and myself flying through the air. Then everything went black.

When I came to, I was underneath my car, lying prostrate and facing the rear wheel. I lifted my head enough to see my outstretched arms and feared immediately that I was paralyzed. I tried to wiggle my fingers and was amazed when they moved. Then I tried my feet and my toes. They moved too. "I can get out of here," I thought. "I just have to shimmy out."

I tried to drag my body forward, but I couldn't move it. I was under the exhaust system, pinned to the ground, and the muffler was burning away my flesh. Now I realized I had to dig my way out. But it was high desert land, and with all my might, I could hardly make a scratch in the dry, hard dirt.

It was then I realized I was about to witness my own death. A great sorrow filled me at first when I thought of my mother, my family, and friends having to hear I was killed in a terrible accident. Next came the assessment of how I had done with the life I was given. Did I have regrets? No. Was anything unfinished, unforgiven? No. Was I proud of the wake I left behind? Had I done everything I could do to contribute my gifts? Had I given all my thanks to everyone I was grateful for? "Yes," I thought. "I did the best I could do. If there's anyone to report to, I'll be proud to report."

It was time then to let go, but how could I do this? I wanted to live. I started to fear, not so much the unknown, but the known coming to an end. Then I thought of what I'd heard about the Native American elders who went to the mountaintop when their time had come, and they calmly waited and peacefully released. And I thought about the Eskimos I'd heard of, who went off to lie in a drift of snow when they knew the transition was close at hand. "I can do this," I thought. "If they could do it, I can do it." And I closed my eyes, took one last deep conscious breath, and began to slip backward, into the silence, into the Source. I was going home.

Then I heard the frantic shouts, "Is anybody there? Is anybody alive?" Suddenly I was back under the car again. The voices continued to call, "Is there anybody there? Is anyone alive?"

"I'm here," I called back, barely audible.
"I'm alive."

I heard the sound of running feet.

"Where are you?"

"Under the car, by the back tire."

I looked up and saw their legs. Two men.

"Oh my God!" they cried out.

"Wait there! We'll go get help!"

"Don't go," I pleaded. "You *are* the help."

New leaders must invent the future while dealing with the past.
MARGARET WHEATLEY

It is in the recognition of the genuine conditions of our lives that we gain strength to act and our motivation for change.
SIMONE DE BEAUVOIR

To learn is not merely to accumulate data; it is to rebuild one's world.
ROBERT GRUDIN

If we go down into ourselves we find that we possess exactly what we desire.
SIMONE WEIL

Not to transmit an experience is to betray it.
ELIE WIESEL

"Just lift up the car."

There was a terrible silence, broken by their fearful announcement.

"We can't! We need help!"

"Yes you can," I cried. "You can. Just lift it up...now!"

And in one miraculous moment, they became the gods we are capable of being. They put their hands under the fender, and on the count of three, lifted the car as if it were an eagle's feather. Then two hands reached down to pull me out. They belonged to the man who had hit my car going seventy miles per hour.

The great gift that this event gave me was two-fold: first, it allowed me the chance to look at my life from a different perspective, to assess it as a whole and determine if I needed any mid-course corrections. Secondly, and most importantly, it taught me a great lesson—that *we* are the help.

When those men approached the wreckage, the first thing they experienced was their helplessness. They did not believe in their own powers and wanted to run off in search of help. They were caught in the story we've been told all our lives—that help is somewhere else, power and strength are somewhere else, the solutions are somewhere else, beyond us, outside of us. But when they heard that voice, *"You are the help,"* some shift happened. Illusions dropped. Doubt was suspended. And in its place rushed a huge and mighty force, a new belief that rippled through every cell in their bodies and infused their beings with whatever strength was called for.

Whatever is needed at this time in history to right this world, to right our own personal and precious lives, we have these things *within* us. We do not need science and technology to save us. We do not need government and religion to save us. We do not need more information and faster computers to save us. What we need is to abandon our notions that solutions exist anywhere but in ourselves.

If I look at my life and find it lacking in adventure or challenge or joy, the solution to that is right inside me, dwelling as a potential, awaiting a decision, a decisive action. If I look at my business, my affiliations, my family and feel uninspired,

> One way to come to say yes is to say no to everything that does not nourish and entice our secret inner life out into the world.
> DAVID WHYTE

> The real moment of success is not the moment apparent to the crowd.
> GEORGE BERNARD SHAW

> The way to have good ideas is to have a lot of ideas and throw away the bad ones.
> LINUS PAULING

> Authentic human existence requires the co-presence of two worlds, the inner and the outer.
> JACOB NEEDLEMAN

unseen, or disconnected, the way to wholeness is inscribed on my heart, written on every cell in my body, waiting for me to look within and turn my ear to the Great Below.

No one becomes a visionary who does not first look within. And none of us can inspire another till we first learn how to inspire ourselves. Coming to grips with the power we have is a necessary step to original thinking. It takes courage. It calls for reflection. It means letting go of the mediocre to create the magnificent. All those voices in your head— let them go like a bunch of balloons. Then remember those men coming upon the wreckage, thinking themselves powerless until they heard the voice coming up from below, and then lifted that car without a thought.

APPENDIX

The 9th Element Group is an organization of creative and visionary evoluminaries who perceive thought leadership as an art form and a practice that links information to inspiration, heart to mind, commercial interests to compassionate action. Recognizing that we, as global citizens, are at a critical point in our evolutionary process—responsible for decisions more serious than humankind has ever faced—we are dedicated to educating leaders who are ready to unleash their imagination, activate their unlimited creativity, and produce positive, productive and profitable changes in their businesses and organizations.

As a product-driven company, the 9th Element Group produces educational programs, publications, and multi-media materials that ignite original thinking, expand global consciousness, and propel businesses and individuals to higher levels of awareness, efficiency, and achievement. Our keynote presentations are upbeat, invigorating, and insightful productions that incorporate music and imagery to touch the heart while they move the mind both forward and inward.

Through its Thought Leadership Institute, the 9th Element Group offers full-day and weekend intensives in the OriginalThink™ Process to move participants from acquired learning habits to original thinking that is evolutionary, inspired, and future based. Using a multi media, multi-sensory approach, we ensure a holistic and full-bodied experience that leads to transformation on a cellular level.

The 9th Element Group maintains an Insight to Action Resource Center on its website (www.9thelementgroup.com), providing connections to a network of agencies committed to serving the public in local, national, and international venues.

For information on our keynote presentations or educational programs, visit our website www.9thelementgroup.com or call 858-431-5003.

9TH ELEMENT GROUP
The Business of Thought Leadership

NOTES

Notes Listed by Chapter

Chapter 1
1. Margaret Wheatley, *Finding Our Way: Leadership for an Uncertain Time* (San Francisco: Berrett Kohler Publishers, Inc., 2005).

Chapter 2
1. Riane Eisler, *The Chalice and the Blade* (San Francisco: HarperSanFrancisco, 1987).

2. Peter Russell, *The Awakening Earth* (London: Routledge & Kegan Paul, 1982), 129.

3. Margaret Wheatley, *Finding Our Way: Leadership for an Uncertain Time* (San Francisco: Berrett Kohler Publishers, Inc., 2005), 121.

4. Elizabeth DeBold, "The Business of Saving the World," *What Is Enlightenment?* (March-May 2005): 75.

5. Peter Senge, *The Fifth Discipline* (New York: Currency Doubleday, 1990), 9.

6. Sinister Wisdom, #7, www.sinisterwisdom.org.

7. Marco Visscher, "The World Champ of Poverty Fighters," *Ode*, (July/August 2005), www.odemagazine.com.

8. Marco Visscher, "How One New Company Brought Hope to One of the World's Poorest Companies," *Ode*, (January 2005), www.odemagazine.com.

9. Joseph Campbell, *Myths to Live By* (New York: Penguin Books, 1972), 266.

Chapter 4
1. Text adapted with permission from Danah Zohar, Ian Marshall, *SQ: Connecting with Our Spiritual Intelligence* (New York: Bloomsbury USA, 2000), 282.

2. G. Jeffrey MacDonald, "A Seal of Approval for Companies' Social Progress," *The Christian Science Monitor* (July 18, 2005).

3. "2003 Report on Socially Responsible Investing Trends in the US," www.socialinvest.org.

4. www.business-ethics.com/what's_new/bestbizschools.html

5. Marjorie Kelly, "Holy Grail," *Business Ethics* (Summer 2005), www.business-ethics.com/current_issue/winter_2005_holy_grail_article.html.

6. "Psychiatric Services," April 2004. Reported in *Our Health News Archive*, "Pill-Popping Pre-Schoolers, Even Toddlers Get the Blues."

Chapter 5
1. Holly Sklar, "CEO Pay Still on Steroids," Knight Ridder/Tribune Information Services, May 9, 2005.

2. Harold Bloom, "In Praise of Consumerism: The Spiritual Fruits of Materialism," *What Is Enlightenment?* (March-May 2005): 46-47, www.wie.org.

3. Viktor E. Frankl, *Man's Search for Meaning* (New York: Simon and Schuster, 1963), 122.

4. Marco Visscher, "How One Company Brought Hope to One of the World's Poorest Countries," *Ode* (January 2005): 40-41, www.odemagazine.com.

5. www.expresscomputeronline.com/20021223/indnews1.shtml

6. C.K. Prahalad, Allan Hammond, "What Works: Serving the World's Poor, Profitably," http://pubs.wri.org/pubs_newsviews_text.cfm?cid=412

7. www.novartisfoundation.com/en/about/25_years/speek_leisinger.html

8. Alexis de Tocqueville, *Democracy in America* (Chicago: University of Chicago Press, 2000).

9. Willis W. Harmann, *New Traditions in Business*, (San Francisco: Berrett-Kohler, 1992), 226.

10. Coleman Barks, *The Essential Rumi* (San Francisco: HarperSanFrancisco, 1995), 191.

11. www.unicef.org/media

12. www.globalissues.org/Geopolitics/ArmsTrade/Spending.asp#USMilitarySpending

13. Shantayanan Devarajan, Margaret J. Miller, and Eric V. Swanson, World Bank Policy Research Working Paper, "Development Goals: History, Prospects and Costs," www.worldwatch.org.

14. Michael Scherer, "Make your Taxes Disappear," *Mother Jones* (April 2005): 74.

Chapter 6
1. Marge Piercy, *The Moon is Always Female*, "The low road" (New York: Alfred A. Knopf, 1980).

2. www.npr.org/thisibelieve/guide.html

Chapter 7
1. www.census.gov/PressRelease/www/releases/archives/income_wealth/002484.html

2. June Gould, *The Writer in All of Us: Improving your Writing through Childhood Memories* (New York: E.P. Dutton, 1989).

3. www.wfs.org

4. www.globalschoolnet.org

5. Elizabeth Debold, "The Business of Saving the World," *What Is Enlightenment?* (March-May, 2005): 83, www.wic.org.

6. www.csuchico.edu/sage/cdeberg@csuchico.edu

Chapter 8
1. James Surowiecki, *The Wisdom of Crowds* (New York: Anchor Books, 2005).

2. Ibid., 30.

3. Ibid., 276.

4. Sharon Begley, "Science's Big Query: What Can We Know and What Can't We?," *Wall Street Journal Science Journal* (May 30, 2003), B1.

5. Jean Lipman-Blumen, *The Allure of Toxic Leaders* (New York: Oxford University Press, 2005), 73.

6. Joan Chittister, "Now They See Us As We Are," *National Catholic Reporter* (September 30, 2005), www.nationalcatholicreporter.org/fwis/fw093005.html.

7. Henri Bergson, *The Two Sources of Morality and Religion* (Notre Dame: University of Notre Dame Press, 1977 [1935]).

8. Robert Jay Lifton, *The Protean Self: Human Resilience in an Age of Fragmentation* (Chicago: University of Chicago Press, 1993).

Chapter 9
1. Stephanie Pool, "Wal-Mart: What a Bargain!," *Utne* (September-October 2004): 28.

2. Devon Leonard, "The Only Lifeline Was the Wal-Mart," *Fortune* (October 3, 2005).

3. www.adage.com/news.cms?newsid=45260

4. Paul Krugman, *The Great Unraveling: Losing Our Way in the New Century* (New York: W. W. Norton & Company, Inc., 2003), 117.

5. Ibid., 118.

6. Ann Coulter, *How To Talk to a Liberal (If You Must)* (New York: Three Rivers Press, 2005), 157.

7. *Common Boundary* magazine, 1990.

8. Robert Grudin, *The Grace of Great Things* (Boston: Ticknor and Fields,1990), 191.

9. James A. Autry, *Love and Profit:The Art of Caring Leadership* (New York: Avon Books, Inc., 1991), 19.

10. Ibid., by permission.

Chapter 10
1. www.globalpolicy.org/socecon/bwi-wto/sumers99.htm

2. Sander G. Tideman, "Mind Over Matter. Towards a New Paradigm for Business and Economics," www.gpiatlantic.org/conference/papers/tideman.

3. Ibid.

4. Kristin Ohlson, "It's Good to Be Good," *Case* (Spring 2004), www.unlimitedloveinstitute.org.

5. Marilyn Schlitz, Ph.D., "Let Go and Prosper: Updates from the Science of Foregiveness," *Spirituality and Health* (September-October 2003): 12.

6. Willis Harmann, www.worldbusiness.org/wharman.cfm.

7. www.spiritinbusiness.org

8. www.paecon.net

9. Paul Fullbrook, *Post-autistic Economics Review* 19 (April 2, 2003), www.paecon.net/PAEReview/issue19/Harvard19.htm. For further information about the PAE, see *The Crisis in Economics: The Post-Autistic Economics Movement: The First 600 days*, Edward Fullbrook (editor), (London: Routledge, 2003).

10. www.gsreport.com/articles/art000171.html

11. Willis Harmann and Maya Porter, *The New Business of Business* (San Francisco: Berrett-Kohler, 1997), www.worldbusiness.org/wharman.cfm.

12. Warren Bennis, *Leader to Leader,* "The Leadership Advantage" (Spring 1999): 18-23.

13. Ian Mitroff and Elizabeth Denton, *A Spiritual Audit of Corporate America* (New Jersey: Jossey-Bass, 1999).

14. Patricia Aburdene, *Megatrends 2010: The Rise Of Conscious Capitalism,* (Charlottesville: Hampton Roads Publishing, 2005).

15. M Raja, "Vipassana Changes the Spirit of Business,"*Asia Times* (July 30, 2003)

16. Frederica Saylor, "Businesses Benefit from a Low-key Spirituality," northernway.org/workplace.html.

17. Michelle Conlin, "The Growing Presence of Spirituality in Corporate America," *Business Week,* www.businessweck.com/1999.

18. David Zweig, World Business Academy, Merchants of Vision, "George Zimmer," April 29, 2004, www.worldbusiness.org.

19. Jane Lampman, "A New Spirit at Work," *Christian Science Monitor* (November 17, 2003), www.csmonitor.com/2003/1117/p14s03-wmgn.htm.

20. www.sandiegometro.com/2004/dec/coverstory.php

21. Dermot Tredget, OSB, "Beyond the Obvious–Benedictine Spirituality in the Workplace," www.grahamwilson.org.

Chapter 11
1.Henri Bergson, *The Two Sources of Morality and Religion* (Notre Dame: University of Notre Dame Press, 1977[1935]), 40.

2. www.heartmath.org/research

3. Joseph Chilton Pearce, *The Biology of Transcendence* (Rochester: Park Street Press, 2002), 80.

4. www.heartmath.org/research

5. Image by Dean Radin, www.noosphere.princeton.edu/terror.html.

6. John Hagelin, *A Manual for a Perfect Government* (Fairfield: Maharishi University of Management Press, 1998), 79-80.

7. Paul Pearsall, *The Heart's Code* (New York: Broadway Books, 1998).

8. Thomas Berry, *The Great Work–Our Way into the Future* (New York: Random House, 1999).

9. Candace Pert. *The Molecules of Emotion* (New York: Scribner, 1997), 287.

Chapter 12
1. Bambi Francisco, "Sequoia Capital's Moritz on how to be the next Google," August 10, 2004, www.investors.com/breakingnews.asp?journalid=22597809.

NOTES

2. Amy Rottier, "Gen 2001: Loyalty and Values Workforce," *Workforce Management* (October 2001).

3. Kevin Salwen, "Making a Difference," *Worthwhile* (October 28, 2005), www.worthwhilemag.com/entry/2005/10/28/.

4. US Census Bureau, Dynamics of Economic Well-Being: Poverty 1996-1999, July 2003.

5. Briefing Paper #165, Economic Policy Institute, September 1, 2005, www.epi.org/content.cfm?id=2091.

6. "Rent, utilities, transportation, food, health care: Consumer Expenditures Survey," US Department of Labor, Bureau of Labor Statistics, February 2004; "Child care: Expenditures on Children by Families," US Department of Agriculture, Center for Nutrition Policy and Promotion, April 2004; "Poverty threshold: US Census Bureau, Current Population Survey 2004 Annual Social and Economic Supplement.

7. www.wsws.org/articles/2005/jun2005/pove-j01.shtml

8. Sylvia A. Allegretto, The Economic Policy Institute, www.epi.org/content.cfm/webfeatures_snapshots_06232004.

9. Robert Greenstein, Sharon Parrott, Isaac Shapiro, "CBO Information Shows House Budget Bill Passed Last Night Would Hit the Poor Hard," Center on Budget and Policy Priorities, November 18, 2005, www.cbpp.org.

10. Karen W. Arenson, "Tufts Is Getting Gift of $100 Million, With Rare Strings," The *New York Times* (November 4, 2005).

11. www.economist.com/surveys/displaystory.cfm?story_id=5104911

12. Text adapted from "Inventing Modern America," web.mit.edu/invent/www/ima/.

13. Paul Polak, "The Big Potential of Small Farms," *Scientific American* (September 2005), 88.

14. David Armstrong with Naazneen Karmali, "Trickle-Up Economics: How low-tech, low-cost designs are helping the poorest farmers on Earth grow their way out of poverty," *Forbes* (June 20, 2005), www.forbes.com/business/global/2005/0620/040.html.

15. Kevin Bullis, "Generating Hope", *Technology Review* (October 5, 2005), www.techreview.com/BioTech/wtr_14867,312,p1.html.

16. Paul Hawken, Amory Lovins, L. Hunter Lovins, *Natural Capitalism: Creating the Next Industrial Revolution* (New York: Little, Brown, 1999).

17. Amory B. Lovins, "More Profit with Less Carbon," *Scientific American* (September 2005), 77, www.sciam.com/media/pdf/Lovinsforweb.pdf.

18. Amory Lovins and L. Hunter Lovins. "Harnessing Corporate Power to Heal the Planet," http://www.worldandi.com/specialreport/2000/april/Sa19071.html.

Chapter 13
1. Danielle Sacks, "It's Easy being Green," *Fast Company* (August 2004): 50.

2. Mathis Wackernagel and William Rees, *Our Ecological Footprint: Reducing Human Impact on the Earth* (Gabriola Island, British Columbia: New Society Publishers, 1997).

3. Sustainable Development International Corporation,

http://www.smartoffice.com/gb3.htm.

4. Elisabet Sahtouris, PhD, "Biology Revisioned" *Noetic Sciences Review* (December-February 2002): 21.

5. www.rolltronics.com

6. www.smartoffice.com/gb4.html

7. www.euractiv.com/Article?tcmuri=tcm:29-117413-16&type=Interview with bjorn

8. Geoffrey Colvin, "Should Companies Care?" *Fortune* (June 11, 2001).

9. Marc Gunther, "Tree Huggers, Soy Lovers and Profits," *Fortune* (June 23, 2003).

10. Livio D. DeSimone and Frank Popoff, *Eco-Efficiency: The Business Link to Sustainable Development* (Cambridge, MA: MIT Press, 1997).

11. www.redefiningprogress.org/bluegreen

12. www.globalexchange.org/campaigns/fairtrade/coffee

Chapter 14
1. Wendy Kopp, Interview with Gwen Ifill, May 31, 2001, Online Newshour, www.pbs.org/newshour/bb/education/jan-june01/teach 05-31.html.

2. Margaret Wheatley, *Finding Our Way: Leadership for an Uncertain Time* (San Francisco: Berrett-Kohler Publishers, Inc., 2005), 171.

3. Thom Hartmann, *Unequal Protection: the Rise of Corporate Dominance and the Theft of Human Rights* (New York: Rodale, 2002), www.thomhartmann.com/unequalprotection.shtml.

4. Alice Z. Cuneo, "Award Recipient Lashes Out At Wireless Industry," *Ad Age* (November 30, 2005), www.adage.com/news.cms?newsId=46964.

5. Chris Mercogliano and Kim Debus, Interview with Joseph Chilton Pearce, *Journal of Family Life*, 5, No.1999, www.ratical.org/many_worlds/JCP99.pdf.

6. Ron Kaufman, Review of Jerry Mander's *Four Arguments for the Elimination of Television*, www.netreach.net/~kaufman/Jerry.Mander.html.

7. www.ourmediavoice.org

8. Robert W. McChesney and John Nichols, "The Making of a Movement," *The Nation* (January 7, 2002), www.thenation.com/doc/20020107/mcchesney.

9. www.bdavetian.com/salonhistory.html

10. J. Brown and D. Isaacs, "Conversation as a Core Business Process," *The Systems Thinker*, Pegasus Communications, Cambridge, MA (December 1996/January 1997): 1-6, www.theworldcafe.com/aboutdi.html.

11. Ibid.

12. Leif Utne, "The Radical Middle," *Utne* magazine (September–October 2004).

INDEX

INDEX

INDEX

INDEX

INDEX

INDEX